The Scottish Romance Tradition c. 1375 – c. 1550

KV-579-016

Scottish Cultural Review
of Language and Literature

Volume 14

Series Editors
Rhona Brown
University of Glasgow

John Corbett
University of Glasgow

Sarah Dunnigan
University of Edinburgh

James McGonigal
University of Glasgow

Production Editor
Ronnie Young
University of Glasgow

SCROLL

The Scottish Cultural Review of Language and Literature publishes new work in Scottish Studies, with a focus on analysis and reinterpretation of the literature and languages of Scotland, and the cultural contexts that have shaped them.

Further information on our editorial and production procedures can be found at www.rodopi.nl

The Scottish Romance Tradition c. 1375 – c. 1550

Nation, Chivalry and Knighthood

Sergi Mainer

Rodopi

Amsterdam - New York, NY 2010

Cover image: Detail from *Histoire de Merlin*
(BnF, Manuscrit, Français 95 fol. 167) © Bibliothèque nationale de France

Cover design: Pier Post

The paper on which this book is printed meets the requirements of "ISO 9706: 1994, Information and documentation - Paper for documents - Requirements for permanence".

ISBN: 978-90-420-2975-0
E-Book ISBN: 978-90-420-2976-7
©Editions Rodopi B.V., Amsterdam - New York, NY 2010
Printed in The Netherlands

To my parents

Als meus pares

Ara et penso — tan lluny! —
i t'invento un posat
expentant, perquè m'omplis
aquest buit de la tarda.
 (Miquel Martí i Pol, 1929–2003)

Contents

Acknowledgements 9

Preface Contextualising Medieval Scottish
Romance 11

Introduction Late Medieval Scotland and the
Romance Tradition 27

Chapter One National Constructs in the Medieval
Scottish Romances 41

Chapter Two The Hero's Progression 103

Chapter Three The Historical Romances 157

Chapter Four The Arthurian Romances 193

Chapter Five The Alexander and Charlemagne
Romances 223

Conclusion The Scottish Romance Tradition 257

Bibliography 265

Index 281

Acknowledgements

I would like to show my gratitude to, first of all, R.D.S. Jack and Philip Bennett, who supervised my MSc and PhD dissertations, giving constant, patient advice, which has helped me in every piece of research I have completed ever since.

I would also like to thank Cordelia Beattie, Sarah Carpenter, Ruth Evans, Gavin Miller, David Salter, and all the other people who have contributed in one way or another to the writing of this book. Many thanks also to Sarah Dunnigan, Rhona Brown and James McGonigal for their priceless comments and to Ronnie Young, who patiently and diligently dealt with my numerous queries in the production of this book.

Last but not least, I would like to acknowledge my family and friends who have always been very supportive – many thanks to all of them.

Preface

Contextualising Medieval Scottish Romance

It is almost impossible to devise a whole acceptable characterisation of romance owing to its different generic manifestations throughout the Middle Ages and beyond. How can the same classification embrace the Old French *romans d'antiques* of the mid-twelfth century and *Squyer Meldrum* (c.1550–55) by the early modern Scottish writer, Sir David Lindsay? A four hundred year gap divides the two which gives rise to the cultural and historical particularities which make each work distinctive. Critics of the novel, or of cinema, do not seem to share the obsessive desire to create definitions which will encompass all the novels ever written and all the films ever made. How many different definitions of romance are therefore needed? Can or should we group together a certain number of texts to enable the task to be made easier; and, if so, how artificial or valid might such potentially anachronistic or arbitrary divisions prove? After all, in Scotland, the first preserved romance – or at least the first romance with strong links to the country – is the early thirteenth-century *Roman de Fergus* by Guillaume le Clerc, who has been identified with William Malveisin, bishop of Glasgow and subsequently of Saint Andrews (Owen ed. 1991: 162–69). *Fergus* is a comic Arthurian romance written in Anglo-Norman and set in southern Scotland.

This preface attempts to give some answers to these questions but by no means seeks to be definitive or comprehensive. I will begin by approaching romances in general from a diachronic and synchronic perspective and by alluding to the most common generic and modal classifications. Their reciprocity with other contemporary literary forms such as epic or saints' lives will also be examined. I will then question "romance" by suggesting why the most productive approach to medieval Scottish romance is one based on linguistic, territorial, and national concerns as well as the broader premises of medieval aesthetics.

Medieval Romance: a critical overview

Linguistically, the evolution of the term "romance" has undergone major changes. In the twelfth century, the word was initially applied to any translation from Latin into a romance language: *roman, romanz* or *romanç*, and *romanzar* or *romançar* as a verb. Its function was therefore to make a text available for a larger audience. The language of prestige and learning, Latin, was translated into the language of the vast majority of the population, the vernacular. Romance rapidly developed into a term not only to designate a translation but any narrative in a romance language. This broad sense of the word was maintained during the late Middle Ages. Now, university students of literature would think of Chrétien de Troyes' texts or, in English, *Sir Gawain and the Green Knight* as exemplary medieval romances. Chrétien, who lived in the second half of the twelfth century, is regarded as the single most influential figure in the development of *romans courtois*, a sub-genre which idealises knightly and courtly manners (but which can also satirise and critique those values), and where *fin'amors* (uninspiredly adapted as "courtly love") tends to be the moving force. Chrétien wrote four Arthurian romances: *Erec et Enide, Cligès, Le Chevalier de la charrette, Le Chevalier au lion* and *Le Conte du Graal* (all composed between c.1170 and c.1190). They were later employed as the basis from which the corpus of Arthurian literature expanded all through the Middle Ages and beyond. Nevertheless, rarely do students first think of the equally influential and masterful thirteenth-century *Roman de la Rose* in French or the remarkable *Sir Gawain and Dame Ragnell* in English. The implications of such assumptions have relevance for the approach to Scottish romance taken in this study. In the case of the medieval French romance canon, both the works of Chrétien and the *Roman de la Rose* have received significant scholarly attention. Yet Chrétien's narratives are labelled as *romans courtois* whereas Guillaume de Lorris and Jean de Meun's long poetic narrative is defined as an allegorical romance. In the examples from the English corpus, the prominence of the *Sir Gawain and the Green Knight* romance over *Sir Gawain and Dame Ragnell* is seen in the way in which university syllabuses favour the former in general introductions to medieval English literature. Although the superior aesthetic value of *Sir Gawain and the Green Knight* could be argued, such syllabuses, while surely designed to offer students the best possible introduction to medieval literature and romances, condition their perception and understanding of the genre. Rather ironically, however, in late medieval England, the figure of Gawain was more well-known owing to the so-called popular romances dealing with his prowess than through the courtly Gawain-poet; these embrace Gawain's *proeza* fully, that is, his excellence not only on the battlefield but also in the courtly, feudal and religious realms. Therefore, what is now the most famous and highly praised English romance was hardly regarded as such in its own time.

These two illustrations raise important issues about the reception and perception of medieval romances in the Middle Ages and now. Even when the term romance is used in its most general sense, most students assume – probably because they have been trained to think in such a way – that it refers to what Gaston Paris classed as *roman courtois* in the nineteenth century (Paris 1883: 518–19) rather than any other manifestation of the mode. In Scotland, the situation is different but not better: at universities the historical romances Barbour's *Bruce* and Hary's *Wallace* are the most broadly known and studied, even more so in history than in literature departments, whereas the remaining corpus of Older Scots romances are rarely part of the syllabus. Conversely, medieval Scottish literature modules tend to centre on the great fifteenth- and sixteenth-century makars Robert Henryson, William Dunbar, Gavin Douglas and Sir David Lindsay. Consequently, when students pursue postgraduate studies the great makars and not the romances tend to be favoured. Only during the last few years has there been a growing interest in the Older Scots romances. But they still remain on the periphery of the periphery of medieval literature.

The influence and relevance of Chrétien's Arthurian narratives in the general conceptualisation of romance was critically established even before Erich Auerbach wrote his highly influential *Mimesis: The Representation of Reality in Western Literature* in the mid-twentieth century. Auerbach, however, regarded Chrétien de Troyes' works as the archetypal *roman courtois*. Following Auerbach, scholars identified the shared features of romance in a rather restrictive manner. They concluded that the common elements consist of: a challenge to the hero, the physical journey through a mysterious landscape, the single-handed combat against the arch-villain, who might be related to the supernatural world, a highly idealised beloved lady, and a happy ending. Although such characterisation accords with most early romances in French, it would certainly exclude most Older Scots romances. That is, the definition only works in a particular place at a particular time. Indeed, to include not only the Scottish narratives but also other European texts and traditions such as the early Spanish, the Anglo-Norman or the English, in which, as a general rule, *fin'amors* is not one of the basic features, a much more general selection of shared motifs must be made. The vast majority of romances contain an aristocratic male hero (either a knight or a king unless it is a comic text) and there is an *avanture* involving a challenge to the hero. This is as far as the definition can go if it is to encompass most (not even all) of the medieval romances written in Europe – a definition which does not take us very far. Therefore, having Chrétien as the archetype creates problems since it presupposes that the quality of the other romances should be measured against the Frenchman's texts. This creates difficulties for a broad analysis of the genre insofar as both the intellectual and socio-political contexts as well as the aesthetic values of a romance composed in Champagne in the late twelfth century cannot be judged in the same way as one written, for example, in late fifteenth-century Scotland such as *Eger and Grime*. This would be as artificial a comparison as to examine a novel by Paul Auster according to eighteenth century literary standards or to expect a contemporary film to respond to the artistic precepts and political anxieties of the expressionistic German films mode during the Republic of Weimar.

A definition must be found which justly encompasses the majority of romances but which, at the same time, allows for fundamental differences between them. The obvious divergences between Chrétien's narratives and the Middle Scots *Eger and Grime* or Lindsay's *Squyer Meldrum* (composed in a very different socio-political and cultural milieu) suggests the need for careful and subtle qualifications within a single, overarching definition. The overall designation should be general and, as Gillian Beer suggests and most critics agree, inclusive (Beer 1970: 24). Owing to the difficulty in identifying the genre or mode through clear and easy theoretical assumptions, the most general, inclusive and completely acceptable definition which can be given is that romance is a narrative of a certain length. The problem is that this does not take us very far since exactly the same can be said about *chansons de geste*, novels and films. During recent years there has been a tendency to define romance not on the basis of shared literary motifs but according to its recreational function (Field 1999: 152) or the prospective audience of the texts. Rosalind Field's approach is particularly enlightening since it focuses on the genre's main purpose and contrasts romance with purely didactic texts. At the same time, it includes the action-centred works such as *romans courtois* and the popular and allegorical romances, which are habitually the two poles most difficult to reconcile in a broad classification. This definition on the basis of different audiences is particularly useful in differentiating the French *romans courtois* from Anglo-Norman romances, or within England, the sophisticated romances of the Ricardian period (including *Sir Gawain and the Green Knight*) from the apparently less sophisticated peripheral texts of the same, previous and later periods, known as popular romances; these have been regarded as minor texts because of the negative connotation of the adjective "popular" in contrast to "courtly" and "aristocratic" (Putter and Gilbert eds 2000: 2–3). Only during the last few years have studies such as *The Spirit of Medieval English Popular Romance* reinstated these works' value. Nonetheless, as this book argues, this procedure is less effective in the context of the Scottish romances which are not straightforwardly analogous to the French and English narratives; Scotland's socio-political particularities can be shown to influence the composition of literary romance. For instance, the probable Middle Scots text, *Eger and Grime*, is commonly termed as a popular romance, yet the first record of its existence alludes to its audience, which is not only courtly or aristocratic, but the King of Scots himself, James IV (Dickson and Paul eds 1877: 1: 330).

In his *English Medieval Romance*, W.R.J. Barron reverts to Aristotelian philosophy in order to outline a workable definition of romance not as a *genre* but as a *mode*. Employing Aristotle's *Poetics* to romance, Barron attaches mythic (the hero is superior in kind), romantic (the hero is superior in degree) and mimetic (the hero's actions are liable to the criticism of others) characteristics (Barron 1987: 2). All three modes are present in romances, varying in emphasis on every occasion. Barron points out that the search for an ideal common to most romances has been present from Ancient Greek literature to our present day (Barron 1987: 4). The narrative of medieval romance combines mimetic and symbolic overtones (Barron 1987: 5). These premises allow for a very flexible approach to the numerous manifestations of the romance mode in which elements from saints' *vitae*, epic, comic literature or lyric poetry fluidly intermingle. Barron's approach is particularly good in helping to disentangle the symbiotic nature of medieval literature in which there are extensive correspondences and analogues between genres. In Scotland, owing to the later development and survival of romance, its dialogue not only with other genres but also other traditions is even more palpable.

Like any literary genre, romance is constantly changing, challenging and recreating itself (Gaunt 2000: 46). The transformations of the main characteristics of the broad-spectrum definition should then be studied within more concrete classifications of the genre. The latter should go beyond, but not ignore, the typical differentiations between *roman courtois*, popular romance, allegorical romance, hagiographical romance or historical romance. Each text should be examined in accordance with the appropriate parameters of place and time of composition: its historical, cultural, intellectual, and aesthetic contexts. This book seeks to achieve that goal in relation to a series of Scottish romance texts, many of which remain relatively unknown and are both critically and culturally undervalued. In exploring early Scottish romance through the lens of the relationship between history and changing aesthetic values, it shows the ideological role played by literature and culture in the construction of national identities. In order to help convey the cultural distinctiveness and singularity of Scottish romance and to enable the reader to gain a broad sense of some important comparative contexts, the remainder of this Preface offers a brief account of the French, Anglo-Norman, and Middle English traditions. Although numerous romances such as the Old Occitan *Jaufre* (written between 1160 and 1250 depending on different theories) elude exact dating, some assumptions about their political and aesthetic environments can still be made which enable useful comparison to be made with those other romances written in the same region about the same time as well as to those written elsewhere in Europe. This necessarily involves some "labelling"; and, as with most labelling, it might seem arbitrary and artificial. Yet because the following definitions are based upon late medieval literary paradigms and historical contexts they are more likely to avoid the pitfalls of those definitions based on too wide-ranging approximations of romance.

The French *chanson de geste* and *roman courtois*

For the purpose of this book, the kinds of romances which directly influenced the Scottish corpus are those in French, Anglo-Norman and English. Before examining the development of the *roman courtois* in France, it is necessary to give a brief account of the *chanson de geste*. This is important not only because of its influence on, and interchanges with, the *roman courtois*, but also because it will provide necessary background for the understanding of Scottish conceptions of romance.

Historically, the *chanson de geste* originated in oral tradition and had a large number of *formulae*. For many years, the later emergence of romance presupposed that it was a more literary genre which led to the assumption that the appearance of romances meant an improvement or, as Sarah Kay affirms, "development" (Kay 1995: 2) in literature. This was regarded as a reflection of the changes in the mid-twelfth century which saw the transition from a more bellicose society to those created out of the establishment of royal and aristocratic courts which had a growing interest in culture and courtliness. This is known as the so-called twelfth-century Renaissance. Kay, however, rejects this traditional opposition between the two genres, arguing that it is based on "a generic convention of literary history" which favours the existence of an immature stage of literary culture against which a new, maturer, and apparently "better" culture can be assessed. In this way, the *chansons de geste* become the primitive Other of the sophisticated *roman* (Kay 1995: 3). Ironically, by supporting such a conjecture, some medievalists were creating the very form of alienation and exclusion which medieval studies in general opposed. In the same way as the *chanson* is undervalued by romance, so arguably have the Middle Ages been by later periods. Enlightenment conceptions of historical progress have biased a perception of the Middle Ages as anchored and compressed in the *middle* of nowhere: between the knowledge of the Classical period and the rebirth of the Renaissance; a hiatus in the evolution of western history; a time in which superstition and faith were at the core of society and thinking. Thus, if for more than one hundred years medievalists have demonstrated that the Middle Ages are not so *middle*, Kay is also restating the importance of the *chanson de geste* far beyond the mid-twelfth century.

Manuscript evidence shows that *chansons*, lais, didactic texts, hagiographical stories and *romans courtois* were compiled together from the twelfth up to the early fourteenth century. This reveals the synchronicity of these genres as well as their reciprocating inter-changes (Gaunt 2000: 48; Kay 1995: 4–5). Foreign writers and scholars travelling through France would have had access to *chansons de geste* for a longer period than that strictly confined to the 1150s. Therefore, their influence on literature in other languages can be more largely attested. The English Charlemagne romances demonstrate how writers translated and appropriated the *chansons* into the English ver-naculars, taking the name of romance even if the basic traits of the epic were preserved. As well as this obvious correspondence with English literature, textual evidence suggests that there were other, more subtle ways in which *chansons* impinged on European literary traditions.

Despite the obvious individual divergences between them, *chanson de geste* are easier to categorise as a genre than romance since the vast majority of them share decasyllabic stanzas (*laisses*; either rhyming or based on assonance), and problematise the discordant nature of French history in a way very different from contemporary historiography (Kay 1995: 8). In contrast to the European dimension of romances, the confinement of *chanson* to the French or Anglo-Norman speaking communities – with very few exceptions such as the Old Occitan *Girart de Roussillon* – helps to establish more common motifs in a less vague manner. Most critics agree that male heroes dominate the action and the women appearing are not the highly idealised and venerated ladies typical of the *roman courtois*, but their role is much more politically-centred, expanding from a means to attain power and land to being the instigators of revenge (a recurrent theme in the genre). Heroic battle scenes are frequent and loyalty to a leader or one's own people takes precedence over personal *pretz* (knightly and courtly reputation) or amatory self-realisation. All these epic elements are also characteristic of most Scottish romances, a fact which raises questions about the later influence of *chansons*, and the survival and transformation of the epic.

Around the year 1150, as far as extant evidence is concerned, the literary cultures of the territories which presently constitute France were dominated by the *chanson de geste*, saints' *vitae*, and the poetry of the troubadours (with its different genres ranging from the love lyric *canso* to the political or moral *sirventes* or the debating *tenso*). In this context, romance began to take shape and flourish under the secular patronage of the nobility. The influence of the martial action of the *chanson*, the allegorical framework of the *vitae* and the stylised *fin'amors* and *cortesia* of the troubadours help the formation, development and establishment of the *roman courtois*.

By the mid-twelfth century, political, social and cultural changes had occurred which are associated with the birth of romance. Socially and economically, the growth of cities and the expansion of trade helped the proliferation and strengthening of the middle classes. Centres of government and courts were also expanding and spreading. Culturally, the first universities were being established which facilitated the access of lay people to knowledge. Consequently, literacy was no longer confined to clergymen, administrative workers and a few members of the laity, but was gradually developing among the nobility and middle classes at courts and cities. All these phenomena, commonly known as the twelfth-century Renaissance, created a new and larger audience with different aesthetic tastes. Romance was one of the responses to such cultural innovation.

With the appearance and consolidation of the *roman courtois*, a dialogue is set up between the epic *chanson* and the courtly romance. One genre does not suddenly supplant another but a series of correspondences and mutual exchanges takes place. Kay illustrates this by alluding to the Saxon episode in the early thirteenth-century *Roman de la violette* taken from *Les Saisnes* (c.1200), an epic piece, and to the Arthurian motifs deployed in the *Bataille Loquifer* (c.1200), a *chanson*. Following Fredric Jameson's approach to genre, Kay also asserts that the *chansons* reveal the "political unconscious" of romance, which underplays or veils the social-political conflicts of symbolic order in the epic; the *romans*, in contrast, problematise some of the repressed historical aspects of the *chanson de geste* (Kay 1995: 5–6).

There are a few romances in Old French earlier than those of Chrétien de Troyes. The most well-known are *Floire et Blacheflor*, whose *amor vincit onmia* story encouraged many different versions and translations into most European languages, and the three *romans d'antiques*, *Roman de Thèbes*, *Roman d'Enéas*, and Benoît de Sainte-Maure's *Roman de Troie* written between 1150 and 1165. Chrétien composed his first preserved work, *Erec and Enide*, slightly later, about 1170. Owing to Chrétien's influence in the establishment and development of the genre, it is convenient to start the examination of the *roman courtois* with his Arthurian narratives. The historical and pseudo-historical setting of *chansons de geste* and the preceding *romans d'antiques*, or even of *Floire et Blacheflor*, is replaced by the mythical territories, mysterious forests and unreal kingdoms of King Arthur. Although these places might still be in Britain, they lack the pretended historicity of Geoffrey of Monmouth's *Historia Regum Britanniae*. The allegorical construction of the narrative is made possible through a potentially symbolic location. The more blatant political motivations of the *chansons*, in which the destiny of a collective is at the core of the narrative, are replaced by the individual quest whose politics concern the private arena: the position and aspirations of the knightly class. The figure of the *chevalier errant* is idealised even when it responds to the real conditions of some landless nobles, who perceived martial success as one of the few ways to progress in society. For one of these knights, another way to achieve a more stable financial situation was by marrying a lady, an heiress of sizeable wealth (Knight 1983: 81–82). *Fin'amors* was the transcendental realisation of such longing. Chrétien, who was probably acquainted with the great troubadour Bernart de Ventadorn (Topsfield 1981: 50), adapted the sophistication of *fin'amors*, which, in the absence of a shared political motivation, becomes the moving force for the action (Auerbach 1953: 141). At the same time, however, *fin'amors* concealed the social ambitions of these lesser noblemen. Under the appearance of the perfection of love and *cortesia*, real tropological issues (ethical, political, or moral) of relevance to the audience were scrutinised. If, in the epic, the masculine aspects of knighthood are emphasised in its heroes, the *roman courtois* creates the need for an equilibrium between masculine and feminine attributes. Similarly, the divergences between dual opposites, such as *sofrirs* (humility) and *orguel* (pride), or between *mesura* (courtly and knightly moderation as governed by reason) and *foudatz* (foolhardiness and submission to human appetites), are assessed in order to create the ideal attitude and conduct of the perfect knight in each situation, whether at court or on the battlefield. The interaction of the different virtues is also necessary: *proeza*, for instance, must be counterbalanced with *mesura*, otherwise it can lead to *foudatz* and defeat when in conflict.

Stylistically, as in most verse romances of the period, the octo-syllabic couplet replaces the epic decasyllabic *laisses*. The inclusion of *fin'amors* and *cortesia* also brings about the selection of particular linguistic expressions. The martial-centred and formulaic language of the *chansons* gives way to the courtly expressiveness of the trouba-dour lyric within which the psychological intricacies of *fin'amors* can be debated. The narrative is designed through episodes which lead to a climax. In less stylish romances than those of Chrétien, however, the episodic division is just cumulative, and the sense of progression becomes rather blurry. Romances are also self-referential and inter-textual in relation to other romances and other genres. Such interplay enriches meaning, adds new interpretations, or is deployed to ironic effect. A good illustration is found in the parallel structure of Chrétien's *Cligès* to the Tristan story, which allows Chrétien to con-demn and comment on Tristan and Iseut's illicit love at the same time as he celebrates the marital love of his story. *Entrelacement*, or the interlacing of different stories in the same text, is a recurrent technique of the mode. The *conjointure*, or the organised arrangement of all these distinct elements and techniques, elucidates the *sen* [meaning] of the romance.

Chrétien's late twelfth-century *Chevalier de la Charrette* and *Conte du Graal* are not just excellent examples of the sophistication of early *romans* but are also the two pillars supporting the later prose cycles of the Matter of Britain; that is, the romances dealing with Arthur and his court. *Lancelot* synthesises and merges elements from hagiography, epic poetry and troubadour lyrics. The combination of such different literary modes allows for multiple, and sometimes contradictory, meanings. Lancelot and Guenevere appear to incarnate the perfect *fins amants* to the extent that, as Kay asserts, their love is regarded as the monolithic and codified approach to the medieval conception of *fin'amors*, when there are many other manifestations of it (Kay 2000: 81). Even so, Chrétien's subtle narrative permits the reader to interpret the sublimation of love in discordant ways. The Christological features attributed to Lancelot can either be regarded as the ultimate mystical experience of the *fins amants* or as a demoni-sation of a pseudo-heretical feeling which aspires to rival *caritas*. Moreover, the ironic intertextual reference to the *Fause Morte* of Tristan and Iseut questions how seriously *fin'amors* should be taken. The ending of the *Chevalier de la Charrette* is problematic and rather open. In terms of authorship, Chrétien is reputed not to have finished his work but to have passed it on to a certain Godefroi de Leigni. One critical tradition maintains that Chrétien refused to conclude the *roman* owing to his dislike of a story about extramarital love, a view which would be supported by his previous *Cligès*. At any rate, there seems to be an intended problematisation of the idea of authorship and attribution of a work of art, maybe alluding to the multi-authorial nature of the *chansons de geste*. Even the name/pseudonym of Chrétien de Troyes (Christian of Troy?) urges us to question issues of medieval authorship (Kay 2000: 87). Its relatively open ending allows the same fundamental plot devices to be employed in future romances. The very nature of romance composition is therefore challenging and polysemic both for author and audience.

The *Conte de Graal* also gives rise to other interpretative problems. The *entrelacement* of the adventures of Perceval and of Gawain has opened a debate as to whether Chrétien was writing one work or two separate romances with intertextual allusions, as he had already done with the *Chevalier au Lion* and *Lancelot* (Riquer ed. 1990: 23–24). Traditionally, it is believed that Chrétien died while writing the *Conte*, leaving the story of the Holy Grail and the Fisher King unfinished. Whether it is true that he passed away or simply that he did not complete the romance (or romances) for another reason, both the narrative and its figurative possibilities rapidly inspired numerous continuations of the story. The first of them was the basis for the Middle Scots *Golagros and Gawane* more than two hundred years after the composition of the original continuation. Yet the flexibility of the romance form can be seen in the fact that the Middle Scots romance relocates the narrative in a completely different interpretative context, one in which its relevance to late medieval Scottish political anxieties is underlined.

In the early thirteenth century, the first romances in prose appeared. Verse romances did not, however, disappear as a consequence. In Scotland, for example, *Lancelot of the Laik* adapted the *Prose Lancelot* in verse. Indeed, all the surviving Older Scots romances are written in verse. R.D.S. Jack suggests that the makars preferred verse to prose because of its artificiality which forced them to develop their rhetorical skills further (Jack and Rozendaal ed. 1997: xvii–xviii). Rather, as Lacy suggests, specialisation occurred: works in verse, as well as being obviously briefer, tended to be episodic and to relate the adventures of one or two knights during a limited period of time. Prose romances, on the other hand, are normally much longer, concentrating on a long period of time, which often encompasses generations or, in the case of cycles, a *historia universalis*. Although the written word in prose is often associated with private reading, prose romances were also intended to be recited in front of audiences. Lacy suggests that the adoption of prose was due to the developing idea that non-rhymed writing was closer to truth that the necessary artificiality of verse (Lacy 2000: 167–68). The use of prose helped to extend the length of romances. Many different story-lines could be developed at the same time. The technique of *entrelacement* allowed narrative plots to be left in suspense: to be returned to many pages later, thereby enhancing and augmenting the expectations of the audience.

Many of the French prose romances of the thirteenth century deal with the Matter of Britain, elaborating on original material from Chrétien's *Chevalier de la Charrette* and *Conte du Graal*. The first of these prose texts, *Perlesvaus*, based on the *Conte*, already bestows an overtly Christian value on the story of the grail, far beyond the different suggestions and interpretations of Chrétien. With the cycle of the *Lancelot en prose*, the Arthurian legend acquires the dimension of a *historia universalis*. Through the first three romances of the cycle, the *Lancelot propre*, *La Queste del Saint Graal* and *La Mort le Roi Artu*, the narrative shifts from the courtly tone of the *Lancelot* to the profoundly spiritual and religious Cistercian-influenced ideology of the *Queste*, which questions the superficiality of the courtly world through the *fin'amors* of Lancelot and Guenevere, and moves towards the pessimism of the Arthurian dream's final destruction in the *Mort*.

Anglo-Norman Romance

The different historical and social contexts of Anglo-Norman England conditioned the development of romances. After the Conquest, the Norman kings simply extended the same form of feudal system into England that they maintained in their lands and possessions in the Continent; yet when Henry II assumed the throne in 1154, the Angevin dynasty supplanted the Norman one. Under the new rule, England was progressively differentiated and isolated from continental France. From the twelfth century, the baronial class became an

idiosyncratic group in England. Susan Crane gives two main reasons
for this: firstly, the barons' status was intimately connected with their
control over land; secondly, their financial and social status worsened
between 1066 and 1400, a fact which "altered their cultural engage-
ment with literature" (Crane 1986: 6–7).

In this context, although the influence of *roman courtois*,
chansons de geste and hagiography is manifest, most of the romance
literature produced in Anglo-Norman England has a particular flavour
to suit the interests of the baronial class. As a consequence of this
transplantation, Field remarks that the subject matter of the Anglo-
Norman texts favours the martial-centred and shows the more
politically overt impact and prolonged life of the *chansons* than in
their French counterparts (Field 1999: 154). Even romances in which
the theme of *fin'amors* is central or thoroughly elaborated, such as
Thomas's *Tristan* or *Ipomedon*, differ considerably from similar ones
written in France. The insular treatment of *cortesia* diverges from the
social refinement of Old French romances to reconsider its value as a
source of heroic feats of arms (Crane 1986: 221). Mostly, however, as
in the Scottish romances, the love motif is displaced and its central
role in the development of the narrative is replaced by more urgent
political issues – in the case of Anglo-Norman England, those affecting the baronial audience. There is no room for the idealisation of
fin'amors and *cortesia* but the most realistic setting of contemporary
political, social and religious tensions is essential to the narrative. The
thematic and structural composition of Anglo-Norman texts profoundly influenced the later development of the English romances up
to the end of the Middle Ages.

Middle English Romance

Most romances written in Anglo-Norman, such as Thomas's *Roman
de Horn* (c.1170) or the *Lai of Havelok* (c.1200), were subsequently
translated or adapted into Middle English. Although the first language
of the barons was progressively shifting from Anglo-Norman to
English, through the re-elaboration of these romances, it becomes
evident that their ambitions remain essentially the same. A good
example of this is *Havelok the Dane* which suggests that the authority
of the King should lie in the consent of the barons so that it does not

deteriorate into tyranny (Barron 1987: 71). As in the vast majority of Older Scots romances, politics play a central role in the texts.

By the close of the fourteenth century in Ricardian England, authors such as Chaucer and the Gawain-Pearl-poet gave a new and more rhetorically sophisticated inflexion to English romance. *Sir Gawain and the Green Knight* displays a refined approximation to chivalry and *cortesia* almost impossible to find in any other English Arthurian verse romance. The author's *entrelacement* of the main three plots, the beheading, the temptation and the interchange of winnings, reveals both his familiarity with the *roman courtois* tradition and his complete mastery in dealing with archetypal themes of the mode. As in many French romances, there is a subtle underlying critique, questioning the validity of the knightly code. Any sort of *amors*, on the other hand, is merely hinted at through the temptation scenes, which could be catalogued in Andreas Capellanus's terminology as *amor mixtus*: purely sexual desire, rather than *fin'amors*. Only the resistance of Gawain to Lady Bertilak's advances saves his head from being cut off. Chaucer's equally elegant "Knight's Tale", as well as exhibiting the sophisticated knowledge of the norms of *cortesia* and chivalric behaviour, does deal with love, adapting and reworking Boccaccio's *Teseida*. Chaucer's acquaintance not only with Boccaccio but also with Machaut's love poetry allowed him to elaborate on the vicissitudes of the imprisoned lovers. Like Petrarch in Italy, Machaut in France had transformed the troubadours' *canso*.

Together with the *Roman de la Rose*, Derek Pearsall suggests that the love poetry of Machaut (c.1300–77), which so influenced troubadour love lyric poetry in France, causes Arthurian romances to become unfashionable. Consequently, when they were adapted into English, the love plot was rendered as archaic and superseded. *Ywain and Gawain* is a very good illustration of this (Pearsall 2003: 62). The particular character of the romances written in England is determined not only by the socio-political reasons mentioned earlier but by aesthetic choices. After the Ricardian period, the English authors of romances did not follow in the steps of Chaucer and the Gawain-poet but reverted to the earlier models. Those narratives were predominantly popular among provincial audiences, and are generally labelled as popular romances in contrast to the sophisticated courtly texts of Gower, the Gawain-poet, Chaucer or Malory. As discussed in the opening to this preface, their designation as "popular" led to their critical neglect, though recent studies have reassessed the richness and literary value of the so-called popular romances. An excellent illustration of the coexistence of different romance traditions in late medieval England is the alliterative *Morte Arthure* and the stanzaic *Morte Arthur*, both written about 1400. Both narratives concentrate on the decadence of the Arthurian court and the death of King Arthur, but their approach is completely different. The alliterative poem responds to the native English and Anglo-Norman tradition: as well as being alliterative, it is centred on martial and heroic action. As in the *chansons de geste*, female roles are confined to givers of power through lineage. The love affair between Guenevere and Lancelot is not exploited at all. By way of contrast, the stanzaic romance is heavily influence by the French tradition. As in the *Lancelot en prose*, the downfall of the Arthurian dream is instigated by the extramarital love of Lancelot and Guenevere which is central to the development of the action. With the exception of the text *Clariodus* and some passages in the Alexander Romances, the elegant courtliness of the stanzaic *Morte* did not take root in the Scottish tradition owing, as I will argue, to the idiosyncratic and singular development of romance in Scotland, the subject of the rest of this book.

Introduction

Late Medieval Scotland and the Romance Tradition

The period after the Wars of Independence in Scotland was mainly presided over by the Stewart Kings. Although during Robert I's reign the English recognised Scotland as an autonomous country by the Treaty of Northampton (1328), the Anglo-Scottish conflicts lasted all through the late Middle Ages. Both Robert I and his son David II faced the renewal of war instigated not only by the English but also by the Balliols and their followers. After their deaths, the mode of action of the first Stewarts, Robert II and Robert III, was closer to that of a ruthless noble family trying to accumulate as many lands and as much power as possible, than to the image of medieval kingship. James I was assassinated by members of his own household (1437) and his son, James II, endured the rebellion of the powerful and influential Douglases in the 1450s (Lynch 1997: 133–34).

Political agitation may appear as an impediment to either economic or cultural development. This was not always the case. Generally, the nobility and the royal house tended to work together despite the tensions that such a partnership created. James I is regarded as the monarch who established the groundings of royal authority which his successors were going to follow (Lynch 1997: 134–35). Within this political panorama, although the court was comparatively smaller than those of England and France, the country developed economically. Geographical remoteness from continental Europe did not result in underdeveloped and restricted financial status either. There was increasing trade between Scotland and France, the traditional ally, and the Low Countries and other nations along the coasts of the Baltic and Northern Seas (Bawcutt 1976: 23).

Before the building of the University of Saint Andrews, Scottish scholars went to Oxford, Cambridge or prestigious continental centres such as Paris, Padua or Bologna. Even after that, they continued to attend foreign universities such as Cologne or Louvain to complete their studies. Hence, Scottish men of letters had the opportunity of being acquainted with an enormous range of philosophical and literary schools all over Europe. This "highly developed sense of scholarship was both self-consciously patriotic and northern European" (Lynch 1993: 19).

The scanty surviving evidence indicates that romances, presumably in Scots, were recited in the Scottish court before the fourteenth century. Out of the ten parts of the fullest version of the Old Norse *Karlamagnús saga*, part II *Olif and Landres* was translated from a romance recited in Scotland. In the Prologue, the author claims that: "Lord Bjarni Erlingsson of Bjarkey found this saga written and told in the English language, in Scotland, when he stayed there during the winter after the death of King Alexander" (I: 178). As with any other centre of power in late medieval Europe, in Scotland there existed the promotion of cultural activities; either written, oral or theatrical, a long time before Barbour composed *The Bruce* (c.1375), the first romance, and clearly literary text, preserved in Scots. In their edition of *The Bruce*, McDiarmid and Stevenson, as well as referring to the Charlemagne romance, translated in the *Karlamagnús saga* which an envoy of the Maid of Norway acquired in 1286, also allude to the existence of a Tristram and Iseult romance by Thomas Rimour (c.1300), which is now lost (McDiarmid and Stevenson ed. 198–85: III: 14). Barbour, as a cultivated man of letters, may have been familiar with both of these and with other works from which no evidence has survived. Therefore, it can be regarded as an accident that no other poem or romance has been preserved in Scots, which was the language of the Scottish court much earlier than the late fourteenth century. In the late twelfth or early thirteenth century, Guillaume le Clerc wrote the Anglo-Norman *Roman de Fergus*, a comic Arthurian romance. Although there are no surviving manuscripts of this romance in Scotland, textual evidence suggests that Guillaume knew the country quite well (Owen ed. 1991: 162–69).

The emergence of Scots as the language of politics and of literature in the late medieval period was a consequence of the gradual establishment and centralisation of power of the royal house. When Robert II commissioned Barbour to write *The Bruce*, notwithstanding the existence of previous Scots compositions, the makar created the literary basis for a new vernacular tradition after the Wars of Independence. As he was writing shortly after those wars, when Scottish nationalism was growing, he realised the need to establish a new and distinctive literary identity. When measured against other European literary traditions in the vernacular, *The Bruce* is a rather late text. Its relatively late date of composition allows *The Bruce* to be a very eclectic romance, borrowing elements not only from previous French, Anglo-Norman, and English romances but also from epic literature both classical and French, chronicles and saints' *vitae*. *The Bruce*, then, is a romance in the broadest, most inclusive sense of the word.

In using Early Scots, originating from the Old English spoken in Northumbria and Southern Scotland, he deploys some elements of English literature such as alliterative verse, especially in set phrases like "wycht and wys" (I. 22). From romance, first of all the makar borrows the name: "Lordingis quha likis for till her, / Ye romanys now begynnys her" (I. 445–46). After the historical and political contextualisation, by "romanys" Barbour probably means a heroic narrative, without further connotations with regard to genre. He also deploys the octosyllabic couplet, the form of expression typical of the French verse *romans courtois*. Thus he associates *The Bruce* with the prestigious French tradition. As well as the makar's knowledge of fourteenth-century French romances, there are traces of his familiarity with *Le Roman d'Alixandre* in Bruce's pre-battle speeches (McDiarmid and Stevenson ed. 1981–85: I: n44). As for Anglo-Norman, Legge points out that the version of the romance of *Fierabras* recited by Barbour, when Bruce and his men are crossing Loch Lomond, corresponds to the Anglo-Norman text (Legge 1969: 9–10). From chronicles, Barbour makes use of the historical setting and evidence, sometimes being even more realistic than some chronicles by dismissing the supernatural – a feature that most future Middle Scots romances will emulate. From epic literature, the makar takes the martial, masculine and male-centred narrative, in which the virtue of loyalty is valued over any other. The end of *The Bruce* also deploys topoi of saints' legends when the King of Scots is preparing for death. Another conventional element of the mode present in the Scottish work is the hero's progression from youth to maturity. Nonetheless, as in most Anglo-Norman and English romances, *The Bruce* places *fin'amors*, the courtly world and, consequently, women, in the background. The focus on the martial and the political did not allow the language and the manners of *cortesia* to develop fully. Barbour also had access to a large amount of book resources in Scotland itself. As Legge remarks, Sir Thomas Gray of Heton started his *Scalachronica* while in prison at Edinburgh Castle, which demonstrates that either there was an important library in the castle, or books were easy to obtain by anyone dwelling there, including noble prisoners (Legge 1969: 9–10). Therefore, even if one discounts the time he spent in France, Barbour could make use of texts in Scots, French, Latin, Anglo-Norman and English in Scotland.

The fifteenth century witnessed the composition of the majority of existing medieval Scottish romances. The patronage of literature fluctuated: under the reigns of James I (1406–37) and James IV (1488–1513) there is evidence that the royal house promoted the arts, whereas in the times of James II (1437–60) and James III (1460–88), most of the literary production took place outside the court and was therefore devoid of the king's influence (Mapstone 1991: 416–19). Royal and noble patronage also encouraged the erection of churches, which are still preserved, in places such as Stirling or Perth, whereas the burghs promoted drama in places such as Linlithgow, Perth and Lanark (MacQueen 1977: 198; Lyall 1989: 34). In the North, the preservation of stone carving in the Western Isles suggests the existence of artistic vitality at the northern courts, whilst the contemporary Gaelic poems (c.1310–1500) come mainly from Perthshire and Argyllshire (Thomson 1993: 130).

James I enjoyed the company of artists, writers and craftsmen at his court. One of his favourites, Robert Cochrane, designed the Great Hall of Stirling Castle (MacQueen 1967: 206). James I, being the most probable author of the *Kingis Quair*, introduced in Scotland a kind of literature very different from that of Barbour. His eighteen-year imprisonment in England permitted him to familiarise himself with both Chaucer and English post-Chaucerian and European writers (MacQueen 1977: 187). The *Quair* evinces these influences. He could be considered as the establisher of a courtly tradition in Scotland, which later makars such as William Dunbar, Walter Kennedy, Robert Henryson in his *Testament of Cresseid* or Gavin Douglas would follow. Considering their minorities, James II and James III were more preoccupied with re-establishing royal authority than with the promotion of the arts. At the same time, however, cultural life at court was very rich, but not necessarily sponsored by the sovereign. Instead, great magnates such as the Sinclairs promoted the arts through the patronage of writers and the acquisition of books for their libraries (Mapstone 1991: 414–15). With James IV, the court recovered its pivotal position as the centre of Scottish cultural life. He promoted the arts and especially literature, William Dunbar being the most representative figure of this cultural flourishing at the royal court.

During the reigns of the Stewart kings, the ambivalent attitude towards Arthur may have contributed to the popularity of Alexander Romances in Scotland. Carol Edington suggests that the Greek origin of the mythological founder of Scotland, Gaythelos, may have galvanised the fame of the Alexander legend in Scotland (Edington 1998: 71). In a period of less than thirty years, two Alexander romances were produced in Scotland, the anonymous *Buik of Alexander* (c.1438) and Gilbert Hay's *Buik of King Alexander the Conquerour*, commissioned by Lord Erskine and probably written about 1460, shortly after his chivalric and political treatises (Cartwright 1986: 229).

The *Buik of Alexander* is a translation of two episodes habitually included in the late twelfth-century Old French *Roman d'Alexandre*, the *Fuerres de Gadres* and Jean de Longuyon's *Voeux du Paon* (1312). The Middle Scots romance has survived in just one copy printed in Edinburgh around 1580 by Alexander Arbuthnet. John MacQueen suggests that James I might have been the patron of the translation under the auspices of a literary programme that was interrupted by his murder in 1437 (MacQueen 1977: 193). The contrast between the two translated episodes, the *Forray* being eminently epic and the *Awovis* being overtly courtly, enhances the deployment of different rhetorical and narrative strategies. The *Avowis* deals with courtliness and *fin'amors* more profusely than most Scottish romances, whereas the *Forray*'s agile, bellicose narrative complies to Scottish romance practices more closely. Its nowadays disregarded attribution to John Barbour in the edition by R. Graeme Richie for the Scottish Text Society (1921–29) demonstrates the extent to which the Archdeacon influenced the anonymous makar in the composition of the *Buik*. In more recent times, Matthew P. McDiarmid has attributed the authorship of the *Buik* to Gilbert Hay, proposing that the actual *Buik of King Alexander the Conquerour* is a c.1500 summary in metre from the original octosyllabic couplets of the *Buik*, which would have survived just partially (McDiarmid 1993: 45). However ingenious McDiarmid's suggestion might be, it is not easy to sustain. While he might have a point with the transformation from octosyllabic couplets into metre, its attribution to Hay does not completely work (see McDiarmid 1993: 37, where he convincingly argues that the pentameters used in the Conquerour were not yet in vogue during Hay's lifetime). The *Buik* as it is preserved operates as a self-contained romance with a meaning of its own. Its author does connect both episodes by replacing the "duc Melchis" (*Voeux*, 1) of the original by "duke Betys" of the *Forray* to give unity to both texts. Moreover, in his prose treatises, Hay acknowledges his patron. If the *Buik*, which has been preserved in its entirety, had been written by Hay, the name of Lord Erskine should have appeared.

Textual evidence suggests that Lord Erskine, whom Joanna Martin identifies with Thomas, second Lord Erskine (Martin 2006: 86 and 2008: 76), commissioned Gilbert Hay to write the *Buik of King Alexander the Conquerour*.[1] Even if we agree that the two c.1500 preserved manuscripts of Gilbert Hay's *Conquerour* (British Museum, Additional MS 40,732 and Scottish Register House, MS GD 112/71/9) were based on an original written in octosyllabic couplets, the existing text would most probably be a rephrasing, rather than a profound alteration of the original. There is no reason to believe that the copier attempted to modify the whole work of an established author apart from the stylistic adaptation to c.1500 tastes. The *Conquerour* is similar, as far as the concatenation of adventures is concerned, to the cumulative prose romances of fifteenth-century France. Even if Hay's purpose is didactic rather than celebratory, he would certainly have been familiar with the abovementioned French works during his more than twenty years of living in France. Hay, however, does not seem to have written the somewhat mysterious "excusatioun" at the end of the poem, which prompts more questions than it actually answers:

All this that followis is bot the excusatioun
Of him that maid the first translatioun,
Bot in this buike sone eftir ʒe sall sie
Quha causit this buike agane to wreittin be,
Quhair and be quhome, quhat tyme it wreittin was,
In termis schort to ʒow I sall rehears –
I will wreit furth befoir me as I find,
His excusatioun I will not laife behind:
Translaittit it was forsuith, as I hard say,
At the instance off Lord Erskein, be Schir Gilbert þe Hay,
[…]

---

[1] I shall adopt the same convention as McDiarmid by referring to Hay's *Buik of King Alexander the Conquerour* as the *Conquerour* to avoid confusion with the *Buik of Alexander*, which I shall refer to as the *Buik*.

That þis great storie wreit as he [Hay] vndirstuide –
Richt sua he wreit with his awin proper hand,
Was neuir befoir translaittit in this land. (ll.19,311–20; 19,331–33)

At first the conclusion to the poem could even be seen as a literary game in which Hay alludes to himself in the third person. Nonetheless, it soon becomes clear that another person, the scribe, re-writer or new *translator*, must have written this. Even as a formulaic phrase, "As I hard say" would have been a rather unflattering manner to allude to one's patron. Similarly, Hay is reported to have written a first translation (l.19,312), a different text from this version, which someone else, who is never explicitly named, seems to have commissioned (l.19,314). Owing to the problematic authorship of the *Conquerour*, Joanna Martin prefers to talk about this version of the poem as anonymous (Martin 2006: 77). What is clear from these lines is that whoever wrote the "excusatioun" was unaware of the existence of the earlier *Buik of Alexander* (l.19,333), which by 1550 might have been replaced in popularity by Hay's *Conquerour*.

Barbour's *Bruce* is often placed alongside Blind Hary's *Wallace* (1476–78). Owing to Barbour's and Hary's fictional constructions of the Wars of Independence, comparison between them has been unavoidable. Moreover, textual borrowing from Barbour and his thematic influences on Hary are widely acknowledged (Duncan ed. 1997: 32; McDiarmid ed. 1968: I.xxxvii; Wilson 1990: 190). Ideologically, however, the two makars start from contrasting premises. While they are both nationalistic, Barbour envisages a pro-royal Brucean and Stewart perspective, unlike Hary who embraces a critical position towards the royal house. The latter proudly affirms that he has received no money for the writing of *The Wallace* (XII. 1433–35), creating the image of an independent Scot who stands for the interests of the nation. Although there is no reason to believe that he was lying, he was quite possibly far from being an independent thinker. According to McDiarmid, he may have had sympathies with powerful border magnates such Alexander, Duke of Albany, James III's alienated brother or Archibald Douglas, Earl of Angus. The border lords did not like James's approach to England through matrimonial policies. One of Hary's consultants was indeed James Liddale, who was the Albany's steward (McDiarmid 1968–69: I. xix–xx; Lyall 1976: 17). Later in life, however, the evidence of two payments to Hary in 1490 and 1492 suggests that he probably recited the poem for

James IV at the royal court (MacQueen 1977: 195; McKim ed. 2003: viii). *The Wallace* is preserved in a 1488 manuscript (MS Advocates 19.2.2) written by John Ramsay which enjoyed great popularity for centuries. As well as being one of the first texts printed by Chepman and Myllar, it was partially reprinted after the Reformation by Robert Lekpreuik in 1570, and adapted and translated to post-Reformation and eighteenth-century tastes by William Hamılton of Gilbertfield in 1722.

Arthurian romances can be found in almost any medieval European language. In Scotland, the attitude towards King Arthur was ambivalent. In the chronicles, Andrew of Wyntoun's *Orygynale Cronykil of Scotland* (late fourteenth century) follows the established English tradition in which Modred betrays his uncle Arthur: "And off tresowne till hyme [Arthur] done / Be Modred hys systyr sone" (V, xii, 4359–60). Conversely, John Fordun, Walter Bower (following Fordun) and Hector Boece regard Arthur as a usurper of power, viewing Modred in a more favourable light. Bower's *Scotichronicon*, for instance, explains that

Arthur succeeded to the kingdom through the machinations of certain individuals. The kingship was not strictly his by right since he had been born out the wedlock, the son of Ygerna wife of Gorlois duke of Cornwall in the castle of Tintagel by the unheard art of the prophet Merlin, [...] whereas the kingdom should rather had gone to Aurelius's sister Anna or her children. For she was born of the lawful wedlock and had married the Scottish earl Loth lord of Lothian and king of Norway, who was descended from the noble line of Duke Fulgentius. By her he had two sons the noble Gawain and the elder Modred. (III, xxiv)

The anti-Arthurian myth responds to what Claude Lévi-Strauss describes as the need for cultural differentiation: "In order for a culture to be really itself and to produce something, the culture and its members must be convinced of their originality and even to some extent, of their superiority over the others" (Lévi-Strauss 1978: 20). It makes sense, therefore, that broadly at the same time that Fordun was promoting the distinct origins of Scotland through Gaythelos, Scota and the Arthurian myths, Barbour was establishing the basis of a distinct literary tradition in the vernacular, too.

Politically, however, the Stewart monarchs envisaged the possibility of appropriating the Arthurian legend. According to Steve Boardman, the Stewarts saw themselves as the restorers of the "British" Arthurian dynasty. Robert II, for instance, could imagine himself as the lawful heir of the legacy of the Britons as much as any English sovereign (Boardman 2002: 55; 60). Thus ideologically, there was a contrary double attitude towards Arthur: one of rejection of the myth through which the English could claim overlordship over Scotland: for instance, "Edward I of England, in a letter to the Pope, argued that Arthur, King of Britons, has held the Scots in subjection" (Alexander 1975: 19); whereas many late medieval Scottish chronicles refuted Arthur's claims over Britain as a whole. The other attitude was the appropriation of Arthur, through which the Stewarts could promote an image in which they were the rightful claimants to a "British" throne.

In literature, the approach is also ambivalent. On the one hand, the makars praise Arthur as one of the Nine Worthies, a literary hero devoid of political implications. On the other, however, when the character is fully developed beyond mere heroic similes, the unavoidable Anglo-Scottish conflicts of the late Middle Ages erupt. This is the case of the two surviving Middle Scots Arthurian romances, *Lancelot of the Laik* and *Golagros and Gawane*, reworkings of the Old French *Prose Lancelot* and *The First Continuation of Perceval* respectively. In the Middle Scots texts, in a context where Scottish reference is present, Arthur's expansionistic ambitions are questioned.

Both Arthurian romances are anonymous and very difficult to date. *Lancelot of the Laik* has conventionally been dated from 1470s by trying to connect Arthur's pernicious government with James III's rule. Nevertheless, textual evident is not conclusive (Mapstone 1991: 412). From a stylistic perspective, W.W. Skeat and Margaret Gray in their editions of the poem try to establish that whoever wrote *Lancelot of the Laik* may have been the author of *The Quare of Jelusy* and also that there are parallels between the romance and the poetry of William Dunbar and Gavin Douglas, which will place the poem after 1488 (Lyall 1976: 13). So far, then, the only possibility would be to place *Lancelot of the Laik* broadly in the last quarter of the fifteenth century.

Owing to the unknown circulation of the poem, issues of the production and audience for the Middle Scots *Lancelot* have also caused some controversy. John MacQueen argues that, because of the courtly atmosphere of the romance, whose supposed core is the love affair between Lancelot and Guenevere, it was probably composed for the queen or any other lady at court (MacQueen 1977: 193). Yet other scholars such as Sally Mapstone suggest that other legalistic and moral material of the only preserved manuscript in which the romance appears (CUL Kk.I.5) shows that *Lancelot of the Laik* was visualised as a piece of moral teaching from an early stage (Mapstone 1986: 153–54). Following a similar line of argument, Joanna Martin proposes that, as with other contemporary works such as Hay's prose manuscript and Hary's *Wallace*, the Middle Scots *Lancelot* may have been commissioned by a member of an aristocratic household or by a member of the lesser nobility (Martin 2002: 170). Although no conclusive evidence exists, the poem's highly politicised subject matter would have, in all probability, been of interest to the great Scottish magnates involved with the governing of the country or with the king himself. The romance, even if not commissioned by the royal house, could have easily found its way into the palace. MacQueen's suggestion should not been completely disregarded, either. The Prologue and most probably the lost ending, in which Lancelot and Guenevere interact and kiss for the first time, would have attracted an audience with a taste for courtly sophistication and *fin'amors*. A wide audience would have reacted to the romance in different ways: whereas the king and great magnates may have been attracted to the politicisation of Lancelot and the debates on kingship, other members of royal or aristocratic households may have preferred to concentrate their attention on the love story between Lancelot and Guenevere.

Like *Lancelot of the Laik*, *Golagros and Gawane* transformed the French source, *The First Continuation of Perceval*, to its own advantage, changing the narrative focus and *sen*. All attempts to give a definite date of composition must be approached with caution. The only surviving copy is Chepman and Myllar's 1508 printed edition, which does not offer much evidence with regards to the time the romance was written. The only certainty is that *Golagros and Gawane* was composed some time between the early fifteenth century and 1508 (Purdie 2005: 95). As well as being published by Chepman and Myllar, it is one of the missing texts of the Asloan manuscript (NLS 16,500). That the romance was compiled first in a manuscript and then for printing production indicates its popularity in the late Middle Ages.

Its authorship also remains a mystery. William Dunbar was the first person to give an author for the texts in his "Timor Mortis Conturbat Me" (also known as the "Lament for the Makaris"): "Clerk of Tranent eik he has tane / That maid the anteris of Gawane" (stanza

10. 1–2). If we assume that the *The Anteris of Gawane* is in fact *Golagros and Gawane*, a certain Clerk of Tranent would be its writer. Presumably, being a younger contemporary of the author of *Golagros and Gawane*, Dunbar's attribution should be taken seriously. The problem is that nothing else is known about (the) Clerk of Tranent – the name itself being elusive. "Clerk" could either be his real name or just a way to refer to him as, for instance, Barbour is sometimes referred as the archdeacon of Aberdeen. Because of thematic and textual parallelisms with *The Wallace* and *Rauf Coilyear*, McDiarmid regards Blind Hary as the author of all three romances (McDiarmid 1991: 329–33). Nevertheless, such intertextuality suggests the existence of a common literary tradition and influences between the texts, much more than common authorship.

Probably written in the second half of the fifteenth century, *Rauf Coilyear* is the only preserved romance in medieval Scotland dealing with the Matter of France (apart from John Stewart of Baldynneis's *Roland Furious* (1583–84), also written in Older Scots, which nevertheless belongs to a different literary tradition from that of the medieval romances). As opposed to most English Charlemagne romances, which have a French source, *Rauf Coilyear* is originally Scottish, even if the author must have been familiar with the king-in-disguise folkloric motif and the story of the converted Saracen (Walsh 1979: 17). Therefore, the author did not have any of the constraints an existing source may have implied. The anonymous author employs the same complicated thirteen-line stanza as in *Golagros and Gawane*, which could indicate a similar date of composition. To be able to make use of such a demanding literary form and still keep the pace of the narrative shows the makar's poetical dexterity. He may either have been a professional writer (that is, someone who was paid for his writings even if that was not his only or main professional activity) or someone with a university education. The text only survived in a rather late 1572 printed edition by Robert Lekpreuik, but it is, together with *Golagros and Gawane*, one of the missing texts of the Asloan manuscript. MacQueen suggests that, like Henryson's *Morall Fabillis*, *Rauf Coilyear*, together with other works such as *The Three Priests of Peebles*, *The Talis of the Fyve Bestis* and *The Freiris of Berwick* may have been intended for the growing non-courtly audience of the fifteenth-century (MacQueen 1977: 199). Although MacQueen's claim makes perfect sense, these texts may not exclusively be written for the non-courtly public. The Scottish courtly poet par excellence, William Dunbar, indiscriminately created highly sophisticated poetry such "Ane Ballat of Our Lady" and comic tales such as the *Tretis of the Twa Mariit Wemen and the Wedo*, and even the short comic romance *Schir Thomas Norny*. Therefore, *Rauf Coilyear* could have pleased not only professional but also courtly audiences.

In Scotland, the first half of the sixteenth century is dominated by three major happenings in the political, cultural and social spheres: the disastrous Battle of Flodden (1513), the consolidation of humanism, and the Reformation. Just before Flodden, Gavin Douglas completed *Eneados*, his monumental translation of Virgil's *Aeneid* from the original Latin into Middle Scots – a masterpiece confirming the maturity of Older Scots as a language of literary prestige, able to compete with any other vernacular. John Bellenden's translation of the first five books of Livy's *Roman History*, the Latin histories of John Major and Hector Boece and the Neo-Latin texts and translations of George Buchanan, even if most of them were completed in France, also contributed to secure a typically Scottish humanism. The aftermath of Flodden coincided with the emergence of Protestantism in Europe. Works such as *Ane Satyre of the Thrie Estaitis* and *The Dreme* by Sir David Lindsay expose the corruption of the Church and a need for its reformation, even if, in the case of Lindsay, reformation must come from within.

Sir David Lindsay's (1486–1555) only romance, the *Historie of Squyer Meldrum*, deals with the historical figure of William Meldrum, whom he knew personally. Although the earliest existing copy was published in 1594 by Henry Charteris, a printer and bookseller from Edinburgh, it was composed towards the end of the poet's life between 1550 and 1555, not long after Flodden, at a period marked by skirmishes in the Borders. Thus even if as Felicity Riddy points out, transforming a friend into a romance hero is very different from composing a heroic narrative about established national leaders such as Robert Bruce or William Wallace (Riddy 1974: 27), the use of the same or very similar romance motifs and the burden and popularity of *The Bruce* and *The Wallace* generates a series of thematic affiliations between the three historical/historicised texts. It is not surprising that Lindsay wrote counselling literature for the king, since he had been the tutor of the young James V (Lyall 1976: 21). Indeed in all Lindsay's texts there is a kingly figure, apart from in his *Squyer*

Meldrum, in which the monarch is mentioned en passant, not playing a central role in the narrative. At any rate, in this romance there is room for social comment, criticising the chaotic political situation in Scotland during James V's minority. Lindsay does not do that by the narration of the great magnates' lives, but as in *The Tragedie of the Cardinal*, through the lives of his neighbours in Fife (Edington 1995: 125).

There are a few more romances surviving in Middle Scots, most of them short or fragmentary. In narrative terms, the vast majority offer a lively development of events rather than concentrating on the vicissitudes of *fin'amors* and courtly demeanour. *Eger and Grime*, for instance, expresses the same detached, ironic approach to love as Lindsay's *Squyer Meldrum*. However, owing to its fragmentary or short composition, the ideological features common to the romances analysed in this book are not developed. The anonymous *Clariodus* (c.1500–50), a translation of the French *Cleriadus et Meliadice* (c.1450–70), deserves special notice. Following the original, the makar develops the themes of both *fin'amors* and courtliness, probably attempting to build a bridge between the Scottish romance tradition and that of the great makars.

In this book, however, I shall argue that the historical romances, *The Bruce*, *The Wallace* and *Squyer Meldrum*, the Alexander romances, the *Buik of Alexander* and the *Buik of King Alexander the Conquerour*, the Charlemagne romance, *Rauf Coilyear* and the Arthurian romances, *Lancelot of the Laik* and *Golagros and Gawane*, belong to the same literary tradition. This tradition is different to but consistent with that of the great makars.

Chapter One

National Constructs in the Medieval Scottish Romances

The eleventh-century kingdom of the Scots was a somewhat uneasy amalgam of several different peoples, languages and cultures. It had been drawn together by a combination of circumstances and was to prove remarkably resilient as a political entity, despite its internal diversity. [...] The line of Kenneth MacAlpin, albeit its different branches, was well established as the ruling house. [...] The kingdom of Scotland familiar to later ages was beginning to emerge from the early medieval mists.

(Barrell 2000: 11–12)

The idiosyncrasies of Scotland during the late Middle Ages suggest that notions of self-government and kingship created a specific political milieu which conditioned and contextualised ideas of identity, freedom and nationhood. The concepts and historical particularities of the kingdom are enacted in most late medieval romances, aiding the creation of a shared national experience which purported to amalgamate the different peoples of Scotland. Historical events were subsequently reconstructed and codified in official documents such as the Declaration of Arbroath, to forge a discourse of a unified Scottish identity, through historical chronicles and literary texts. All of this written evidence indicates the internalisation of a national consciousness. The external pressure exerted by the English during the period seems to be the fundamental *primum mobile* giving weight to the term "nationalism".

In this chapter, I shall examine the representation and interrelation of kingship, identity, freedom and nationhood in the late medieval Scottish romances, drawing on Barbour's *Bruce* and Hary's *Wallace*, Hay's *Buik of King Alexander the Conquerour* and the anonymous *Lancelot of the Laik* and *Golagros and Gawane*. Although *The Bruce* and *The Wallace* seem to be the most valuable texts for a discussion of these concepts by virtue of their obviously historical roots, the authors of the *Conquerour*, *Lancelot of the Laik* and *Golagros and Gawane* also scrutinise the nation's anxieties through the medium of the pseudo-historical character of Alexander and the representation of the mythological Arthurian world. The texts' masterly deployment of rhetorical devices permits them to unify these themes despite the diverse characteristics of each narrative. The erudite use of rhetoric should not be overlooked when referring to the Scottish tradition, since R.D.S. Jack has argued successfully for Rhetoric as one of the major unifying elements (if not the main one) present from *The Bruce* up to at least 1707 (Jack and Rozendaal eds 1997: xxv).

Notions of national identity in medieval Scotland

Concepts of nation and national identity are not always easy to define in pre-capitalist societies. Scholars such as E.J. Hobsbawm and Benedict Anderson claim that nations and also nationalism are the result of the changes that came about with the French and Industrial Revolutions. Capitalism, industrialisation, urbanisation, the seculari-sation and bureaucratisation of the state and the printing press gave rise to the creation and development of nations and nationalism. The creation of these "imagined communities" through the dialectics of grouping the whole of society to defend the interests of the ruling classes may seem to be an invention of the bourgeoisie (Anderson 1983: 46; Hobsbawm 1990: 9–13). Anything prior to them can be regarded as a proto-nation or proto-nationalism; the "nationalism of the nobility" or "the elites" at most. Nevertheless, this "nationalism of the nobility" to which these scholars allude is not so different from the "nationalism of the bourgeoisie". The dominant classes with political and economic power are in both cases those who promulgate the nationalistic views. Moreover, these "imagined communities" to which Anderson refers, are already constructed (or "imagined") in medieval political writings. In the case of Scotland, the Declaration of Arbroath (1320) is an excellent illustration of this. Not only does the Declaration symbolically rather than realistically confer the sovereignty of the kingdom on the nobility, but more importantly it also re-codifies the Wars of Independence (1296–1314) as a collective struggle of the Scottish people, involving all social strata, against the invader. Therefore, documents such as the Declaration of Arbroath show conscious attempts to create clearly defined concepts of the Scottish nation under an ideological agenda much earlier than the Industrial Revolution.

Medievalists and early modernists refer to nations before the capitalist transformation of western societies took place. Bernard

Guenée asserts that the idea of nation in the Middle Ages originates from Cicero's definition, which was later recast by Isidore of Seville: "a nation was defined by its birth – [...] it is a group of men of common origin, bound together by ties of blood" (Guenée 1985: 52). Such an approach goes beyond views exclusively based on the socio-economic changes brought about by industrialisation. Anthony D. Smith, for example, suggests that factors other than the purely economic exist in the birth of nations. The fundamental elements in Smith's conceptualisation of nation are the growth of myths and memories of a shared origin and history; a common cultural heritage, in which language and religion play a central role; the delimitation of frontiers; and the unification of the legal, economic and social systems (Smith 1995: 14 and 1998: 175–76). Not only does this approach allow us to envisage medieval nations, it also includes a range of ethnic, historical and social features which convey a more far-reaching definition of nationhood.

As opposed to other Western constructions of national consciousness, in medieval Scotland the issue of Scottish identity does not stem from an idea of racial, territorial or linguistic unity:

As a land, Scotland is thoroughly diverse, divided rather than united by geography. It was the land of many peoples, Scots, Picts, British, English and Norse in the Dark Ages, with later additions of Norman-French and Flemings. Nor is there a single "native" Scottish language: there are at least two – Gaelic and Scots. (Webster 1997: 2)

Bruce Webster here implies a non-essentialist genesis of the origins of Scottish identity. The mid-ninth century is considered the time in which the kingdom of Scotland was beginning to take shape when Kenneth I, king of the Scots of Dál Riata, also became king of the Picts. By the early eleventh century, the kingdom of Scotland had expanded southwards with the absorption of Edinburgh (954–62) and Strathclyde (1018). For this reason, Malcolm II is often regarded as the first king of what now broadly corresponds to Scotland. The two factors which facilitated the emergence of a shared sentiment of unity among the Scots were much more pragmatic than its future redefinition:

Two things very gradually worked to bring disparate peoples together: first the increasing acceptance of a single faith, as Christian missionaries in the sixth to ninth centuries gradually converted the different tribes; and the even more gradual ascendancy from the ninth century of a single line of kings, who ruled over Picts and Scots as the kingdom of Alba. (Webster 1997: 3)

This constitutes the gradual process of recognition of a unifying commonwealth. During the thirteenth century, the expansion and consolidation of royal authority secured the association of the ruling dynastic house, the Canmorcs, with the Scottish nation (Watson 1998: 18). The Wars of Independence latterly helped the rise of nationalism when Edward I threatened the personal and national liberties of Scotland and its inhabitants.

It is no coincidence that Edward planned and executed his invasion of Scotland immediately after the deaths of the last representatives of the Canmore dynasty – of Alexander III in 1286 and Margaret in 1290. This menace to national survival is encapsulated by G.W.S. Barrow: "Even today a country's freedom may mean its independence from external powers" (Barrow 1979: 16). This was exactly the situation of Scotland during the Wars of Independence. Scotland had to defend its freedom as an autonomous nation against England: "the external power".

The conceptions of identity and nation were to be disseminated in the literature of Scotland soon after the Wars of Independence. Although Bannockburn is popularly regarded as the definitive battle which secured the Independence of the kingdom up to the Act of Union, during the late Middle Ages the successors of Robert I had to confront threats to their sovereignty more often than they would have liked. In 1346 David II was vanquished, being taken as prisoner by the English. As a consequence, he probably had to pay fealty to Edward III. A year later, only the castles of Edinburgh, Stirling and Dunbar, which were in possession of the Scots, prevented the English occupation. As well as military confrontations throughout the fourteenth and fifteenth centuries, the tensions between England and Scotland reappeared in a new way. In a letter from 1328, Henry IV, reverting to the mythological origins of Locrine and Brutus, claimed overlordship over Robert III's Scotland. Similarly in 1456, Henry VI, calling himself King of Scotland, wrote a letter to James II, demanding his homage. Finally in 1480, in preparation for a military campaign, Edward IV also regarded himself "as soverain of Scotland" (Nicholson 1974: 148; 219; 394; 491). Hence it is evident that literature, as an expression of human activity, would exhibit such political fears by means of a thorough treatment of the nature and requirements of freedom, nationhood and identity through representation of kingship.

Historical chronicles, as well as the romances treated here, played a decisive part in the dissemination of both a historical and mythological past, amalgamating the experiences of all the inhabitants of the realm. The chronicles of John Fordun, Walter Bower and Hector Boece and the romances of Barbour and Hary recreated overtly, as the Scottish Arthurian and Alexander romances did more implicitly, the Scottish past, establishing a conception of nationhood which set the basis for later developments of Scottishness until the present day.

Representations of Kingship in the Scottish Romances

At a basic level the medieval notion of kingship stems from the classical tension – and necessary reconciliation – between strict justice and mercy. The rediscovery of Aristotelianism in the thirteenth century deeply influenced Thomas Aquinas's thought, not only in theological and philosophical matters, but also in political theory. He might be considered a rather distant source for ideas of kingship in late medieval Scotland, yet Edward Cowan suggests that political concepts appearing in Aquinas's *De regimine principum* coincide with those expounded in the Declaration of Arbroath (Cowan 1998: 57). Even if those ideas were not directly taken from Aquinas, it is quite likely that the redactors of the Declaration were following texts which were inspired by the philosopher. The latter's definition of kingship, then, offers a starting point:

> The king should recognise that he has a duty to act in his kingdom like the soul in the body and God in the world. If he recognises this, he will be driven by a zeal for justice when he considers that he has been appointed to exercise judgement over the kingdom in God's place, and he will acquire kindness and mercy when he regards the individuals under his rule as members of his own body. (*De regimine principum*, ch.12)

Essentially, Aquinas sees good government as *Rex imago Dei*; that is, as the terrestrial mirror of the divine synthesis of justice and mercy ordained by God. The Scots romances problematise different conceptions of this subject in order to provide an ideal solution to the suitable royal government required by Scotland.

In *The Bruce*, the hero's first intervention already specifies the particularities of kingship within the general ideas expressed by Aquinas. When Edward I offers Bruce the possibility of becoming King of Scots in exchange for paying fealty to him, the Earl of Carrick's speech establishes the national discourse of the romance:

"Schyr," said he, "sa God me save
Ye kynryk hharn I nocht to have
Bot gyff it fall off rycht to me,
And gyff God will yat it sa be
I sall als frely in all thing
Hald it as it afferis to king,
Or as myn eldris forouth me
Held it in freyast rewate". (I. 157–64)

Bruce's first words state his position and the kind of kingship which he is advocating. First, he implicitly discredits Edward as the arbiter of the succession conflict by referring to God as the only one with sufficient authority to choose the rightful king. As John of Salisbury affirms, a king "is subject only to God and those who exercise His office and represent Him on earth" (*Policraticus* V.ii.65). Edward, then, has no right to nominate the Scottish monarch. Moreover, Barbour represents the English king as a foreign invader who aims to subjugate and oppress the country and, consequently, as totally inadequate for the role. Again, in accordance with the political theory of both Aquinas and John of Salisbury, Edward responds to the image of the tyrant in direct opposition to that of the ideal Christian sovereign. Secondly, Bruce defends the autonomy of the kingdom and its monarch against any foreign subjugation or, in the case of Edward I, abuse and aggression. Finally, he refers to the old ancestry of rulers in Scotland, which, on being intimately related to the notion of tradition, legitimises its autonomy. Therefore, in his first declaration, the hero sets up the basis for future government of the country. Although his plans for the nation are not already defined, his apostrophe to national independence based on divine and racial premises would have been very appealing to his audience. One of the poet's main goals appears to be that the romance should serve as an example to the courtly Scottish audience of his time: "the weak nobles at Robert II's court in the mid 1370s are imaginatively returned to the example set by the predecessors at the turn of the fourteenth century" (Jack and Rozendaal eds 1997: 2).

In the Arthurian romance tradition in Scotland, both in *Lancelot of the Laik* and in *Golagros and Gawane*, Arthur and Golagros advance similar views to *The Bruce* on kingship and national autonomy. In the Middle Scots *Lancelot*, Arthur's answer to Galiot's envoy when the British King is asked to submit his kingdom to a superior force is closely constructed along the lines of the *locus communis* of regal discourse in the late Middle Ages:

> "Schir knycht, your lorde wondir hie pretendis
> When he to me sic salutatioune sendis;
> For I as yit, in tymys that ar gone,
> Held never lond excep of God alone
> Nore never thinkith til erthly lord to yef
> Trybut nor rent, als long as I may lef". (ll.559–64)

What makes this response exceptional is that both the cyclic and non-cyclic *Prose Lancelot* relate this episode in fewer words than the Scottish text. In Kennedy's edition of the non-cyclic romance, these are Arthur's words:

> "Biaus sire, fait li rois, ge ne tign onques terre de nului fors de Deu, ne ja de cestui ne la tandrai". (264)

> ["Sir," the king said, I have never held my land from anyone except God, and I will never hold from this man" (212)][1]

In the cyclic text edited by Sommer, spelling differences are the only ones which can be appreciated:

> "biax sire fait li rois ie ne ting onques terre de nului fors de dieu. ne ia chestui ne la tendrai". (III. 202)

The two Old French versions allude to the divine origin of kingship, but do not refer to the ancestry of the lineage, which is the makar's amplification. The latter designs a symbolic image which his audience could easily identify as being of significant political relevance to the Scottish state, the parentage of the Stuarts as heirs of the Canmores, through the Bruces, forging an idea of the same long standing family

---

[1] Whenever possible I am using Corin Corley's abridged translation, which is indicated by the page number. When no page number is given, it is my own translation.

governing the nation. At the same time, it is reasonable to assume that at least some of the listeners, who might be familiar with the preeminent Scottish national poem of the time, *The Bruce*, would analogically connect Bruce's and Arthur's situations at this juncture. The arguments employed by the legendary British king echo those used by Bruce: each is in favour of the sovereignty of his land, whose ruler should pay fealty to God alone, and both also problematise the tension of being under the menace of a foreign superior power. The text places Arthur in a favourable position before his audience, even if they will soon realise that his attitude is not the ideal one for a king.

Thus, notwithstanding the obvious thematic differences between the two works, their starting points parallel the critical state of a king-dom endangered by the imperialistic ambitions of a militarily superior rival. This tension will create, among other things, the perfect atmosphere in which to debate the mechanisms of kingship at different levels: for Bruce, it will be a process of learning the way in which a king should act, whereas for Arthur it will be a question of recovering the old policies he has forgotten.

In the other Arthurian romance, *Golagros and Gawane*, it is again Golagros's sovereignty over his lands that is challenged (in this poem, Arthur himself is the aggressor):

"If I, for obeisance or boist, to bondage me bynde,
I war wourthy to be
Hingit heigh on ane tre,
That ilk creature might se,
To waif with the wynd.
"Bot savand my senyeoury fra subjectioun,
And my lordscip unlamyt, withoutin legiance,
All that I can to yone King, cumly with croun,
I sall preif all my pane to do hym plesance,
Baith with body and beild, bowsum and boun,
Hym to mensk on mold, withoutin manance.
Bot nowthir for his senyeoury, nor for his summoun,
Na for dreid of na dede, na for na distance,
I will noght bow me ane bak for berne that is borne.
Quhill I may my wit wald,
I think my fredome to hald,
As my eldaris of ald
Has done me beforne". (ll.436–53)

Golagros's arguments are the same as those deployed by Bruce in *The Bruce* and Arthur in *Lancelot of the Laik*. His domains are threatened without any apparent reason other than the invader's obsession with power. In this text, the disposition of the narrative transforms Arthur's justifiable attack on the Riche Soudoyer, who has imprisoned Gyflet fils Do, into an unlawful menace to national liberty only grounded on Arthur's arbitrary and senselessly aggressive attitude. Without alluding to any particular historical circumstance, Arthur's threat emphasises the Scottish reference by representing a situation analogous to the Anglo-Scottish tension of the late Middle Ages. In 1385, for example, Richard II invaded Scotland, and in 1482, Gloucester did the same. Generation after generation of Scots experienced or knew from first hand witnesses about English invasions of the country. Furthermore, in contrast with the *First Continuation*, in which the name of the stronghold itself, *Chastel Orgueilleux*, presupposes Arthur's role as an eradicator of sin, in the Scottish poem the castle is not given a name at all. Therefore, owing to his general tenets, the makar obliterates the two chivalric and religious requirements which justify Arthur's military intervention.

Tonally, Arthur's opponent, Golagros, intermingles dramatic love of his land with an understanding of his duty. He asserts that if he gave himself into subjection, he would deserve to be hanged (ll.436–39) and, despite Arthur's menace, he is determined to hold his territories freely according to his refined sense of *cortesia*. In just fifteen lines, then, Golagros proves to be an excellent ruler who combines his duty towards his subjects with the necessary *cortesia* and refinement a lord is supposed to possess. Constance S. Kelly notes: "Golagros is portrayed as an honorable, peace-loving individual forced by an outsider's greed into a struggle for supremacy" (Kelly 1975: 252). His image contrasts with that of Arthur in all respects; he wants to impose martial superiority regardless of right and law. Historically, Arthur acts "at a level at which the Scottish audience can see him sharing the political ethics of the hated Edward I" (Jack 1974–75: 11); spiritually, both Arthur and Edward have relinquished a pilgrimage or a crusade with the purpose of enlarging their material possessions. In *The Bruce*, in a fictitious episode elaborated by Barbour, Edward is said to have abandoned a crusade to get hold of Scotland: "Yat [Edward] was yan in ye haly land / On Saracenys warrayand" (I. 139–40). In a parallel situation, in *Golagros and*

Gawane, Arthur completes his pilgrimage to the Holy Sepulchre as quickly as he can to come back to conquer Golagros's lands. This attitude places them in an even more indefensible position both in the romance and in the eyes of the audience. Golagros's *cortesia* and his intelligent use of rhetoric persuade the listeners of his right to be the ruler of these lands: "the hearers themselves become the instruments of proof when emotion is stirred in them by the speech; for we give our judgements in different ways under the influence of joy, of liking or of hatred" (*Rhetoric* I.ii.5). In *Golagros and Gawane*, then, it is the oppressor, Arthur, who will have to learn to be a good monarch again. The exercise of his *privata voluntas*, leading to a pernicious conception of kingship, supersedes the idea of *Rex imago Dei* – according to medieval philosophers, the attitude which should be expected from a Christian sovereign.

In Gilbert Hay's *Buik of King Alexander the Conquerour*, Alexander's right to become not only king but the ruler of his empire is constructed along similar lines as those of the other romances. Just before starting his instructive book the *Regimen of Princis*, Aristotle puts forward the reasons which support Alexander's sovereignty. The philosopher first praises God's omnipotence:

[God] gouernes all þe warldit in generall,
The quhilk is weill of wourschip and gudnes,
That all thing ledis and in powar has.
Traist wele, þi conquest and þi hie renovne
Cummys of His tholance and permissioun,
And nocht of þe, bot of þare ordinance,
That vndir Him has all þe governance. (ll.9391–98)

Aristotle's words postulate that the ultimate power of Alexander's government is celestial in origin – even Christian in origin, as Hay makes Alexander a Christian king. Thus Alexander has the responsibility of applying the law not according to his *privata voluntas* but by following the dictates of God. The significance of God's "permissioun" goes beyond its customary apostrophe in late medieval treatises dealing with political theory. Like Arthur, Alexander's conception is somewhat problematic. God Ammon (Zeus) is said to be his father. Philip adopts him (l.9420–22), but then marries Cleopatra. As a consequence, Alexander's succession is, on occasion, jeopardised. Being directly chosen by Ammon legitimises his divinely-ordained accession to the throne. Aristotle also makes clear that human law is on Alexander's side because:

He [Philip] made þe are in-till his testament –
Thus art þow king by richtwis iugment;
Syne was þow chosin be þe commintie –
Thow may nocht falȝee richtwis king to be;
Syne throw conquest þe warld þe obeyis –
Thus thrinfald richt into þi ballance weyis. (ll.9423–28)

Mapstone outlines the threefold nature of Alexander's right to the throne: inheritance, choice by people (or more specifically the nobility), and conquest; all of them endorsed by God's election (Mapstone 1986: 109). At any rate, it is noteworthy that the direct appointment from King Philip in his testament does not seem to be enough; the nobles are required to ratify the decision. The equilibrium of power suggests that a good monarch will be supported by the nobility, with whose approval important issues should be agreed. Even so, this is not sufficient: Alexander is the *rightful* king beyond birth (or adoption in his case) and consent; he needs to fulfil his duties. He has to deserve his position as the head of the communal body. In this, he resembles the eponymous character in Barbour's *Bruce*: both demonstrate by merit on the battlefield, and not by blood ascendancy, that each is the *proper* leader of their people. Both romances, as well as more indirectly *The Wallace*, advocate a sort of kingship in which accomplishment of the kingly obligation is prioritised over birth.

In *The Wallace*, owing to the absence of a monarch, the same concepts are introduced in a different manner. Hary, instead of amalgamating the figures of Robert Bruce and his grandfather, only refers to Bruce as one of the competitors for the Scottish crown: "Off quhilk thre com Bruce, Balȝoune and Hastyng" (I. 47). Goldstein also remarks that at a time when the Brucean ideology was completely assimilated in Scotland, Hary paid even less attention to legal accuracy than Barbour (Goldstein 1993: 234). In this way, the makar at once avoids contradictions with historical evidence and *The Bruce*. In Hary's romance, the one who repudiates the country's submission to Edward is not one of the three competitors for the Crown but the Bishop of Glasgow:

Byschope Robert, in his tyme full worthi,
Off Glaskow lord, he said that "we deny
Ony our-lord bot the great god abuff". (I. 65–67)

At a time when there was not a clear royal figure to withstand the
English king, the author significantly chooses one of the leading
members of the Church to gather support for the national independence of Scotland against a foreign intervention. Not only does Hary
underline the role of the clergy in the Wars of Independence, but he
also elucidates the close relationship between the Church and the King
and its importance in Hary's construction of Scottish identity:

The Church could be a formidable support to the royal authority, since it was to the
crown that the church always looked for protection. Monasteries were important land-
owners; bishops were men of education and served often as officials in the royal government. Without the church, most of the developments in royal government would
have been impossible. (Webster 1997: 34–35)

Some forty lines later, Balliol is deposed and Edward nominates
himself "Roy full ryk" (I. 120). At this critical moment, Hary alludes
to the mythological origins of Scotland to legitimise the nation's
autonomy according to tradition:

The croune he [Edward] tuk apon that sammyne stane
At Galados send with his sone fra Spane,
Quhen Iber Scot fyrst in-till Irland come.
At Canmor syne king Fergus has it nome,
Brocht it till Scwne and stapill maid it thar,
Quhar kingis was cround viii hundyr ӡer and mar
Befor the tyme at king Eduuard it fand. (I. 121–27)

In the later Middle Ages the symbolism and mythology of a nation's
origins, as well as being one of the touchstones of the formation of
national consciousness, also constituted a justification of legitimacy
and sovereignty. For example, in the *Pleading*, addressed to Pope
Boniface in 1301, Baldred Bisset mentions Scota as the mother of the
free Scottish nation, refuting English versions in which Brutus is the
founder of Britain and when he divided the kingdom between his three
sons, Albanactus (Scotland) became subject to Locrinus (England). In
The Wallace, as soon as the English monarch takes effective
possession of the government, Hary negates Edward I's right on the
grounds of mythological history and tradition.

All five narratives, *The Bruce*, *The Wallace*, the *Buik of King Alexander the Conquerour*, *Lancelot of the Laik* and *Golagros and Gawane*, deal with the representation of good kingship along the lines of those proposed by late medieval thinkers. In developing this conception, the authors refer to the conflict of a nation's autonomy threatened by an external aggressor, the shared components of identity and of the national and dynastic discourse. This places a particular emphasis on the Scottish political realities of the time.

By way of contrast with other traditions, in the French *Chanson de Bertrand du Guesclin* (late fourteenth century), the debate on possible submission to the enemy is treated in a very different manner to that found in the Scottish romances. When the Duke of Lancaster asks Bertrand (not a king, but a national leader nonetheless) to join the Anglo-Normans in return for "terre et gant avoir" (1.1897), Bertrand's response is devoid of the dramatic and solemn gravity of the Scottish texts. While in the Scottish romances national and personal enterprises cannot be detached from each other, in the French text the personal fealty of Bertrand and national identity are not necessarily the same thing:

"Sire, ce dit Bertran, foy que doy Saint Remy!
Se tant premierement vous avoie servi,
Tenir me devriez vo mortel ennemi
S'a un autre seigneur je m'estoie parti". (ll.1899–902)

["Sir," said Bertrand, "By Saint Remy! If I had agreed to serve you, you should regard me as your mortal enemy, since I would have left another lord."]

Although Bertrand's words imply a refusal to submit to another lord together with an affirmation of his loyalty to the French sovereign, the hero's language is that of *cortesia*. This stylistic device is even more evident if the Duke's reaction is analysed: "Quant li dux vit Bertran parler si sagement, / En son cuer le prisa le duc moult grandement" (ll.1909–10) ["When the Duke saw Bertrand speaking so wisely, his heart shook greatly"]. This likely historical scene is fictionalised along the lines of the courtly tradition. Chivalric attitudes and behaviour redefine Bertrand's nationalistic and royalist dialectics. The effect of this formal disposition, albeit equally appealing, demonstrates a set of implications alternative to those of the Scottish romances. As inheritor of the rich and ancient tradition of *chansons* and *romans courtois*, the

French author has no qualms about applying notions of chivalry and *cortesia* even in these overtly political scenes. Conversely, while coming from a French-influenced background, the Scottish authors prefer to make use of less ornamented courtly language and attitudes when themes concerning Scotland's political situation are debated. This underlines the instructive and ideological functionality of the texts.

Freedom and nation

The pre-eminence of freedom in these texts interweaves with, and sometimes becomes impossible to dissociate from, the need for the good exercise of kingship. In the context of Barbour's *Bruce* and Hary's *Wallace*, the theme of national liberty is traditionally regarded as the main concern and leitmotiv of the romances. In the Arthurian texts, the term "nationalism" would not completely apply to the mythological world of the Matter of Britain, where feudal and territorial conflicts do not necessarily correspond to contemporary power and national struggles between European countries. However, the assertion of the autonomy of a lord or a king's territories in the face of a foreign invasion is one of the key subjects in both *Lancelot of the Laik* and *Golagros and Gawane*.

As early as 1290 the Treaty of Bingham, although it did not explicitly mention freedom or liberty in general, made reference to "liberties in particular": rights, laws, liberties (Barrow 1979: 22). However, as soon as Edward I deposed Balliol, he dismantled the "Scottish state apparatus" (Goldstein 1993: 47). The abolition of Scottish institutions is considered to have given rise to the first signs of Scottish nationalism among the nobility. For this reason, Goldstein equates the defence of Scotland with the defence of secular and ecclesiastical centres of government. These institutions represented not only the actual mechanisms of power through which the king and the Church exercised their authority but, according to Webster, they were also the pillars of Scottish identity at a symbolic level. The importance of symbolism in the creation and development of a national consciousness should not be ignored. It was not a gratuitous act of authoritativeness and domination when Edward I took the Stone of Destiny to England – the Stone being a symbol of Scottish independence. In the late Middle Ages, myth was almost as important as history for the birth and consolidation of national identities:

The three Scots compilations [...] develop an appeal to natural law by stressing the familial aspect of their pretended history. The nation, when it arrived in a northern region of Spain, before its settlements in Ireland and Scotland, had an original mother-queen Scota and an original father-king Galados. These names refer respectively to a hypothesised Scythian eastern origin and the Gadelic and Gaelic language spoken by the family or tribe. (McDiarmid 1979: 7–8)

During the Wars of Independence, Baldred Bisset composed another fundamental document which shapes the Scottish attitude towards national freedom. In the *Pleading*, Baldred protests that "it is almost against natural law and astonishing for someone who enjoys legal independence to be subjected to the authority of someone else" (Cowan 1998: 46). Baldred also alludes to mythology to refute Edward's claim to the Scottish throne: whereas the English king put forward an argument based on his ascendance from Arthur, Baldred claimed that the Scots descended from Scota, therefore dismissing the Arthurian claim. Fordun would elaborate on this myth in his *Chronica Gentis Scotorum* about seventy years later.

Goldstein claims that, although the lowest classes came to sympathise with and support the rebellion, they began to back the Scottish nobility because they offered the possibility of better living conditions than those they possessed under the English yoke. In his opinion, nationalistic ideals had little to do with the motivations of the Third Estate (Goldstein 1993: 51). Yet it seems logical to consider that there should have been a growing sense of nationalism among the soldiers who fought with Wallace and Bruce since "they did fight, like their leaders, in circumstances when it would have been simpler and safer not to do so" (Webster 1997: 89). Whether they essentially fought for social reasons or for their country's autonomy (or for both, as I believe), Barbour and Hary ingeniously adapt such actions in order to present a united nation confronting its enemies.

In "The Idea of Freedom in Late Medieval Scotland", Barrow claims that the Declaration of Arbroath (1320) is the best illustration of Scotland's desire for freedom in that period. The Declaration points out that "we [Scots] are fighting for freedom – for that alone, which no honest man gives up but with life itself" (Barrow 1979: 28). His interpretation of these lines underlines that the only freedom a person would prefer to wealth and honour must be his or her personal liberty. Hence, for the first time in Scottish history the independence of a kingdom from the domination of a hegemonic foreign invader began to be firmly linked with the concept of individual freedom (Barrow 1979: 32). It might be striking for a modern reader, who tends to relate personal freedom to democracy, to find such an assertion in feudal times. However, this did not mean that after 1320 each Scot enjoyed personal liberty as understood nowadays. It is one thing to express an ideal in a written document, but it is a very different one to put into practice. As Barrow himself concludes, a free kingdom started to be regarded as a community of free men, even if such a conceptualisation did not reflect reality (Barrow 1979: 32).

In *The Bruce*, the apostrophe to national freedom has been traditionally regarded to be at the core of the romance. Yet this is not the only exclusive meaning present in the Scottish romances. The various definitions of freedom given in the *Middle English Dictionary* (Kurath et al. eds 1952–: III: 874–76) and in the *Dictionary of the Older Scottish Tongue* (Craigie et al. eds 1931–2002: V: 562–63) can be summarised as follows:

1.– National independence.
2.– Class or group (such as a guild) privilege.
3.– Personal freedom.
4.– The participation of citizens in a nation's political affairs.

"National independence" is the predominant sense all through *The Bruce*. In so far as Barbour's main ideological discourse corresponds with Scotland's fight for independence, the other three senses should be fully understood only when contrasted with the former. As David Daiches asserts, when John Barbour exhorts freedom, he is primarily concerned with the independence of the realm (Daiches 1977: 8, 10; cited in Barrow 1979: 18). This does not negate the existence of the other meanings, but suggests that the other three depend on the first one in the makar's textual and political composition of the text. Barbour, however, redefines meanings 2 and 3 in the context of national freedom. In this way, as the narrative evolves, the national cause, the class privileges and the personal interest are impossible to dissociate from one another.

As Hans Utz also highlights, Douglas's adherence to Bruce's party in order to avenge himself on the English and recover his lands is seen as the defence of "class privilege" (Utz 1969: 156). Bruce's loyal comrade-at-arms is the perfect illustration of this conceptual evolution during the narrative. His first steps in the romance are led by his wish to recover his father's properties:

Ye bischop led him to ye king [Edward I]
And said, "Schyr heyr I to ʒow bryng
Yis child [Douglas] yat clemys ʒour man to be,
And prays ʒow par cheryte
yat ʒe resave her his homage
And grantis him his heritage". (I. 415–20)

At the beginning of *The Bruce*, then, James Douglas, second only to Robert Bruce as a hero, is disposed to submit to Scotland's greatest enemy, Edward I, in return for his possessions. Douglas articulates an eminently feudal discourse: he merely defends his individual/class interests. Inasmuch as his concerns are merely personal, for him the national struggle is simply a means to accomplish his objective, never an end in itself. As his behaviour exhibits the habitual noble code of conduct in a manner appropriate to his hierarchical position, he leaves the particularities of Scotland aside. This passage also serves to portray the origins of James Douglas's confrontation with Edward I and, at the same time, it parallels Bruce's first argument with the King of England (I. 154–67). In both cases, Douglas and Bruce stand for what they think is right to defend (possessions and the freedom of Scotland respectively), whereas Edward I is characterised as the tyrannical aggressor who causes the confrontation.

Again, when Douglas joins Robert Bruce, he is motivated by the intention of recovering his lands at first, not by Bruce's defence of the interests of Scotland:

And Iames off Dowglas preuely
Said to ye byschop, "Schyr ʒe se
How Inglis-men throw yar powste
Dysherysys me off my land,
And men has gert ʒow wnderstand
Als yat ye erle off Carryk
Clamys to govern ye kynryk,
[…]
Yarfor schir giff it war ʒour will
I wald tak with him gud & ill.
Throw hym I trow my land to wyn
Magre ye Clyffurd and his kyn". (II. 98–104; 109–12)

Anne McKim claims that the relationship between Douglas and Bruce is that of "remunerative recognition of service proffered" in exchange for Douglas's loyalty (McKim 1981: 169). Nonetheless, by becoming one of Bruce's men, he also becomes a supporter of his cause: the liberation of the realm. As in the English romances,

> conflict between a hero and his society is not central and problematic. Rather than locating the human drama in self-discovery, the insular romances propose that the human drama is collective, a communal search for stability that takes place through the hero's search. (Crane 1986: 83)

Although as a nobleman he continues to persevere with the idea of recovering his properties, he progressively attaches more importance to the national struggle than to his class privileges.

The first instance in which this shift becomes evident is found in Book VIII. 15–73. Douglas and his men attack Sir Philip Mowbray and his troop, because they were looking for Robert Bruce to kill him. Douglas places Bruce's security and cause before his own. There is a progression from the personal to the national in his conduct. He comes to identify with Bruce's cause, leaving his own ambitions in the background, though not forgetting them. The makar was completely aware of his knightly audience; for this reason, if Bruce's image serves as an example of good kingship (Ebin 1971–72: 222), Douglas's image illustrates the attitude that the Scottish nobility listening to the romance should adopt towards their king and their country.

Goldstein approaches the poem from a diametrically opposed perspective. He regards freedom only as the defence of "class privilege", dismissing the presence of national and personal liberty. For him, this concept only concerns "the Community of the Realm of Scotland", that is, "the highest strata of Scottish society" (Goldstein 1993: 164). Hence, the exhortation: "A, fredome is a noble thing" should be interpreted as freedom that is something exclusively for the nobility: "Past readers have neglected to consider the literal meaning of the word "noble" here, though the poet's presentation of Edward's violation of property rights gives us every reason to take Barbour at his word". To draw such a conclusion, as well as referring to the loss of property of the members of the upper classes, Goldstein also alludes to Barbour's privileged position. His main objection is that the makar was one of those who took advantage of the institution of serfdom; therefore, he would never have cast doubt on its existence. Barbour, as an archdeacon and a poet at court, obviously profited from the institution of serfdom (Goldstein 1993: 163–67). Nonetheless, the writer was also within his rights to praise the pre-eminence of freedom for all, no matter to which social strata they belonged. One thing need not necessarily exclude the other. Neither can Barbour be branded as a hypocrite when he praises freedom, and, at the same time, has serfs working for him. It would be helpful to distinguish between Barbour, the Archdeacon, a member of the Community of the Realm, and Barbour, the makar, exploring a narrative voice.

Historically, in the late Middle Ages, the personal freedom of Scottish subjects was to be respected within the limitations of their vows of loyalty to lords. The oath of loyalty presupposed certain obligations on the part of the lords, too:

A duty of protection, moreover, did not lend itself so well as services to such precise definition. The vassal was to be defended by his lord "towards and against all men that may live or die;" first and foremost in his person, but also in his property and more especially in his fiefs. Furthermore, he expected from this proctector – who had become […] a judge – good and speedy justice. (Bloch 1961: 224)

Furthermore, the particular political situation of Scotland both during the Wars of Independence and at the time the romance was composed did not discourage oppression of both class and personal liberties. Although Isaiah Berlin surely refers to more contemporary conflicts, the following statement is also applicable to late medieval Scotland:

What they [oppressed classes and nationalities] want, as often as not, is simply recognition (of their class or nation) as an independent source of human activity, as an entity with a will of its own, intending to act in accordance with it […] and not to be ruled, educated, guided, with however light a hand, as being not quite fully human and therefore not quite fully free. (Berlin 1958: 41–42)

In *The Bruce*, both the upper classes and the Third Estate would constitute the "oppressed classes and nationalities". The English deprived the Scottish nobility of their institutions and also of their possessions, if they did not submit to Edward I. They also abused their authority and exploited the lower classes. If Barbour's highlighting of the "common folk" is united with Berlin's assertion, the logical conclusion is that the praise of freedom in *The Bruce* is addressed to all Scots.

> When the Narrative [Barbour's] says that the churchmen and lords chose Bruce, "the people consenting", "people" almost certainly refers to the commons, the intent being merely to cite the three constituents of the community. In such context "community" is more than a convenient legal phrase and does carry authority, but the emotive force referred to reside in other words, the synonyms "land", "country", "nation", "people", "folk", "Scots". (McDiarmid 1979: 8–9)

Both shortly before and after Barbour's praise of freedom, the nobility and the peasantry are said to suffer alike owing to English tyranny: "Thus-gat levyt yai & in sic thrillage / Bath pur and yai off hey parag" (I. 275–76). "Thus-gat" refers to the sufferings undergone by the Scots as expressed in the two previous long sections. From its purely grammatical structure, the apostrophising of freedom included in the previous section also alludes to both the "pur" and "yai off hey parag". Barbour extols an ideal situation, in which everyone might enjoy personal as well as national freedom, in just such terms as the Declaration of Arbroath proposes. As R.D.S. Jack affirms: "the hierarchical context which exacerbates this tension between ideal and actual is accepted throughout by narrator and heroes. [...] The narrator's ideal is not the destruction of that order but the perfect society in which each individual loves his brother" (Jack and Rozendaal eds 1997: xxvi).

In addition to this, had Barbour not wanted to include the commoners in his praise of freedom, he would not have bestowed on them such a relevant role in the liberation of the country. The representation of their active participation in the Wars of Independence challenges and subverts several literary and chivalric conventions. Therefore, although Goldstein's arguments are convincing, *The Bruce* as a unifying literary and ideological piece of art epitomises the concept of freedom on personal and national levels, not as an ethereal ideal but as the practical respect of the boundaries, duties and rights between lord and vassal. This notion operates as one of the main tools which will bring all the Scots to fight together.

The same thematic tension between selfish defence of feudal properties and national commitment is present in *The Wallace*. At the time of its composition, the Brucean and Stewart monarchies had been legitimised for more than one hundred years in the people's minds, which favoured a freer treatment of the figure of Robert Bruce than in *The Bruce*. Matthew P. McDiarmid summarises the historical climate in the following way:

The interest of the Crown in securing a genuine treaty that would allow it to deal firmly with a difficult aristocracy was obvious, and the burgesses and more commercially minded nobles of the fifteenth century could also see their profit from it. [...] It was not surprising, therefore, that schemes of matrimonial alliance with the English royal House and even the eventual union of the crowns began to be contemplated. (McDiarmid ed. 1968–69: I.xvii)

If in *The Bruce* the poet had to make use of several fictive and rhetorical strategies to silence Bruce's desertion of the national cause and adherence to the English party, Hary was able to develop his Bruce in a distinct manner. While Barbour constructs Bruce as a *speculum principis*, Hary first condemns and then regenerates the figure of the King of Scots through the intervention and guidance of Wallace. As a result, the contrast between feudal and national tensions is even more dramatic than in Barbour's narrative, since it is the future King of Scots himself who has to reinstate his priorities.

In the early stages of the narrative, the two main pretenders to the Scottish Crown, Balliol and Bruce, are characterised as traitors to the national cause in so far as their priorities focus on personal promotion: they are differentiated only by audience awareness of Bruce's future as the liberator of Scotland. It is only the extradiegetic competence of the listeners that places Bruce in a favourable light. They could not fail to recognise Bruce as the Elect. The audience knew Balliol would remain a traitor, whereas Bruce would eventually rejoin the national struggle and replace Wallace as Scotland's leader.

At Falkirk, when Wallace observes that Bruce is fighting on Edward's side, he makes a disheartened and severe assertion: "Allace," he said, "the warld is contrar-lik!" (XI. 210). As a champion of the national cause, Wallace finds it difficult to come to terms with such a situation: in a strange and absurd world, the theoretical leader of the nation is literally killing his subjects. This scene endorses even more the image of Wallace as a tragic hero who has to face all kinds of adversities. Now Wallace will have to instruct Bruce on how to lead his country. As one who has lost the right way, Bruce is unable to understand Wallace's position at first: "Quhy wyrkis thow thus and mycht in gud pes be?" (XI. 457). Like Boethius in *De Consolatione*, his question reveals at once an unawareness of the situation and an attachment to mutable earthly possessions. Both need a guide to learn what they have to do. God's mysterious ways are transferred into the spiritual incapacity to comprehend the political realities of Scotland.

At this juncture, Bruce is corrupt and can see only the materiality of the world: he cannot grasp the meaning of high ideals such as national freedom or good leadership. In his narrow vision, he cannot see beyond the selfish but short-lived advantages he is offered. Symbolic blindness motivates his question: he wonders why Wallace does not want to sell his soul to the devil (Edward I) in return for material gold. Wallace's answer clearly refers to the country's urgent need far beyond personal egotism: "I cleym no rycht bot wald this land defend, / At thow wndoys throu thi fals cruell deid" (XI. 460-61). This assertion defines the tone of his reprimand and later lesson to Bruce:

Throuch thi tresson, that suld be our rycht king,
That willfully dystroyis thin awn off-spryng."
[...]
"I cleym no thing as be titill of rycht,
Thocht I mycht reiff, sen god has lent me mycht,
Fra the thi crowne off this regioun to wer,
Bot I will nocht sic a charge on me ber.
Gret god wait best quhat wer I tak on hand
For till kep fre that thow art gaynstandand.
It mycht beyn said off lang gone her off forn,
In cursyt tym thow was for Scotland born.
Schamys thow nocht that thow neuir ȝeit did gud,
Thow renygat deuorar off thi blud?" (XI. 471–72; 483–92)

Wallace severely reproaches the future king for his inability to come to an understanding of his country's realities and needs. His rhetorical discourse is structured and founded upon two basic themes: treason and Bruce's destiny. The hero finds the two concepts impossible to reconcile. Bruce will now have to make an ultimate decision: his choice between English gold or Scottish loyalty can no longer be postponed.

Wallace's harsh oration makes no concession to ambiguity. Although his words may seem rather too aggressive when talking to his king, there are three factors which justify his course of action: first, after Falkirk, the political and national stability of Scotland was hazardous; secondly, at a rhetorical level, the use of powerful and direct language is meant to move both Bruce and the audience of the romance; and thirdly, at a symbolic level, he is morally obliged to act in this manner insofar as he is the Elect (XI. 484–85). Therefore, the Elect, who is justified by God himself, addresses and corrects the other Elect, who is not yet aware of his *avanture*. Wallace becomes the mature father figure and teacher/guide leading Bruce (symbolically, young prodigal son and pupil) from ignorance to knowledge. Should Wallace be successful, the succession will be effective: the Guardian/leader/liberator of Scotland will be replaced by the reborn King/leader/liberator. The final image is dramatically and visually striking: "Schamys thow nocht that thow neuir ȝeit did gud, / Thow renygat deuorar of thi blud?" (XI. 491–92). Wallace resorts to the image of Saturn, a father who was willing to devour his own children (Goldstein 1993: 246). The direct question together with the iconographic force of "thi blud" and the pertinent mythological reference are the final rhetorical devices used to teach the future sovereign. In his *History of Sexuality*, Michel Foucault points out the emblematic significance of blood in feudal societies:

> The blood relation long remained an important element in the mechanisms of power, its manifestations, and its rituals. [...] A society of blood – I was tempted to say of "sanguinity" – where power spoke *through* blood: the honor of war, the fear of famine, the triumph of death, the sovereign with his sword, executioners, and torturers; blood was a *reality with a symbolic function*. (Foucault 1990: 147)

The "symbolic" image of blood reappears some lines further, and is a persistent image throughout the narrative. According to Goldstein, its presence is never gratuitous: "the vivid presentation of gore to satisfy the audience's desire for revenge seems to occur in proportion to the scale of the English aggressors' provocation" (Goldstein 1993: 224). He concludes that "blood is endowed a symbolic significance that is truly remarkable for a poem that is not expressly about Christ" (Goldstein 1993: 232). In the English camp, Bruce begins to have his dinner without washing: "Ane said, 'Behald, ȝon Scot ettis his awn blud'" (XI. 536). Edward I asks for some water for Bruce to wash his hands:

> "This blud is myn. That hurtis most my thocht."
> Sadly the Bruce than in his mind remordyt
> Thai wordis suth Wallace had him recordyt.
> Than rewyt he sar, fra resoun had him knawin
> At blud and land suld lik all beyn his awin.
> With thaim he was lang or he couth get away,
> Bot contrar Scottis he faucht nocht fra that day. (XI. 540–46)

Biblical intertextuality imposes an allegorical interpretation here. The
Bible refers several times to sins being metaphorically forgiven by
hand washing.[2] Allegorically, Bruce realises that no matter how much
he washes his hands, he will never clear from his conscience all the
Scottish blood he has already spilled. Like Lady Macbeth in
Shakespeare's play, innocent blood will forever besmirch his hands.
Bruce will no longer remain inactive and blind towards his nation and
his people. He does not and will not accept Edward's *water* again.
Nothing which might be offered by the English monarch will buy his
loyalty. He sincerely adheres to the national cause to defend all his
subjects and to liberate the country, "At [that of every single Scot
seems to be implied] blud and land suld all lik beyn his awin" (XI.
544). Bruce starts to see his country as part of himself, with him as the
head and the rest of society as the body. In the traditional association
of society with the body, the members exist interdependently. For its
perfect functioning, all of them must be harmoniously complemented:

> The place of the head in the body of the commonwealth is filled by the prince. [...]
> The place of the heart is filled by the Senate, which initiates good works and ill. The
> duties of the eyes, ears, and tongue are claimed by the judges and governors of prov-
> inces. Officials and soldiers correspond to the hands. [...] Financial officers and keep-
> ers are compared to the stomach and the intestines. [...] The husbandmen correspond
> to the feet. (*Policraticus* V.ii.65)

Wallace's rhetoric has been effective: as his power begins to decline,
the national cause is perpetuated and renewed in the figure of Robert
Bruce. Their final reconciliation takes place in their next meeting:
"'Wallace," said Bruce, "[...] rabut me now no mar. / Myn awin dedis
has bet me wondyr sar'" (XI. 595–96). This serves to restore the natural order "with the subject kneeling [XI. 596–97] before his rightful
king, a fitting resolution to the topos of the world turned upside down"
(Goldstein 1993: 246). In fact, this is also a reversal of a *locus
communis* of epic poetry, in which there is a conflict between the king
and the hero:

---

[2] In *Deuteronomy* 21: 6-8, for instance, "all the elders of that city nearest to the slain
man shall wash their hands over the heifer whose neck was broken in the valley; and
they shall testify, 'Our hands did not shed this blood, neither did our eyes see it shed.
Forgive, O Lord, they people Israel, whom thou hast redeemed, and set not the guilt of
innocent blood in the midst of thy people Israel; but let the guilt of blood be forgiven
them.'"

It is the business of the king to maintain his dominion. [...] If the only way to do this is to sacrifice his property or his life, he must do so. The hero, on the other hand, is under no such restraint. Whatever his social rank, even if he is the son of a king, he has no responsibility for the society into which he intrudes. He has only one object, the establishment of his own reputation. (Jackson 1982: 12)

Therefore, as with Douglas in Barbour's narrative, the Bruce in Hary's text evolves from the personal to the national. As in *The Bruce*, the liberty of a nation supersedes "class privilege". Despite a similar treatment, Hary adumbrates this progression from a more elaborately rhetorical framework than his predecessor. While the evolution of Barbour's Douglas is one of political awareness, that of Hary's Bruce is an internalised process of self-realisation. The different epochs in which they were written might also explain their dissimilar approaches. The archdeacon of Aberdeen composed *The Bruce* at an early period when he had very few Scots rhetorical models to follow, whereas Hary, a contemporary of the greatest makars in the golden age of Scottish medieval literature, had those vernacular rhetorical models Barbour lacked: "Such rhetoric as Walter Bower cultivates in his *Scotichronicon* and such strongly imagined creations as Hary's Wallace or Henryson's Cresseid are quite alien to Barbour's time" (McDiarmid and Stevenson eds 1981–85: I: 51).

In Wallace's final renunciation of the guardianship, once the continuation of the national struggle has symbolically been handed on to Bruce, the knight still expresses the same concern with national freedom:

"Gud men," he said, "I was ȝour gouernour.
My mynd was set to do ȝow ay honour
And for to bryng this Realm to rychtwysnas.
For It I passit in mony paynfull place.
To wyn our awin my self I neui spard.
At the Fawkyrk thai ordand me Reward.
Off that reward ȝe her no mor throu me.
To sic gyftis god will full weill haiff E". (XI. 763–70)

The tragic hero's words return to Hary's main theme. The tired Wallace provides a sacrificial example, pointing to the kind of altruism his fellow nobles should show in serving Scotland's cause. The defeated Wallace of history is reconstructed as an invincible hero, whose renunciation of the guardianship is not the anticlimactic speech of a vanquished knight but rather a triumphant oration in favour of national freedom. Of course, the pseudo-sacred figure of Hary's Wallace knows that such an unselfish disposition will be rewarded in heaven. Again, the Wars of Independence against the English are elevated to sacred territory.

Barbour and Hary posit the national and individual consequences of foreign invasion through the occupation of Scotland. In Book I of *The Bruce*, the author explains the barbarities of the English in Scotland, the way in which they abuse power and the defenceless position of his kinsmen. The poet suggests that, together with the Scots' lack of freedom on the national level, they are also deprived of any kind of human dignity. To recover their fundamental rights, there is a need for a fair government, which will apply justice correctly. This point is even clearer when the famous apostrophising of freedom is contextualised.

After deposing Balliol, Edward I hastens to occupy and oppress Scotland. His proceedings are rapid and effective, which tacitly implies that the occupation follows a premeditated plan. The rapidity with which the invasion takes place confirms Barbour's suspicions in I. 91–110 when Edward I is chosen as the arbiter of the succession to the Scottish Throne. Historically, however, the situation was different:

to present the dispute over the succession as a conflict of freedom and thraldom, Barbour considerably alters the history of 1286–98. In the first place, Scotland was not helpless in 1286 as Barbour suggests. Six guardians, appointed less than a month after Alexander's death by a convention at Scone, ruled in the name of the king's lawful heir, the infant Margaret of Norway. (Ebin 1971–72: 226)

In *The Bruce*, then, the humiliations suffered by the Welsh and Irish are also going to be faced by the Scots. The English offensive is systematic. First, the English troops take all strongholds: "Sa hale yat bath castell & toune / War in-till his possessioune" (I. 185–86). This ensures the control of the country and makes resistance impossible. Subsequently, Edward bestows all important public positions on Englishmen "for to gowern land afferis / He maid off Inglis nation" (I. 192–93). After taking these two steps, Edward has the dominance of Scotland.

Despite the historical gap and differences between colonial Africa and late medieval Scotland, Frantz Fanon's comments on the former are also applicable to the Scottish situation as denounced by Barbour:

The colonial world is a world divided into two. The dividing line, the frontiers, are shown by barracks and police stations. In the colonies it is the policeman and the soldier who are the official, the instituted go-between, the spokesmen of the settler and his rule. (Fanon 1980: 29)

Scots can no longer confront the English militarily (the latter possess the strongholds) or legally (the reins of power are in English hands). Barbour's nationalistic and dynastic discourse becomes prominent here. Those referred to as English are not only the lords or soldiers who were born in England, but anyone either from England or Scotland supporting Edward I, whereas Scots are only those who fight with and for Robert Bruce (Goldstein 1993:195). This distinction will be maintained during the rest of the narrative. A symptomatic example is that of Sir Ingram Umphraville, who is first called English at the beginning of the romance; then, when he joins Bruce, Umphraville is regarded as Scottish. Finally he is again considered to be English on leaving Robert I's court for that of Edward II. Barbour's tenets comply with an identification of the King of Scots with the nation itself. The makar's dialectics disseminate the existing royal ideology. As Fiona Watson remarks, with the consolidation of kingly authority during the thirteenth century, national identity began to be conceived along the lines of the ruling family's political aspirations (Watson 1998: 18).

When presenting his initial account of English tyranny in *The Wallace*, Hary contrasts the heroes and the villains. Nevertheless, the distinction is different from that drawn in *The Bruce*: the opposition is between the English invaders and the "trew Scottis" whom Edward "gert sla hastely / Off man and wiff vii thousand and fyfty" (I. 93–94). This allows for a more dramatic and hideous representation of disloyal Scots: "Whereas Barbour avoids calling Bruce's Scottish opponents 'Scots' insofar as that is possible, Blind Hary does not hesitate to present Amer as both Scottish and traitor" (Goldstein 1993: 248). In the more combative and Anglophobic language of *The Wallace*, the specific construction of "traitors" enhances the virulence of the nationalistic message.

In the lines following the submission of Scotland, both poets relate and denounce the demeanour of the English towards the defenceless people of Scotland. In *The Bruce*, they are accused of doing whatever they please: they rape women and their daughters (I. 199–200) and steal (I. 208–210). Similarly in *The Wallace*,

Both wiffis, wedowis, thai tuk all at thar will,
Nonnys, madyns, quham thai likit to spill.
King Herodis part thai playit in-to Scotland
Off ʒong childyr that thai befor thaim fand. (I. 163 66)

Thus, they oppress the Scottish community in every possible manner: on physical, psychological and economic levels. Hary incorporates a typological comparison with Herod with which he intensifies the horror occasioned by the English. The allegorical correspondences of the war against the invaders as a holy enterprise are also established. At the same time, he denounces the English behaviour in a chivalric society since "office of knychthede is to mantene and defend wedowis, maidenis, faderles and moderles barnis, and pore miserable personis and piteable, and to help the wayke agayne the star" (Haye 1901–14: II. 27). Insofar as the English knights are harming those that they should respect, their conduct can only fall into the category of bad knighthood. Hary's accusation works at two different levels: typologically, in its relation to sacred history, and chivalrically, in its connection with the techniques of the *roman courtois* tradition.

The thematic strategies of *The Wallace* and *The Bruce* include a portrayal of the intervention of ecclesiastical institutions in the Wars of Independence. In *The Wallace*, for example, the author devotes some lines to the enemies' atrocities committed against the properties of the Church to conclude that "Thai tuk in hand of thar archybyschops haile" (I. 168). Then, both Hary and Barbour denounce the loss of secular institutions of power and the English appropriation of the centres of faith. This double seizure threatens both Scotland's survival as a nation and its identity, which was closely associated with King and Church. According to John Pocock, as well as a common ancestry, history and tradition, nations are constructed as communities sharing an inherited "institutional past" (Pocock 1975: 99). In this light, with the abolition of native legal institutions, Edward I deprives Scotland of one of its defining national symbols. Both authors deploy the loss of the "institutional past" as a weapon in favour of national autonomy and against foreign invasion.

The worst thing of all, however, is that the Scots cannot even defend their rights. Barbour tells us twice in twelve lines what happens if anybody dares to protest: the invaders would find – or invent, if necessary – any reason to deprive them of their land or life, or else, they would live in misery (I. 203–4; 210–12). The logical conclusion makes explicit reference to legal mechanisms of justice: "For yai dempt yaim efter yar will, / Takand na kep to rycht na skill" (I. 213–14). There is an implicit demand which goes beyond national or individual freedom. Barbour clamours for the necessity of equity, which would permit the inhabitants of Scotland to live with dignity. The kind of legal impartiality expressed in these lines can only be recovered through the good administration of government. This is what Bruce offers to his subjects.

The next passage focuses on the praise of freedom: the most frequently quoted section of *The Bruce*. However, when it is cited in anthologies, the quotation tends to begin with I. 225: "A, fredome is a noble thing", not mentioning the previous six lines, which again stress the pre-eminence of justice:

[Alas] yat folk yat euer wes fre,
And in fredome wount for to be,
Throw yar gret myschance and foly
War tretyt yan so wykkytly
Yat yar fais yar iugis war,
Quhat wrechitnes may man have mar. (I. 219–24)

Immediately after the exposition of the English cruelty and subjugation of Scotland, the beginning of the famous apostrophe to freedom is introduced and related to the lack of justice in the framework of law:

A, fredome is a noble thing,
Fredome mays man to haiff liking,
Fredome all solace to man giffis,
He levys at es yat frely levys.
A noble hart may haiff nane es
Na ellys nocht yat may his ples
Gyff fredome fail3he, for fre liking
Is 3harnyt our all oyer thing. (I. 225–32)

Barbour highlights the need for justice to safeguard freedom. In this milieu, equity can only be interpreted, not as an ideal, but through its everyday application according to the mechanisms of royal and legal

power. Barbour's praise of liberty thus becomes a plea for a benevo-
lent application of justice. Therefore, the two major aspects which
Barbour associates with freedom, happiness and free choice, are necessarily dependent on the correct administration and functioning of the
mechanisms of Scottish royal authority.

Although this is "the first address to Freedom in medieval
literature" (Utz 1969: 152), Barbour's idea of liberty is constructed
along foreseeable scholastic lines. The pillars on which the poet places
freedom – free choice and the possibility of happiness – coincide with
Aquinas's analysis of the concept. According to the medieval philosopher, people can choose to act freely: "every act of free choice is
preceded by a judgement of reason". So far, this approach is not
peculiarly medieval. But Aquinas also states that "man is free in
choosing this or that particular good. The choices of some particular
goods may be necessary as a means to the acquisition of the final end,
happiness" (Copleston 1991: 193–98). In *The Bruce*, in one of the
climactic moments of the narrative, then, Barbour, as man of his times
and an archdeacon, conflates the idea of national freedom with
Christian thought. This anagogic interpretation of attaining earthly
happiness by choosing good things, which, at the same time, should
lead us to eternal felicity, *beatitudo*, in the transcendent afterlife, is
what is really medieval about this theory.

In *Squyer Meldrum*, although there are no explicit references to
freedom, Sir David Lindsay also offers a negative image of the
English after Flodden. He centres his narrative on Meldrum's military
and amatory adventures in Scotland, France and England, depicting
the English as enemies but also the French as allies. The portrayal of
France and the French is the least problematic. Meldrum visits the
French court, where he meets King Louis. The encounter serves to
revive the Anglo-Scottish tensions, which climax in a confrontation
between the English and the Scots at King Louis' court (ll.601–72). In
The Bruce, the battles in Ireland serve the same purpose, with the
English and Scots taking their disputes beyond the confines of their
frontiers. As did many other Scottish nobles of the time, such as Sir
Gilbert Hay, Meldrum enters the service of the French sovereign
(ll.673–79). The narrator argues that the squire's bravery against the
English won him a place in Louis' retinue. Meldrum's chivalric
exploits for the French monarch are dealt with in a few lines, not
devoid of courtly overtones, with a lady of high rank wanting to marry

him, whom he refuses to return to Scotland (ll.680–87). As in most Scottish romances, the choice between love and nation is resolved in favour of the latter. Within his maturation process, Meldrum is not yet ready to settle down.

However, Lindsay does not give a homogeneous image of the despicable Auld Enemy. Instead, he treats different groups or individuals in a particular manner. The language of epic and romance appropriately shapes the narrative when both nations come into play. The above mentioned confrontation at the French court ends with the English attacking the heavily outnumbered Scots in a house, to which they set fire (ll.624–36). Meldrum fittingly appears in the scene and saves the day (ll.637–55). At this point, Lindsay makes no concession to the English. The deadly sins of "Inuie" (1.624) and "ire" (1.635) rule their actions. There is no justification for this fight in France, which causes numerous casualties on both sides.

In the context of the Scottish Arthurian romances, *Lancelot of the Laik* problematises the boundaries of freedom in relation to kingship and the oppression of the poor, which in more contemporary terms would correspond to Berlin's reference to the "oppressed classes". Amytans, as Arthur's spiritual guide in his regeneration process, warns him that "With gret myschef oppressit ar the pure; / And thow art causs of al this hol injure" (ll.1355–56). The idea is further developed to explore the consequences of aggrieving all strata of society:

May he [a prince] his rigne, may he his holl empire
Susten al only of his owne desyre
In servyng of his wrechit appetit
Of averice and of his awn delyt
And hald his men wncherist in thraldome?
Nay! that shal sone his hie estat consome,
For many o knycht therby is broght ydoune
All uteraly to ther confusioune.
For oft it makith uther kingis by
To wer on them in trast of victory. (ll.1527–36)

Amytans exhorts the dangers of a lord exercising his *privata voluntas*. As the head of the communal body, the king should be the first to commit himself to the laws of the country, serving as an example for his vassals to follow. But more importantly, the stability of his territories seems to depend on the respect of individual liberties as promoted by late medieval Scottish documents such as the Treaty of Bingham. Even if his interpretation is rather adventurous owing to lack of evidence, Bertram Vogel suggests that the precarious state of government under James III might have caused the author to adapt this particular passage from the *Prose Lancelot*, highlighting its political import (Vogel 1943: 5). At any rate, if only in general terms, the makar does disseminate a Scottish concern with the close connection between good government and a country's survival as an independent state with personal liberties.

In the other Middle Scots Arthurian romance, *Golagros and Gawane*, the portrayal of the triad of national freedom, the autonomous nation and national identity differs considerably from those expressed in the historical romances. Although the other three narratives also tackle these issues and their implications in the Scottish political situation of their times, the actions taken by Golagros's court in the Arthurian romance indicate a subtle but nonetheless dissimilar representation of these notions. After his feigned victory over Gawain, Golagros asks his "cumly knightis":

"Say me ane chois, the tane of thir twa,
Quhethir ye like me lord, laught in the feild,
Or ellis my life at the lest lelely forga,
And boune yow to sum berne, that myght be your beild?" (ll.1181–84)

The question very much echoes the Declaration of Arbroath, which established that if a King of Scots did not perform his duties correctly and had to submit to another nation, the Scottish community would be within its rights to depose him in favour of another leader (Duncan ed. 1997: 780). The Declaration is "a manifesto of a united nation, determined to resist English aggression and to oust even Bruce should he show any sign of weakening in the cause" (Dickinson et al. eds 1952: 131). At least ideally, both in the romance and in the Declaration, sovereignty rests on the Community of the Realm in Scotland and Golagros's nobility respectively, who are essentially those that must approve of the king's proper administration of power. The independence of the country and the defence of its interest take precedence over royal ambitions. By way of contrast, national concerns supersede royal and personal desires. Interestingly, in Anglo-Norman and English romances such as *Guy of Warwick* or *Bevis of Hampton*, kings must abide by justice, which cannot be subverted by regal authority (Crane 1986: 69). Yet the spirit is completely different from that of the Scottish romances insofar as, within this ideological framework, the Anglo-Norman and English texts were defending baronial rights and ambitions, whereas the Scottish works prioritised the interests of an independent Scotland.

So far, the sort of kingship proposed by the author is supported by exactly the same arguments as those posited in *The Bruce* and in *The Wallace*. The makars articulate a discourse in which the kingdom's self-government prevails over the figure of the sovereign, at least at an idealistic level. In the historical romances, for example, Balliol cannot be the ruler of the nation in that he is characterised as a weak monarch who eagerly capitulates before Edward I. Therefore, in the Scottish contextualisation of *Golagros and Gawane*, Golagros, whose image is that of an ideal ruler, contrasts with Balliol, who must necessarily place his position and privileges in the hands of his council since he has failed to maintain the independence of his dominions.

Nevertheless, what is strikingly dissimilar from the other narratives is the answer of Golagros's lords, which conveys a fascinating range of implications:

"We wil na favour here fenye to frende nor to fa.
We like yow ay as our lord, to were and to weild;
Your lordschip we may noght forga, alse lang as we leif.
Ye sal be our governour,
Quhil your dais may endure,
In eise and honour,
For chance that may cheif". (ll.1187–93)

The most obvious interpretation of these lines postulates the sense of loyalty felt by these subjects of Golagros towards their lords' fair administration of power. The oath of loyalty, as one of the pillars of late medieval social hierarchy, is the best reward for a good leader. Nevertheless, the response of Golagros's council creates an inescapable tension between fealty and allegiance to one's lord and the concept and maintenance of national/territorial freedom. Although by the end of the romance Arthur releases Golagros from his oath of homage, reconciling both notions, the intricacies of the decision of Golagros's vassals still remain to be analysed. By elevating Golagros to the status of the best possible leader of his people, an implicit assumption of the cult of personality is exhibited. This is at the expense of other criteria such as the future of the country under foreign rule or the effects derived from the coercion of national liberty. Therefore, while, as in *The Bruce* and in *The Wallace*, the nature of Golagros's attitude originates in considerations expressed in the Declaration of Arbroath, the subjects' actions reveal a naiveté absent from the other narratives. They merge the idea of identity with the figure of the ruler. Hence, their blind confidence in him may lead them to the loss of their national and, quite probably also personal, liberties.

In general, then, the Scottish romances explore the national concerns of government through the different attitudes and tenets of their main characters. After the Wars of Independence, the affirmation that "the peculiar pattern of England and Scotland after the [Norman] Conquest seems to have led to the invention of a type of romance which is truly of *origine lignagère*" (Legge 1963: 139), no longer applies. Although the English romances dealt with "issues of insular baronial life" and legality (Crane 1986: 16) thoroughly, the scope of the Scottish texts concentrates on matters affecting the integrity and autonomy of the whole realm. Territorial and national concerns supersede feudal disputes.

Nationhood and nationalistic discourses

The national discourse in *The Bruce* is introduced within the discussion on the relativity of freedom and the necessity of having a sovereign who supports it. Barbour does so not only through the praise of liberty (I. 223–74), but also by means of excoriating Bruce's rivals to the Scottish crown, Comyn and Balliol.

Edward offers the Scottish throne to John Balliol if the latter swears fealty to the English king:

Bot Schyr Iohn the Balleoll perfay
Assentyt till him in all his will,
Quhar-throuch fell efter mekill ill.
He was king bot a litill quhile
And throuch gret sutelte and ghyle
For litill enchesone or nane
He was arestyt syne and tane,
And degradyt syne was he

Off honour and off dignite,
Quheyer it wes throuch wrang or rycht
God wat it yat is maist off mycht.[3] (I. 168–78)

The actions of Bruce's rival demonstrate that he is not good enough to govern and lead Scotland. By strategically juxtaposing Balliol's agreement and Bruce's refusal (I. 157–64), Barbour contrasts their divergent attitudes towards the future of their nation. Balliol dissents from Bruce's plans for the country: he repudiates national freedom and puts that of Scotland at jeopardy, betraying his "eldris". In case it is not sufficiently obvious to the audience that Balliol is not the monarch his nation needs, the narrator explicitly anticipates these events, concluding that: "Quhar-throuch [the agreement] fell efter mekill ill" (I. 170). As King of Scots, Balliol's procedures bind the destiny of the entire country: he is a monarch who submits his nation to an external power. This occasions both the dramatic devastation of his country and the oppression of his people.

Even when Edward deposes Balliol "For litill enchesone or nane" (I. 173), the makar detaches himself from the righteousness of the English king's action: "Quheyer it wes throuch wrang or rycht / God wat it yat is maist of mycht" (I. 177–78). At this juncture, the text's dynastic and nationalistic trends conflate: from a Brucean and Stewart perspective, Bruce and his Stewart descendents are the rivals of the Balliols' cause; consequently, Balliol's position will not be defended under any circumstances. Moreover, from a nationalist standpoint, insofar as Balliol has placed his personal or feudal aims above those of his country, he deserves to be deposed by all available means (even by Edward's intervention). Barbour implicitly attests that Balliol's deposition was brought about through God's wisdom, which presupposes the correctness of the action. The thematic and conceptual composition of *The Bruce* does not leave room for feudal ambitions but only for the defence of the national and the Brucean/Stewart dynastic cause.

As Goldstein notes, John Balliol strategically disappears from the narrative in the remaining nineteen books: "Barbour effectively

---

[3] Historically, however, the circumstances might have been different. Although it is true that Balliol did homage to Edward I, a "letter to Edward I renouncing his homage and fealty [...] suggests the Edward has extorted his homage and fealty by violence". (Goldstein 1993: 42)

silences Balliol himself, a passive figure who never speaks" (Gold-stein 1993: 154). The lack of a voice of his own prevents him from justifying his actions. At the same time, it avoids any tension between his supposed plans for the realm and those of Bruce. In the makar's political conception of the work, the former's silence operates as his symbolic inability to conceive a future for Scotland. As the author has already discredited him as the sovereign of the country, neither his presence nor his words are required (the similar historicised presenta-tion of Balliol as a puppet monarch in Hary's *Wallace* may well be partly derived from *The Bruce*. Hary's portrayal of Balliol is even more exiguous than that of Barbour). Historically, Balliol's inability to fight for the sovereignty and rights of the nation against Edward I obliged the *communitas regni* to take drastic measures. As Fiona Watson declares, for the first (but not last) time in late medieval Scotland, the king was disposed of its power owing to his "incapacity" (Watson 1998: 22). In *The Bruce*, such incapacity is reproduced through John's silence.

Comyn's attitude in the first book also jeopardises the freedom of Scotland since his plans are focused on personal promotion rather than on national interest. By denouncing his agreement with Bruce to Edward, Comyn aims to become king and keep his lands too. Behind his behaviour, there is a total unawareness of his own country's most urgent needs: being a king under these circumstances would mean being another of Edward's puppets just like Balliol. Therefore, he is as inappropriate a leader for Scotland as Balliol was. Of the three of them, only Bruce can be regarded as the ruler Scotland requires. Barbour ignores the great and influential power exercised by the two branches of the Comyns during the later thirteenth century. As in his depiction of Balliol, the makar reduces Comyn's portrayal to his confrontation with the main hero.

As well as his submission to Edward, there is another trait in Comyn's demeanour that makes him unworthy of kingship: his infringement of his previous pact with Bruce is a violation of the oath of loyalty. For a late medieval audience, someone who cannot keep his oath would never be a good monarch, since he is undermining one of the pillars of society. Betrayal in the sphere of royal power is equated with the loss of national liberty. Barbour compares Comyn's treason to the greatest treacheries of pseudo-historical romances: those of Troy, Alexander the Great, Julius Caesar and Arthur (I. 515–62).

Comyn is symbolically transformed into a traitor of comparable renown. The simile also situates Bruce in the same position as those of the Nine Worthies who were betrayed. Crucially, the opposition between treason and loyalty highlights Douglas's role: "Larg and luffand als wes he, / And our all thing luffyt lawte" (I. 363–64). Therefore, in the construction of the Matter of Scotland, a term coined by Goldstein, the monarchical hero is accompanied by his loyal comrade-at-arms. Although the nuances of the relationship between Bruce and Douglas may not have many clear parallels with those of other heroes, Barbour craftily reverts to epic and romance techniques in the creation of this new historically based sub-genre of romance.

In Hay's *Conquerour*, a similar opposition between a suitable king and an inappropriate one is developed. In contraposition to Alexander's idealised image of leadership, Darius is pictured as the example not to follow. If in *The Bruce*, Comyn and Balliol would not be able to lead and govern Scotland, in the *Conquerour* Darius's bad rule of the Persian Empire can be interpreted as the cause of his and its downfall. His death is symptomatic of his misrule. His own men kill him (ll.6770–74) because all his subjects hate him. In his dying moments, he still has time to formulate his last speech in front of Alexander:

Bot Alexander, þow has ane fare myrroure,
To luke to me, and think of my dollour,
[…]
Quhare ar þai castellis and þai fare clething,
The beddis of gold quhare þai bodie lay in?
Quhare ar þai ladyis and þai dochteris dere,
Thay wiffe, þi moder, and þai sisteris clere? (ll.6826–27; 6864–67)

Darius offers himself as a mirror for Alexander; as a negative mirror of how not to act. Unlike Aristotle, however, he does not proffer a lesson on kingship, but concentrates on a more affective vision of humankind from a Boethian perspective. The customary realisation that earthly possessions are ephemeral is given a even more dramatic gravity by the way in which Darius dies, betrayed by those "quhome maist I traistit in" (l.6821). In his *memento mori*, alone, betrayed and humiliated, he comes to realise how important it is to win his people's love, not purely in emotional terms, but also to be able to trust them when things are against the monarch. As in *The Bruce*, contrasting kingly figures, including Edward I, operate as a dichotomy against which the heroes define themselves.

In the *Buik of Alexander*, binary opposition of values and dual relationships between characters stress another vital aspect in the late medieval Scottish romances: loyalty. While treason is not as developed as in *The Bruce* and the *Conquerour*, the import of the subjects' loyalty to his monarch is at the core of the texts' ideological tenets. If Douglas is the epitome of loyalty in *The Bruce*, in the *Buik* all twelve peers display unconditional allegiance to Alexander, thanks to the Macedonian Emperor's love for them and his willingness to reward them. When Duke Betys kills Samson, for instance, Samson claims that he is dying for Alexander, who will avenge his death (*Forray*, 928–36). Out of loyalty, Samson performs the last sacrificial act for his monarch and his cause, not even questioning the reasons for his death. Likewise, Ptolemy's words exemplify the twelve peers' love and respect for Alexander:

> Said Tholomere, "shir [Alexander], wit ye wele
> That your great worship euer ilk dele
> Hes vs effered on sic manere
> That neuer mare in peax na were,
> Nane sall for yow refusit be
> Trauell, thocht it be great to se.
> For ye sa wyse ar and worthy,
> And so fulfillit of courtessy,
> That ye serue to haue full wele
> All that euer may be done ilka dele.
> Ane lord makes worthy men, I wis,
> Or ellis sum folk begylit is! (*Avowis*, 3465–76)

Ptolemy's unreserved loyalty springs from Alexander's behaviour towards his men. Loyalty is represented as a reciprocal commitment which only good monarchs will receive from their subjects. Such a symbiotic relationship is accomplished not only through material rewards, but more importantly through Alexander's "great worship" of his men and his good government. The audience could easily establish a negative analogy with mid fifteenth-century Scotland, a period of political instability and betrayed loyalties under James II, which ended with the Black Douglases' rebellion in the 1450s.

The concept of leadership in which the best possible leader should be the lord is common to two out of the three Scottish historical romances, *The Bruce* and *The Wallace*. In *The Bruce*, Barbour dismisses the importance of the rule of primogeniture through a deliberate obfuscation of succession procedures. If Bruce is the only valid monarch for the country, it is because he is the best king. In the climactic moments before Bannockburn, Bruce's image as a national leader is reinforced: he makes an inspired and inspiring speech to enthuse his men and reaffirm the nationalistic message Barbour wishes to convey. The hero, playing the role of a general according to classical tradition, shows his command of the rhetoric of persuasion. Bernice W. Kliman claims that "Barbour develops the last great exhortations to battle before Bannockburn (XI, XII) more fully than the other rhetorical speeches, bringing to a dramatic climax Bruce's self-realisation of his aims" (Kliman 1975: 156). In the crucial events of the narrative, Barbour deploys the most rhetorically sophisticated language following the rules of decorum. According to Geoffrey of Vinsauf:

Whether short or long, let the discourse always be decorated within and without; but choose among ornaments with discretion. First examine the soul of the word and then its face, whose outward show alone you should not trust. Unless the inner ornament conforms to the outer requirement, the relation between the two is worthless. (*Poetria Nova*, ll.742–47)

Bruce's speech is built around three main topics: the country's freedom, its rights (which are supported by God) and material possessions. First, the King of Scots emphasises that "Ye fyrst [reason] is yat we haf ye rycht / And for ye rycht ay God will fycht" (XII. 235–36). Secondly, aware of his followers' personal interests, Bruce refers to the "ryches" the English have brought with them, so "Yat ye powrest of ȝow sall be / Bath rych and mychty" (XII. 237–44); the monarch contemplates the material profits his men may acquire from the spoils. Through the manner in which he expounds this matter, it seems as though Bruce is addressing the vast majority of his troops (or at least representatives of all the social strata) – again conveying that the national struggle includes every single Scot. Thanks to his command of rhetoric, he manages to conflate the country's interests with those of his followers. Finally, he stands for his cause (the liberation of Scotland) and his subjects. When he refers to "childer" and "wywis", he means not only widows and orphans, but the weak, who, according to chivalric tradition, must be defended by knights. By including all the inhabitants of the country in the King's words, Barbour's Bruce becomes not only a chivalric but also a national hero.

In the *Buik of Alexander*, following the French original, the makar constructs the Macedonian Emperor's speeches along similar lines to those in *The Bruce*, emphasising the king's capacity of leadership:

"Lordingis," said the nobill King,
[...]
"I pray ilk man that he
Nocht couetous na yarnand be
To tak na ryches that thay wald,
Bot wyn of deadly fais the fald.
Fra thay be winnin, all, wit ye weill,
The gudis ar ouris euer ilk deill". (*Avowis*, 7250; 7266–71)

While Bruce appears to talk to all of his men, Alexander's speech is directed to his "lordingis". At any rate, as in *The Bruce*, the booty is important, but not the main reason why they should fight. If in Barbour's romance Bruce tells his men to fight primordially for their right, Alexander wants them to fight with honour – the rewards will come after the battle. Both monarchs, therefore, carefully merge political and chivalric principles with their subordinates' material ambitions. Their command of rhetoric makes them exceptional leaders on the battlefield.

In the elaborate creation of the Matter of Scotland in which the binary opposition between treason and loyalty is highlighted, the representation of Robert Bruce must be revised. Barbour has to tackle a serious problem when projecting young Robert's image: Bruce's adherence to Edward's party. As Barrow asserts, Bruce was the only Scottish leader who deserted the national cause in the period between 1294 and 1304 (Barrow 1996: 109). Historically, Bruce threatens national liberty and favours his personal interests at the expense of his loyalty to Scotland. In *The Bruce*, nevertheless, the makar intermingles the emancipation of his country with Bruce's royal aspirations. The future king is portrayed as the only possible liberator and ruler of the country, even if his own interests are often far from the national policy he dictates. The author conveniently suppresses the years of Bruce's support for Edward. To do so, he makes use of poetic licence. In the 1290s, the Robert Bruce aspiring to the Crown after Alexander

III's death is Robert Bruce, the Competitor, the grandfather of the future sovereign and main character in the poem, King Robert I:

As a genealogist of the Stewarts, Barbour knew that he was conflating three generations to create the image of a perfect leader. But an icon moves the sympathy of an
audience more powerfully than a flawed model and the moving of one's audience to
proper action is the causal end of our discipline as defined by Aristotle and understood by early Christian commentators. (Jack 2000: 29)

Such a deliberate displacement of roles also serves first to avoid explaining or justifying Bruce's adherence to the English party. Sec- ondly, it creates antagonism between Robert Bruce and Edward I from the beginning. Thirdly, the struggle for the Scottish throne between John Balliol and Bruce demonstrates that there is only one suitable king of Scotland. For the author's purposes, then, unifying the figures of the Competitor and his grandson turns out to be very profitable at a literary and political level. Another interesting compatible interpreta- tion is that offered by Kinghorn, for whom this "deliberate confusion of Bruce and his grandfather" serves to "give the impression to posterity that there had been a family resistance of two generations standing" (Kinghorn 1968–69: 141).

Nevertheless, this does not completely solve Barbour's problem, since the succession conflict took place before 1299. Therefore, after Bruce's refusal of Edward's devious proposal that he assume the crown of Scotland, Bruce is not mentioned again for three hundred lines. In the meantime, Balliol is crowned and deposed and the coun- try occupied. After these three hundred lines of desolation, Robert Bruce (historically, the grandson already) appears again:

Thys lord ye Brwys I spak of ayr
Saw all ye kynryk swa forfayr,
And swa trowblyt ye folk saw he
Yat he yaroff had gret pitte. (I. 477–80)

This is the way in which the makar links Robert Bruce, the Competi- tor, and his grandson, the future king. Barbour's Robert Bruce (the one amalgamating the nationalistic virtues of grandfather, father and son) re-emerges as a patriot after his long silence, politically and historically necessary: "Barbour's construction of the fictive Bruce cannot admit of a patriot who placed his duty to his nation behind that of his family" (Goldstein 1993: 150). In these three hundred lines, the

period 1299–1304 is supposed to have elapsed. From a historical perspective, Bruce rejoins the national cause. When peace with England
was no longer advantageous for Bruce, he decided to revive his royal
aspirations in Scotland. At this point, his own interests become difficult to differentiate from those of Scotland (Goldstein 1993: 150–51).
Nevertheless, according to Barbour's account, the hero has never left
the national side. On the rhetorical and literary levels, the fusion of
characters also conveys a symbolic sense of unity to the romance. For
this reason, it is vital to avoid mentioning Bruce's desertion, inasmuch
as the hero's attitude would not have been understood from a nationalistic position and would have damaged the intentionality of the plot
as a whole.

The construction of Barbour's plot is overtly nationalistic. Feudal
concerns remain subsidiary to the main discourse. The delicate political situation of that particular moment did not encourage any other
discursive pattern:

> internal instability increased at Robert II's accession. Not only did Douglas make a
> spurious claim to the throne and have to be bought off, but Robert's eldest son was
> illegitimate. The future line of succession was not secure. It was in this context of
> political instability that Barbour wrote the *Bruce*. (Watt 1994: 93)

In a feudal society, in which a lord may own lands and properties on
both sides of the border, it is at least understandable that, owing to
personal interests, sometimes a noble might support one king and at
other times the other. This was also Bruce's dilemma: he had to
choose between his feudal interests and the national cause.
Circumstances obliged him to opt for his personal and feudal interests.
While the other most important Scottish families remained faithful to
the defence of Scotland, Robert Bruce and his followers adhered to
Edward I twice, first in 1296 and again in 1302. Notwithstanding that,
in the historical context in which he was writing, the poet could not
merely explain the hero's desertion if he wanted the nobles to support
Robert II. To do so would have meant encouraging and justifying
treason among the Scottish nobility in the late fourteenth century; that
is, something completely opposed to Barbour's conceptual
motivations.

Another relevant component of Barbour's ideology relates to the
succession. While Bruce is represented as the ideal King of Scots, the
author has to resolve another serious problem when it comes to the

election of the king. Robert Bruce was not the candidate best positioned under a strict interpretation of the rule of primogeniture. An introduction to the legal matters concerning the succession is clearly presented at first:

Tyll yat ye barnage at ye last
Assemblyt yaim and fayndyt fast
To cheys a king yar land to ster
Yat off awncestry cummyn wer
Off kingis yat aucht yat reawte
And mayst had rycht yair king to be. (I. 41–46)

Likewise, the subsequent main argument defended by Balliol and his supporters remains clear and unambiguous: "he wes cummyn off ye offspryng / Off hyr yat eldest syster was" (I. 50–51). Historically, this corresponds to their main argument, since Balliol was the true heir to the Scottish Crown according to the strict rule of primogeniture.

Yet, when it comes to Bruce and his followers, Barbour's exposition appears to be deliberately vague. Goldstein argues that at first Barbour seems to allude to the historical arguments posited by Bruce. The future King of Scots claimed that the particular nature of kingship should exclude the rule of primogeniture. If this were so, Bruce's thesis at this point in the poem would serve to refute that of Balliol. However, subsequently Barbour obscures the argument by saying that Bruce's claim is in branch collaterate. Since all the competitors claim that they are descended from Earl David, William the Lion's brother, Goldstein concludes that these lines do not fit with Bruce's historical position (Goldstein 1993: 155).

Barbour's audience, on hearing this part of the romance read aloud, could probably reach no conclusion on who should be the rightful monarch in legal terms. They could only continue to listen to the poet in search of further evidence. Nevertheless, none of the other arguments put forward by the historical Bruce are alluded to since they would have worked against him historically, and also against the dialectics of the romance. The author was not really interested in giving much more complementary information about this matter; historically, Balliol was the best positioned candidate, being the son of the daughter of Earl David's oldest daughter, whereas Bruce was the son of the earl's younger daughter. Consequently, "the facts of Scottish history for the past two hundred years were against Bruce"

(Barrow 1993: 41–42). After his seizure of the throne, Bruce's position was less than comfortable. Many Scottish nobles felt obliged to fight against him as he was not the rightful King of Scots. His action was probably seen as a usurpation of the crown as unjustifiable as Edward I's deposition of Balliol. Equally importantly, Robert II would not have liked to see his legitimacy to the throne questioned in a text he had commissioned himself. After the death of Robert I and before becoming King of Scots, the future Robert II fought the rebellion initiated in 1332 by Edward Balliol, John Balliol's son, helped by the English. Thus, a destabilising image of a Balliol as rightful heir in Barbour's *Bruce* was out of the question.

As inheritor of the *roman courtois* and epic traditions, Barbour concentrates on heroic action rather than on presenting a thorough debate concerning the nature of the competitors' argumentation. He makes use of another rhetorical device to persuade the reader about the sort of king Scotland needs: one who is going to lead the country freely and justly. The Archdeacon resorts to the *roman courtois* convention in which the best knight is the Elect because of inherent merit. Although, as buttressed by historical evidence, Balliol was forced to submit to the English king, the invention of a secret alliance between Balliol and Edward (I. 168–78) helps the makar to suit his own ends. In the ten lines about his reign, Balliol's opposition to Edward is not mentioned at all (Watt 1994: 97). Instead, Barbour depicts Balliol as a traitor, comparatively strengthening Bruce's position as a leader. According to chivalric tradition, the military worth of a great lord is of the greatest importance. Therefore, the author's projection of Bruce's image as the champion of national freedom and ideal leader justifies his right to be king. *Per contra*, Balliol, owing to his weakness (historically) and to his treason (in the romance), should not be the King of Scots.

The arguments posited by Barbour might be inspired by (or at least coincide with) those expressed in the Declaration of Arbroath:

We are bound to him [Robert I] for the maintaining of our freedom both by his right and merits, as to him by whom salvation has been wrought unto our people, and by him, come what may, we mean to stand. Yet if he should give up what he has begun, seeking to make our kingdom subject to the king of England or to the English, we would strive at once to drive him out as our enemy and a subverter of his own right and ours, and we would make some other man who was able to defend us our king. (Declaration of Arbroath, Duncan ed. 1997: 780)

Interestingly, in the *Policraticus*, John of Salisbury advocates a similar proceeding in the election of leader, together with Divine Providence:

And so, as has been said, he [the prince] is placed by divine governance at the apex of the commonwealth, and preferred above all others, sometimes through the secret ministry of God's providence, sometimes by the decision of His priests, and again it is the votes of the whole people which concur to place the ruler to authority. (*Policraticus* V.vi.83)

The most important ideas in this extract from the Declaration are the equation of right and merit, which minimises the supremacy of the rule of primogeniture over any other argument. Furthermore, the Scottish lords will oppose and depose the monarch should he betray his country. These views, then, correspond with those expressed in *The Bruce*. Bruce wins his right to be king thanks to merit, inasmuch as he is the leader destined to liberate Scotland; hence, he also gains its people's support.

In Hay's *Buik of King Alexander the Conquerour*, Alexander's accession to the throne is also problematic. When his father, King Philip, marries Cleopatra (ll.2090–93), Alexander realises that his succession is jeopardised. Hence, he puts a plan into practice: he kills Jonas, the Seneschal of Greece and Cleopatra's uncle. Soon afterwards, he defeats Philip, who is forced to apologise to Olympias, Alexander's mother (ll.2199–201). Alexander proves his power, which not even his father can withstand, thus placing himself in a perfect position for the succession. After Philip is killed, the council of lords must choose a new king. Alexander gives a speech to the council:

"And heir-attour I gif ȝow my counsall,
To cheis ane king with haill consent,
To quhome þair is baith wit and wisdome lent,
And power als to keip ȝow and defend –
Ȝe se quhow Dare ȝow has his message send,
To haue tribut or to destroy ȝour land,
And ȝe mon othir obey vntill his wand
Or ellis to cheis ane man of gouernance,
Ȝow to defend fra sic clame and challance." (ll.2436–44)

Even if Alexander will become the most dominant sovereign in the world, at this juncture Darius is the ruler of a much more powerful

empire which threatens to subjugate the Greek people. The Scottish
simile is easy to establish in relation to the English menace to Scottish
autonomy during and after the Wars of Independence. Under such a
situation, the monarch Greece requires responds to Alexander's exposition. He must be someone with enough influence to unite the support
of both Greeks and Macedonians under his leadership beyond internal
disputes; that is, a hero with the same attributes as the Bruce, whom
Barbour creates for his romance. Subsequently, Alexander formulates
his own claim to the throne:

> "And I am bot ane childe heir, as ye se,
> And hes eneuch heretage for me,
> Baith of conquest and of motheris landis,
> Of Armene, þat now cummis in hir handis,
> And thocht I was maid air be testament,
> Yit will I put it in your iugement,
> And heir resingis all my power hale
> To yow lordis, and to your god consall;
> Supois þat I mycht hald it throw puissance,
> I will nocht haue it with your displesance,
> And thairfoir cheis quhom ye think worthiest –
> I sall supple him quhill my lyf may lest,
> For gude loue and seruice to me done". (ll.2449–61)

Alexander puts forward his claim with remarkable humility and
submission to the council. Notwithstanding his right through Philip's
testament, he will respect the council's decision regarding the election
of the most suitable candidate. At least ideally he bestows the powers
to choose and depose the monarch on the lords, very much echoing
the theoretical authority of the Community of the Realm of Scotland
in the Declaration of Arbroath, who reserved the right to depose
Robert I if he could not guarantee the country's independence.
Similarly, by renouncing his right by inheritance, like the hero in *The
Bruce*, Alexander enforces a tacit agreement of a king elected not by
birth, but by merit. If Bruce is the only one capable of confronting
England and the two Edwards, Alexander is the only one capable of
confronting the Persian Empire and Darius. In practical terms,
however, after vanquishing his own father, it is very unlikely that the
council will dare to nominate a leader other than Alexander.

Despite being a cumulative romance, in which some adventures
are synthesised, the text does pay attention to the process of legiti-

mising authority in a foreign land. Alexander marries different women, who carry the inheritance of lands and kingdoms. The most interesting episode regarding the Macedonian Emperor's matrimonial alliances concerns his great enemy Darius. Alexander takes Darius's family prisoner, while Darius is in retreat. Quite conveniently, Darius has a daughter:

Alexander has tald to his priwe
That he wald haue Roxen, his dochter fare,
And hir to spous, quhilk was hir faderis [Darius's] aire, (ll.6313–15)

Hay ignores courtly conventions: there is no need for any attraction between the two; she is not described according to the premises of courtly beauty at all; no feeling is even hinted at. The author does not want to disguise the true meaning of late medieval marriages amongst the nobility with idealised embellishment. The political message is the one that counts. Even more interestingly, Darius, his greatest foe, has no qualms about the marriage arrangement. Not only does he agree, but he also makes Alexander his heir (ll.6378–85). Darius's strange predisposition to succumb to Alexander in such a submissive manner most probably responds to the author's interest in legitimising weddings through female inheritance than to a more logical epic reaction to the Persian Emperor. After the Canmore dynasty, in a period of approximately eighty years the Balliols, the Bruces and the reigning Stewarts all accessed the throne through female inheritance. It is not strange, therefore, that Gilbert Hay, a man preoccupied with the political intricacies of Scotland, elaborates on Alexander's legitimisation of power through marriage.

At the beginning of *The Wallace*, it is William Wallace himself who is the catalyst of nationalistic discourse. Thematically, Hary conflates the hero's personal revenge with the national cause in a similar way to Barbour's intermingling of Bruce's dynastic aspirations with the future of Scotland. Wallace's image as a tragic hero is cemented early on by allusions to the misfortunes of the members of his family together with his escape "till Gowry" (I. 144–54). This perception of incessant pursuit is repeated throughout the narrative. At this point, his affliction on account of the unfortunate fate of his family is ingeniously equated with his suffering for Scotland:

Willhham Wallace or he was man of armys
Gret pitte thocht that Scotland tuk sic harmys.
Mekill dolour it did hym in his mynd,
For he was wys, rycht worthy, wicht and kynd. (I. 181–84)

Even before he became a knight, he had expressed his concern with
the state of his devastated and subdued country. Hary's rhetorical
devices redefine and unite the concepts of personal and national
endurance in the figure of Wallace. From then on, both ideas will form
an inseparable objective in the hero's mind. Wallace is first represented non-naturalistically as a *puer senex* of legend rather than the
youthful warrior. He no longer thinks as a boy does but as a mature
man, an indispensable requisite for leading his nation against Edward
I. This image is further elaborated throughout Book I: as McDiarmid
points out, "he [Wallace] does not make a youthful impression, 'Sad
of contenance he was bathe auld and hing' (201–2)" (McDiarmid ed.
1968–69: I. lxxxviii).

    The type of nationalistic discourse articulated by Wallace is
rendered even before his first appearance in the romance. Unlike
Barbour who, despite his unquestionably partisan dialectics, always
shows a more balanced posture towards the foe, *The Wallace* begins
with a combative attitude towards the Auld Enemy, which echoes
Scotland's situation at the time when Hary was writing:

Till honour Ennymyis is our haile entent.
It has beyne seyne in thir tymys bywent,
Our ald Ennemys cummyn of Saxonys blud,
That neuyr ʒeit to Scotland wald do gud
Quhow gret kyndnes thar has beyne kyth thaim till.
It is weyle knawyne on mony diuers syde,
How thai haff wrocht in-to thar mychty pryde
To hald Scotlande at wndyr euirmar,
Bot god abuff has maid thar mycht to par. (I. 5–13)

This passage refers to the period 1474–78, contemporary with the
writing of the romance. James III and his councillors wanted to reconcile with England through a series of matrimonial alliances. Many
Scots opposed such a policy (McDiarmid 1968–69: II. 124). As a
result, Hary's objective was to incite in his audience hatred of the
English (Jack 2001: 48). Therefore, the kind of nationalism postulated
by Hary is as much a reaffirmation of *Scottishness* as a manifesto

against the English. He "develops a narrative designed to move rather than to instruct, a work intensively nationalistic and anti-English in outlook, organised around the life of a single, almost supernatural hero" (Ebin 1971–72: 235). Nationalism is constructed as a counter-action directed against the traditional enemy:

With the English metonymically transformed into "Sothroun", human beings are reduced to objects that become easy to eliminate without moral qualms. Racist discourse, like other repressive practices of language, generally works this way: the Other is furnished with a label, rendering the person an object not a subject (Goldstein 1993: 222).

The poet, then, recreates the perfect scenario – the Wars of Independence – to arouse the audience's national feeling against the English menace to their identity. Hary's argument is based upon the Scottish past experience, which is consistently *translated* into his contemporary Scotland.

Moreover, the author's reference to English origins as "cummyn of Saxonys blud" anticipates his subsequent legendary contextualisation of right. First, Geoffrey of Monmouth's *Historia Regum Britanniae* (1136) established the common origin of all the inhabitants of Britain through the progeny of Brutus, the mythological founder of the British nation. Wace's and Layamon's translations of Geoffrey's *Historia* into the vernacular also contributed to the development of the myth. Formerly, although Bede did not refer to the mythological founder directly and recognised the existence of "five languages and four nations – English, British, Irish, and Picts", he did state that "at first the only inhabitants of the island were Britons" (Bede 1990: 45).

In the twelfth century, then, Geoffrey re-elaborates the history of the British people already including the figures of Brutus and Arthur, whose political overtones were further developed in later versions of the English *Brut* to accommodate and justify the ambitions of the Plantagenets. *The Brut* or *The Chronicles of England*, from which different editions and versions appeared between 1440 and 1528 (Brie ed. 1906: x), is a perfect illustration of this:

Þe v day afterward they aryued in an hauene of Totenesse, & comen in-to þe Ile of Albion; & þer þey founde neiþer man ne woman, as þe story telleþ, but Geauntz; & þey woned in hulles and in Caues. Brut saw þe land was fayr, & at his likynge, & good also for hym & for his folk […]. Brut & his men anon stertyn vp, & his men foughten with þe Geaunth, & quellyd hem euerychon […]. And þis Brut lete felle adoun wodes, & lete erye & sowe londes, & done mow medes for sustinaunce of hym & his peple. & he departed þe land to hem, so þat eche of hem had a certayn place for to dwelle vpon. And Brut late Calle al þis land Britaigne, atfer his owne name, & his folk he lete calle Britouns. (*The Brut*, 10–12)

The text's political and ideological purposes become patent from the very first lines. As opposed to Bede, who wrote at a time when late medieval kingdoms were not yet consolidated (731), the anonymous author/translator of *The Brut* introduces the criteria of sovereignty and invasion. The Trojan Brutus conquers the whole "island", which would legitimise his descendants' (the Kings of England) claim over Wales and Scotland. Acting as a coloniser, he pulls away the roots of any former inhabitants and their culture by changing the country's name to match his own, Britain. Coryn, the best of Brutus' warriors, also renames "Cornewayle" and the future London is called "þe new Troye" (11). A very typical practice of colonisers throughout history is to rename the newly conquered lands according to their own language. They build their own towns and the lands are divided among Brutus' vassals. Nevertheless, the colonial discourse is sagacious enough to negate any kind of former civilisation since only "Geauntz" lived there. In more recent times, Fanon identifies the same attitude on the part of the coloniser in Africa:

Colonial domination, because it is total and tends to oversimplify, very soon manages to disrupt in spectacular fashion the cultural life of a conquered people. This cultural obliteration is made possible by the occupying power, by the banishment of the natives and their customs to outlying districts by colonial society, by expropriation, and by systematic enslaving of men and women. (Fanon 1980: 190)

The British colonisation of Britain is no longer an invasion but a civilising act. As in a *locus classicus* of chivalric romance, the British become the civilising knights who bring light to a primitive land.

The legend of Arthur as the king unifying the British Isles, first mentioned by Geoffrey in his *Historia*, is also present in *The English Brut*. The surrender of the Scots is of particular interest: after having begged Arthur's mercy on them, "he [Arthur] hade pite of ham, and haf ham lif and lyme; and alle þai felle adoune to his feete, and bicome his lege men, and he toke of ham homages" (*The Brut*, 77). The author's dialectics are unequivocal: the Celtic king shows his mercy by refraining from killing all Scots, in return for swearing everlasting subjection to Arthur, which politically justified the English kings' claims over Scotland. Again, *The Brut* carefully deploys language and action to provide the narrative with a justifiable colonialist discourse.

The Arthurian legend was, by this point, progressively gaining ground. The Celtic/British origin of King Arthur and his claim to rule over the British Isles were very appealing to the English monarchs who saw a double justification for their bellicose aggressiveness towards their Irish, Welsh and Scottish neighbours. If Brutus offered the English the possibility of extolling the common past of those different peoples of Britain, the Arthurian myth was re-adapted to their political claims. Hence, not only was it employed to legitimise the military occupation of England's nearest neighbours but it also served to reinvent the Celtic ancestry of the English kings. By referring to them as "Saxonys", Hary abrogates the English demands for hegemony according to the legendary past of the British people and negates any sort of right they may put forward concerning Scotland. The Scottish chroniclers also refuted the Arthurian legend owing to its political implications. Fordun tries to give some counter-arguments to Monmouth but directly quoting from the latter (III. xxv). The elaboration of the anti-Arthurian argument evolved until the Early Renaissance when Hector Boece rearranged the story to the extent of having Modred transformed into the King of Scots. He is the heroic figure who confronts the treacherous Arthur.

Interestingly enough, if in *The Wallace* the tension between the chivalric and the national discourses is never palpable (although the hero is a knight), in the French *Chanson de Bertrand du Guesclin* the main character's actions reflect the typical attitudes and ambitions of his class. The single combats and skirmishes undertaken by Hary's Wallace are assimilated to the dialectics of Scotland's national independence. His concerns are not individual promotion, but his is a heroic figure as long as he defends the rights of his country. In contrast, Cuvelier's recreation of Bertrand negotiates between the protagonist's aspirations and behaviour as a knight and his role as the emblematic voice of French nationalism. In most cases, his words correspond with those of the defender of the national enterprise:

"qui pour son seigneur en bataille mort prent,
Dieu a de lui pitié, en gloire ou il l'atent;
Car on se doit combatre aventureement
Pour sa terre defendre; […]" (ll.4620–26)

[for someone, who fighting for his lord, dies on the battlefield, God feels great pity and has him in His glory because he combats courageously to defend his land.]

As in the case of Scotland, French nationalist feeling is encouraged by means of opposition to English hegemonic aspirations.

Nevertheless, this is not always the case: in ll.2624–80, after another royalist plea in favour of his king and country, Bertrand accepts a personal challenge from Thomas of Canterbury. Cuvelier problematises the tension between the national and the chivalric discourses through the mediation of the citizens of Dinan. On the one hand, as a knight, Bertrand is forced to defend his honour against Thomas' accusations. At the same time, however, a single combat is going to be fruitless as far as the French cause is concerned. Bertrand's defeat and death (it is a joust for life or death) would be completely counterproductive to the general interest of the realm as he is the natural leader on the battlefield. Conversely, if his antagonist is killed, this would not affect the English army and pretensions at all in so far as he is a simple knight. For this reason, the people of Dinan are concerned about Bertrand's chivalric demeanour:

Adonc s'en est la ville moult durement troublee,
Et prient pour Bertran a la chiere membree
Qu'a joye le ramaint par bonne destinee;
Bourgoises et bourgois en font grant assemblee. (ll.2687–90)

[Then, the city was tremendously worried and prayed for Bertran at the council house so that he could have lasting joy and be successful in his enterprise. The burgesses gather for an important meeting.]

The citizens' intervention highlights the controversy between chivalric conduct and national duties. While the French champion does confront and vanquish Thomas, the resolution offered seems to suggest that there is not a definitive response to the problem: must a knight defend his personal honour above anything else or must he sacrifice his reputation in favour of his country's cause? In the rest of the *Chanson*, he continues to be the paladin of the nationalistic discourse, but the consequences of his unlikely (though not totally impossible) defeat are never answered. Therefore, Cuvelier accounts for the existence of this tension, but leaves the answer for the audience to debate.

In his *Squyer Meldrum*, Lindsay offers a much more critical vision of Scotland than either Barbour or Hary. He is particularly judgmental, refusing to idealise either the country or its people. The author adopts a satiric and critical tone, which, however different in construction, could remind the reader of his *Ane Satyre of the Thrie Estaitis*. The beginning of the romance narrates the atrocities of the Scottish soldiers at Carrickfergus, setting the town on fire, spoiling families and raping women (ll.90–103). The misbehaviour topos is mostly associated with an enemy's invasion of one's country. A good illustration of this is the English ravaging of Scotland in Barbour's *Bruce*, conveniently placed just before the praise of freedom. Rather surprisingly, Lindsay displaces the topos, starting the narrative with a denunciation of his fellow countrymen's brutality in Ireland instead of extolling their deeds of arms. Indeed none of the latter English actions against the Scots matches this one. It is Meldrum himself who has to rescue Irish women, priests and friars from the Scottish soldiers, having to kill two of them in the process (ll.101–61). The squire as an individual emerges as the hero; yet the Scottish army as a whole are accused of heavy misdeeds. With such a displacement, the reader is warned about Lindsay's critical position towards contemporary Scottish politics.

On his return to Scotland after fighting in France, Meldrum falls in love with an unnamed lady. This seems to be the setting for the perfect *roman courtois* ending, the lady being a widow with an inheritance. Nevertheless, Lindsay transforms such an advantageous situation into harsh criticism of Scotland during the minority of James V, to whom he was a tutor. The turbulent political panorama in Scotland is revealed through the adventures and misfortunes of Meldrum. First, the dispensation never comes because it is "miscuikit" (l.1180). Lindsay does not indicate whether the mismanagement of the document was just accidental or completely intentional. Yet he does state that Meldrum had many quarrels and defended his honour often due to other knights' envy and jealousy (ll.1185–90). From the hero's personal experience, the author extrapolates the internal disputes for land and power in his contemporary Scotland. The writer also gives further evidence as to why the dispensation did not reach Meldrum and his lover. Stirling of Keir (a knight, whose name is not given, suggesting that his family was still a well-known and powerful one at the time Lindsay wrote this romance) wants the lady to marry "a

gentilman, within his land" (l.1196).[4] Stirling of Keir's attitude unveils the real nature of the institution of matrimony in feudal times. It
contrasts with romance ideals in which love should precede marriage
as epitomised by Meldrum and his beloved in the narrative. The
unnamed knight contemplates the possibility of extending his domains
by marrying one of his vassals to a rich widow. This rather habitual
practice in late medieval Europe takes a more sinister turn when
Lindsay tells us the way in which the knight plans to carry out his
intentions. He wants to ambush Meldrum and force the then
defenceless lady to comply with his ambitions. The two lovers are
warned in time. Though heavily outnumbered, Meldrum defends
himself, but is seriously wounded. Fortunately for Meldrum, the
Regent, Sir Anthony Darsie, comes to the rescue (ll.1381–83).
Lindsay digresses from the main narrative to give a brief account of
the ruling of Scotland at the time. Darsie was a French knight who
fought with Meldrum in Picardy – hence their friendship. But more
importantly, the King of Scots was only five at the time (ll.1384–
1401). Thus, Stirling of Keir is imprisoned (ll.1421–24).

    At this juncture, this information simply states Meldrum's good
political connections and, in knightly terms, extols the virtues of loyalty and comradeship. Nevertheless, the following event relocates the
importance of Lindsay's previous digression. When Darsie is slain
(ll.1484–88), the instability of Scottish politics becomes evident. With
a five-year-old king, "tyrannis" (l.1494) (a very appropriate word
given the terminology of contemporary political theory) take control
of the country. As a consequence, the unnamed knight is released.
Finally, justice is administered in the least unlikely way, when the
knight is killed at Stirling Bridge (ll.1496–99). Lindsay detaches
himself from any firsthand knowledge of the incident with an
otherwise formulaic "as I hard say" (l.1495). Although this would be a
suitable ending for an epic or a romance, there is something disturbing
about it. The way in which Lindsay constructs his narrative subverts
epic and romance conventions to underline the realities of political life
in Scotland, in which the intrigues of the ruling classes make justice a

---

[4] As Kinsley remarks, when James V fell under the influence of his mother's husband,
Angus, and the Douglases, Lindsay fell out of favour. He was sent several times
abroad on diplomatic missions (Kinsley 1959: 4). Now in the last years of his life
Lindsay did not probably want to anger powerful members of the royal household,
jeopardising his position again.

random matter, leaving personal vendettas as the only possible response.

Among Scottish Arthurian romances, there are some points in *Lancelot of the Laik* and *Golagros and Gawane* which allude to a king's ideal position towards his nation and can be interpreted in connection to the Scotland of the time. In the Middle Scots *Lancelot*, the author discusses a monarch's responsibility towards his kingdom by contrasting Arthur's attitude with that of Gawain. When Gawain decides to seek the Red Knight (Lancelot in disguise), all the members of the Round Table wish to join him in his quest. Arthur reproves his nephew:

"Sair Gawan, nece, why dois yow so?
Knowis yow nocht I myne houshold suld encress
In knychthed and in honore and largess?
And now yow thinkith mak me dissolat
Of knychtis and my houss transulat
To sek o knycht and it was never more
Hard sich o semblé makith o before". (ll.2200–06)

After the lesson on good kingship Amytans taught him, not only has Arthur got a more clearly defined idea of his assigned functions as a sovereign, but he has also nurtured a renewed conception of his court. The makar negotiates the discord between the chivalric ideal as represented by Gawain's demeanour and a nation's priorities. As a noble warrior, Gawain longs for knightly action and adventures. As soon as he contemplates the possibility of looking for the mysterious Red Knight, he hastens to depart in search of him without considering the *national* implications of his decision. The regenerated Arthur has acquired a different insight of things: leaving the country without any knight would debilitate its defence against any possible invasion. Arthur's lands would become indefensible. The King also knows that, after having ignored the government of his territories for a long time, he needs to regain his vassals' confidence through "knychthed, honore and largess". Although this scene is also present in the original *Prose Lancelot*, within the Scottish literary and historical contexts the transcendent role of the nation's destiny becomes more important than that of a single knight (or even king). The transmutation of the passage, therefore, acquires exceptional, dramatic meaning.

Nevertheless, Gawain, who is consistently characterised as the most loyal of Arthur's retinue and as a great warrior and military leader (ll.2631–78), fails to understand his country's pressing urgencies once again. When Arthur permits him to take forty knights to seek Lancelot, his answer could not be both more chivalric and less adequate:

[Gawain] On kneis swore, "I sal the suth duclar
Of everything when I agan repar
Nor never more aghane sal I returnn
Nore in o place long for to sujornn
Whill that the knycht or verray evydens
I have, that shal be toknis of credens". (ll.2237–42)

Following the romance tradition, Gawain makes a solemn promise embellished with the most eloquent rhetoric. While this would be the perfect proceeding in a purely chivalric context, the politicised question of nationhood lying behind the text problematises the implications of such an answer. Being the second time he must express the same idea, Arthur's new rebuke may almost be interpreted in a comic light:

Saying, "Nece, yow haith al foly urocht
And wilfulness that haith nocht in thi thoght
The day of batell of Galot and me". (ll.2245–47)

It is also ironic that Arthur reminds Gawain of the battle that only Lancelot, the absent knight, can win. Gawain's single-minded predisposition towards knightly deeds of arms incapacitates him to comprehend the extremely delicate situation of Arthur's kingdom. Therefore, even in the Middle Scots romance, which supposedly develops the love affairs between Lancelot and Guenevere, the nationally politicised dialectics restrain chivalric ideals and acts.

Similarly, although the portrayal of Galehot is drastically reduced in the Scottish *Lancelot*, there are some subtle elements absent from the original, which highlight political issues typical of the Scottish approach to romances. While in the *Prose Lancelot* Galehot himself tells his knights that it would not be honourable for him to take part in the battle (276), in *Lancelot of the Laik*, Galiot assembles a council, in which his counsellors suggest that to fight with Arthur would degrade him (ll.745–52). Although holding a council to debate important matters was common practice in late medieval countries with hereditary right of counsel (Guenée 1985: 172), the alteration of these passages from the original highlights the Scottish preoccupation with a nation's mechanisms of government, common to the other romances analysed above.

In *Golagros and Gawane*, the politicisation of the original French narrative transforms the Arthurian romance into the perfect forum to debate Scottish preoccupations with the government of a nation. As mentioned earlier, Golagros's feigned victory allows us to see him as the kind of monarch a country requires. He places his sovereignty in his people's hands by asking them whether they prefer to have him as a lord subjected to a king or to choose another lord instead (ll.1168–86). In contrast, in *The First Continuation*, the Riche Sodouyer does not consult his council to deliberate on the submission of his land. His only worry is his beloved, who may die if she learns about his defeat. In this essentially courtly context, she is sent to another castle. The narrator addresses the audience directly:

Savés por coi l'en fist aler?
Por ce qu'il li voloit celer
Coment li estors ert finez.
Si tost con s'en fu delivrés,
Si fu par le castel seü
La fins toute, si com il fu. (ll.6473–78)

[Do you know why has he [the Riche Soudoyer] made her leave? Because he does not want her to know the outcome of the combat. But as soon as he got rid of her, all the city learnt about what had really happened at the end.]

The concerns of *romans courtois* dominate the narrative of the French text. The political dilemmas of the Scottish adaptation are not present. In *Golagros and Gawane*, these ideas situate the text in the same ideological framework as the Declaration of Arbroath. The Declaration extols an ideal – and an idealised situation – intimately connected with the notion of the natural law, in which royal power should rely on the people's approval.

In Hay's *Buik of King Alexander the Conquerour*, the hero can also be connected to the Scottish monarch. While Joanna Martin relates Alexander's image as a *puer senex* to the kings' minorities during the fifteenth century (Martin 2006: 79), Mapstone argues that the insistence on Alexander's youth is easily transferable to the

Scottish situation in the 1460s during the minority of James III
(Mapstone 1986: 112). However inspired and flattering the analogy
might be, Hay's wishful thinking of James III as a new Alexander
failed to materialise. In more general terms, of course, the analogy
could be applied to all fifteenth-century Kings of Scots or could even
go back to 1329, when David II succeeded Robert I at the age of five:
James I even if captured was about twelve when recognised as king;
his son James II was six when he was crowned after his father's
assassination. Even James IV, albeit not a minor, was fifteen when he
accessed the throne in 1488. Therefore, Alexander's youth when he
succeeded Philip was a triumphant and prestigious mirror to which the
young Scottish monarchs could look for inspiration.

There is also in the *Conquerour* a direct reference to Scotland.
When Alexander is in Paradise, he received news that some rebellions
are taking place in India. The narrator takes the opportunity to digress
about the number of kings existing in India and Europe. He concludes
his interpolation with the British Isles:

Quhilkis in auld tymes was in divisioun;
In Scotland, Ingland and till Irelandis,
Thre kingis war, as men vnderstandis – (ll.15,960–62)

In the previous lines, the narrator simply enumerates the different
kings in Christendom but when he refers to the British Isles he lays
emphasis on a territorial and political division which has existed for a
long period of time. Such a remark puts forward the right of Scotland
to stand aside as an independent country regardless of the tensions
with England in the late Middle Ages.

The allusion to the "eldris" in *The Bruce*, *Lancelot of the Laik*
and *Golagros and Gawane* must be understood, then, not as a defence
of familial right, but of national/racial differences between the foreign
menace and the autochthonous inhabitants of Scotland. In *The Wallace*, following Barbour's fictive strategies, Hary denounces the
unhistorical agreement between Balliol and Edward I. Once Wallace
had instructed Bruce, the latter emerges as the ideal king for Scotland,
which again prioritises personal merit in detriment of the rule of primogeniture. The biggest difference between *The Bruce* and *The Wallace* and the Arthurian romances is the necessarily historical contextualisation of the former. The theme of national freedom forces Bruce
and Wallace to fight to attain this ideal. Were they not able to defend

their country's liberty, they would be rejected as leaders. By way of contrast, in *Golagros and Gawane*, the fact that the vassals opt for retaining Golagros as their lord at any price (in fact, the price of national freedom) postulates his excellence as a king in the eyes of his people. Nevertheless, this particular event would never take place in the historical romances since the independence of Golagros's idealised, small, free country completely differs from the portrayed reality of Wallace and Bruce's occupied Scotland.

As well as these indirect analyses of issues to which the Scottish audience would be particularly sensitive, both Arthurian texts make overt allusions to the kingdom of Scotland. In *Lancelot*, the author subtly includes referential elements to generate an extra tension between Lancelot and Arthur absent from the French text. Amytans accuses the monarch of being responsible for king Ban's death and his wife and son's disinheritance, a passage which is also included in the original. What is significantly different from the French *Lancelot* is the name given to Ban's kingdom: the imaginary Benoyc becomes Scotland, under the name of "Albenak" (Gray 1912: xvii), which could be an odd use or misinterpretation of the adjectival form "Albanach" from Gaelic. Not only does this transformation make the romance more appealing to the audience but it redefines the narrative axis in the Scottish political milieu. Again, the question of the Scottish nation either being free or in submission to an overlord is posed. It is extraordinarily significant that the sin Arthur had forgotten was the one corresponding to his duties towards Albenak. On isolating this act of misconduct in a king, the makar strategically examines the problems and paradoxes occasioned by subjection to foreign authority. The country has to wait for the external lord's help, which at the same time happens to be an imposition of non-native patronage. It is not difficult to imagine why this overlord would not be as eager as a native ruler to defend the nation's interests. The Scottish implications in the late Middle Ages are inescapable.

The national component is completed by also *Scotticising* Lancelot who, as Ban's son, is the heir to the Scottish crown. The knight who is supposed to intervene decisively in favour of Arthur is portrayed in the middle of two major tensions: first, he is in love with his king's wife; second, the sovereign himself is indebted to him owing to his own negligence towards the kingdom of Albenak. Again, the correspondences and dissimilarities between the idealisation of

courtly games and *fin'amors* and the more realistic dissemination of
the mechanism of kingship create a very particular progression of the
action.

Nevertheless, the *nationalised* Lancelot does not make any sort
of overtly Scottish statement. On the contrary, his main objective
focuses on his being accepted by the queen in the service of love. At
this point, the national parallelisms with Scotland either fade away or
are too artificially maintained. The existence of the original French
text necessarily imposes a number of constrictions on the thematic
elaboration of the Scottish version, which the author could not ignore.
In the Old French *Prose Lancelot*, the hero is never interested in
recriminating Arthur's violation of his duty towards Ban in so far as
the knight's main concern is attaining Guenevere's heart. Lancelot
must emerge as Arthur's champion to be accepted as Guinevere's *fin
amant*: only the best knight on the field would be good enough to
become the perfect lover. Were the reader to interpret the final scenes
of the narrative in *Lancelot of the Laik* as an allegorical representation
of Scotland, the signs would not work at all. Lancelot as the inheritor
of the throne of Albenak (Scotland) would be the main knight responsible for the victory of Arthur's (the foreign overlord?) victory over an
invader, Galiot. This political allegory would not make any sense at
this juncture. Therefore, the numerous references to the historical
Scottish situation at the time seem to raise different views of the
concepts of freedom, kingship and national identity; but they do not
operate as a national allegory.

In *Golagros and Gawane*, the Scottish echoes are also present
throughout the narrative. Thus, when Spynagros tells Arthur that
Golagros does not pay fealty to any overlord, Arthur's hegemonic
ambitions come to light:

"Hevinly God!" said the heynd, "how happynis this thing?
Herd thair ever ony sage sa selcouth ane saw!
Sal never myne hart be in saill na in liking,
Bot gif I loissing my life, or be laid law,
Be the pilgramage compleit I pas for saull prow,
Bot dede be my destenyng,
He sall at my agane cumyng
Mak homage and oblissing,
I mak myne avow!" (ll.265–73)

Arthur's oath has nothing to do with Gawain's chivalric avowal in *Lancelot of the Laik*. That of the king can only be interpreted as an obstinate menace of invasion of a foreign land without any justifiable reason. Images of death and destruction articulate Arthur's aggressive discourse. He is disposed to wage war against Golagros going as far as necessary to accomplish his objective. By presenting Arthur's future inroads in such a way, the makar creates a conspicuous correspondence between the text and late medieval Scotland: "the introduction of the issue of fealty in the Scottish Romance has inescapable political overtones" (Jack 1975: 9). The audience could easily identify this coercion of national freedom with past and contemporary Anglo-Scottish tensions. Golagros, courteous and valiant, becomes the *speculum principis* for the country's rulers. All the death and suffering occasioned by war deeply move Golagros. His love for his people obliges him to personally defend his possessions and independence before Arthur's knights: "I sal bargane abyde, and ane end bryng; / Tomonre, sickirly, my self sall seik to the feild" (ll.772–73). As a good leader, his double commitment to his people and country reveals his moral and knightly superiority to Arthur, who never considers combat himself. In the national discourse ascribed to the narrative, then, a king must equally love and defend his people and his nation's interests.

Conclusion

At a time when relationships with England generated numerous tensions in the area of identity, nationhood and kingship, the Scottish romances problematise these issues, endeavouring to provide some answers. Although Hary and Barbour convey these notions in a more direct manner than the composers of the Alexander and Arthurian romances, all of them debate the nature and interrelationship of these ideas. The makars offer a conception of kingship which does not leave room for individual aspirations unless they are assimilated within a national discourse concerned with the common good of the nation. The king should guarantee the autonomy of the country and administer his power with the perfect combination of justice and mercy, symbolically mirroring God's divine governing of the world. Through this assurance of equality, all the inhabitants of the kingdom will combine in the national struggle, which aims to create a sense of unity.

The dialectics of both the chivalric and the historical romances intermingle the notions of good kingship and government with national discourse. Nationalism is connected with a country's freedom from the suzerainty of another nation. Inevitably, then, feudal utterances are necessarily assimilated within the national ideal. In the historical romances, good illustrations of this are James Douglas's evolution in *The Bruce* or the mutation of value in Bruce himself through Wallace's guidance in *The Wallace*, whereas in the Scottish chivalric romances, the chivalric and courtly action remains subservient to royal ambitions. This causes a series of alterations in the adaptation of the French originals in the chivalric romances, and emphasises the issues concerning the Kingdom of Scotland.

Chapter Two

The Hero's Progression

One of the most frequent topoi of late medieval romances is the hero's progression from youth into maturity through a series of tests. The Scottish romances are not an exception: it is common practice for the makars to represent their main characters undergoing a learning process – either spiritual, moral or physical – as a part of the accomplishment of their quests both in chivalric and historical romances. The spiritual or ethic education should not be seen as an exclusive and distinctive Scottish characteristic, however, unless some particular elements so define them. I shall argue that national concerns such as nation, identity or kingship are closely connected to the heroes' inner developments.

Yet not all the makars draw their hero's journey in the same way. Thus the Scottish romances offer different layers of interpretation, depending on the disposition of their work. Although referring to sacred texts, Hugh of Saint Victor's "house-bricks" metaphor is an excellent tool to understand the distinct significance of each level of meaning:

> In this question it is not without value to call to mind what we see happen in the construction of buildings, where first the foundation is laid, then the structure is raised upon it, and finally, when the work is all finished, the house is decorated by the laying on of the color. (*Didascalicon*, VI.ii)

Within this structure, the anagogic, the allegorical and the tropological significance are to be unveiled. While this is applicable to holy works in general, when dealing with secular texts, a reader is not supposed to find all the levels of interpretation in each composition.

In the Scottish romances, allegory at its different levels is present in various forms. The makars develop alternative narrative strategies to provide their works with the appropriate referential signs so that an allegorical meaning can be deciphered. Different literary modes are used: Barbour and Hary's accounts of the Wars of Independence constitute two distinct approaches to the elaboration of their romances. In *The Wallace*, a consciously allegorical fabric is devised for the text.

The hero's characterisation is assembled not only through the chivalric adventures typical of the *roman courtois* tradition but also along the lines of a martyr's or saint's *vita*. Wallace's progression becomes a heroic and spiritual pilgrimage, which, through history, is elevated to the mysteries of anagogy. In *The Bruce*, the main character's spiritual maturation is devised through historical events and knightly action. As Dante would define it, *The Bruce*, though not possessing a complete allegorical structure, is polysemous (see Minnis and Scott ed. 2000: 459–60). The two historical narratives culminate with the perfect representation (and glorification) of death.

In the Arthurian and Alexander romances, the heroes' progress is also elaborated in different ways, relocating the narrative focus of the French originals. In *Golagros and Gawane*, the questioning of arbitrary warfare and violence becomes the ideal setting for Arthur's spiritual regeneration. Coming from the advice to princes tradition, *Lancelot of the Laik* and Gilbert Hay's *Buik of King Alexander the Conquerour* concentrate on moral and ethical concerns. In *Lancelot of the Laik*, Arthur evolves from a bad administrator of his realm to possessing an understanding of what a Christian monarch should be, whereas in Hay's romance, an already competent Alexander improves his ruling skills thanks to Aristotle's counsel. In the anonymous *Buik of Alexander*, it is not Alexander's but King Clarus's unjustified invasion of Ephesus that is at scrutiny. In the six texts, the spiritual/ethical significance of the protagonists' self-discovery cannot be detached from the political discourse centred on the good government of a country.

The Wallace's allegorical framework

Hary deploys the allegorical conventions of the time in which dream visions and prophecies adumbrate the spiritual orchestration of *The Wallace*. Wallace's evolution from a knight of low rank to the Guardian and liberator of Scotland goes beyond purely heroic action. He emerges as a martyr of the national cause and is finally conducted to heaven. To complement this allegorical structure, Hary applies a mythical/divine rearranging of events to the disposition of the romance. As Jack and McDiarmid argue, historical events such as the Battle of Stirling Bridge and that of Falkirk are rearranged to conform to a Christian patterning of the romance (McDiarmid ed. 1968: I.lxxviii; Jack 2001: 46).

The hero's life is also reshaped in a manner in which the religious/divine elements are central to his development. The restructuring of events accords with Geoffrey of Vinsauf's notion of reordering the material:

neither transposition of order should cause impropriety, but rather each part should take the other's fittingly, without strife, yielding to the other freely and pleasantly. Expert art inverts matters so as not to pervert them; it displaces material so as to place it better thereby. (*Poetria Nova*, ll.93–99)

By doing so, Hary creates a defined allegorical framework for his romance. When Wallace is imprisoned in Ayr and about to be executed, he becomes completely aware of the importance of his *avanture*, an almost sacred enterprise to set Scotland free:

"All worthi Scottis, all-michty god thow leid,
Sen I no mor in wyage may ȝou speid.
In presoune heir me worthis to myscheyff.
Sely Scotland, that of help has gret neide,
The nacioune all standis in a felloun dreid.
Off warldlynes all thus I tak my leiff.
Off thir paynys god lat ȝou neuir preiff,
Thocht I for wo all out off witt suld weid!
Now othir gyft I may none to ȝou gyff." (II. 198–206)

According to Jack, when the narrator substitutes the nine-line stanza of Chaucer's *Compleynt of Mars* for his customary couplets, the text offers passages of remarkable emotion (Jack 2001: 45). In this concrete instance, the structural change emphasises all the nuances of the hero's passion. Wallace's "compleynt" captures the dramatic agitation of a moment of national and self-realisation.

Allegorically, Wallace's personal vendetta pushes forward and intermingles with the country's imperative necessities. The national and the personal struggle become an inseparable unity (see chapter 3). His face-to-face combats and sporadic skirmishes are allegorically redefined and relocated in the context of Scotland's struggle for emancipation. In Book VI, for instance, when Wallace's wife is killed, not only does Wallace take revenge on his spouse's murderer, but he also expels the English from Lanark. He comes to understand that he is the Elect. The conjunction of his epiphany coincides with his symbolic paralysis – he is imprisoned and seriously injured – intensifying the hero's tragedy. The notion of Wallace's later martyrdom is anticipated in this passage; thus the transcendence of addressing God directly as the one to lead and liberate his fellow compatriots. The national cause and the fight for freedom are seconded by the Lord and will be elevated to the domain of allegory. Wallace is thought to be dead: "thai presumyt he suld be werray ded" (II. 252) and his body is washed: "His body wousche quhill filth was of him past" (II. 267). The hero is constructed as a Christological figure with his passion, and subsequent resurrection. At the same time, his symbolic death as a man leads to his rebirth as the legendary liberator of Scotland. Thus Christological symbolism is deployed to establish Wallace's absolute status as champion of Scotland's liberty. The political significance of the romance is transferred into the field of religious iconography. This transcends the literal world through an allegorical reconstruction of both Wallace and his fight, which, by the end of the romance, will lead the hero to the territory of anagogy with his ultimate entry into heaven.

A common element in the divine, historical patterning employed by Hary is prophecy. When Wallace is thought dead, the visionary figure of Thomas of Erceldoune asserts that Wallace is still alive and that he will liberate the country:

"Forsuth, or he deces,
Mony thousand in feild sall mak thar end.
Off this regioune he sall the Sothroun send,
And Scotland thris he sall bryng to the pes.
So gud off hand agayne sall neuir be kend". (II. 346–50)

The authoritative power of the pseudo-mythical Thomas permeates Wallace's status as the Elect. The choice of Thomas is not gratuitous in this context. The classical *auctoritas* is supplanted by the contemporary and Scottish authority of Thomas. The visionary foretelling of the Scottish struggle is nationalised through the person most likely to play such a role, a Scottish soothsayer. The concepts of allegory, Scottishness and nation cannot be dissociated in Hary's discourse. The prophecy parallels and strengthens the previous one on the English side: "Als Inglis clerkis in prophecys thai fand / How a Wallace suld putt thame of Scotland" (I. 351–52). If this first prophetic allusion to

Wallace may have gone unnoticed amongst the audience, Thomas's prophecy again emphasises the point while structuring the allegorical dimension of the romance.

In *The Wallace*, after the prophetic *visio* which reveals that Wallace is the Elect, there is no further learning process or spiritual progression. The hero acts as a mature and conscientious character up to his death. The text functions in accord with a total allegorical structure:

> All things rest upon the first foundation but are not fitted to it in every way. As to the latter foundation everything else rests upon it and is fitted to it. The first one carries the superstructure and underlines the superstructure. The second one carries the super-structure and is not only under the superstructure but part of it. The foundation which is under the earth we have said stands for history, and the superstructure which is built upon it we have said suggests allegory. (*Didascalicon* Book VI.iv)

Within this allegorical fabric, Wallace can be regarded as a *puer senex*, a figure more typical of a legend or a *vita* than of romance.

Regarding the French *vita* of Saint Catherine, for example, Calin argues in favour of this static, immutable representation of the main character:

> Despite her womanhood, Catherine acts like a man; she conquers clerks as a clerk, dominating them and the spectators by her beauty and her goodness but, even more, by her power of logic, quick wit, and agile tongue. As much as any figure of litera-ture, she partakes of the topos of *puella senex*, a woman with the beauty of a young girl and the wisdom of a sage. (Calin 1994: 104–5)

Hary redefines the saintly characterisation of a *puer/puella senex* in the context of romance. Wallace is the young warrior and leader of the Scottish cause at the same time as his acts are governed by the arche-typal wisdom of an old clerk. His sufferings are those of a martyr. The saintly type, such as that of Catherine, is applied to Wallace and more generically to the romance.

These thematic and structural interchanges between romances and saints' legends were common in the late Middle Ages. As opposed to the archetypal heroes of the genre, Wallace's personality does not evolve through a learning process. Instead, the makar creates different narrative strategies parallel to those of saints' legends and dream visions to provide the reader/hearer with spiritual insights into Wallace's personality. His evolution, therefore, is not through a typical set of tests which lead to maturity, but through the distinct stages of religious revelation.

A vision of Saint Andrew and Virgin Mary reaffirms his role as the Elect at the beginning of Book VII. The patron saint of Scotland gives him a sword:

> "I am," he said, "in wiage chargit with the;"
> A suerd him gaiff off burly burnist steill.
> "Gud sone," he said, "this brand thou sall bruk weill."
> Off topaston him thocht the plumat was,
> Baith hilt and hand all gliterand lik the glas.
> "Der sone," he said, "we tary her to lang.
> Thow sall go se quhar wrocht is mekill wrang". (VII. 74–80)

Then, after the "Inglismen tuk trewis with Wallace" (VII. 2), it is Saint Andrew himself who provides the hero with a sword to continue the war. At this point, the religious and political discourses intermingle. Politically, the *nationalisation* of the knight's guides is palpable once again: first, Thomas of Erceldoune revealed his vision of Wallace as a liberator, now Scotland's patron saint will complement and amplify Thomas's previous intervention.

Religiously, the first words of the passage point to different levels of meaning. These layers accord with the allegorical approach to texts practised in the Middle Ages, deriving from exegesis. First of all, the symbolism of the sword gives the reader/listener a range of different interpretations. The sword was a symbol of justice and of the cross. According to Gilbert Hay:

> And, first and formast, thare is to the knycht gevin a suerd with a crossit hilt, that signifyis that rycht as oure lord Jhesus Crist vencust in the croce the iymy of mannis lygnage, to the quhilk he was dempt throu the syn of Adam, oure first fader, that rycht sa suld a knycht vencuse the fais of the Croce throu the suerd. For the suerd is ordanyt to do justice with; and tharfore is it maid with twa egeis, in takenyng that he suld manetene and defend bathe temporalitee and spiritualitee with the double scherand suerd. (Haye 1901–14: II. 44)

At an ethical/political level, Wallace must take on responsibility for restoring justice in Scotland by the expulsion of the English: war is justified again. At a spiritual level, the symbolism of the sword sublimates Wallace's *avanture* and its quasi-sacred significance. Biblical intertextuality also transcends the holy nature of the vision: the precious gem with which the weapon is forged, topaz, symbolically alludes to one of the foundations of the wall of New Jerusalem (*Rev.* 21.20), which are also seen "gliterand lik the glas" (*Rev.* 21.11; 21.18; 21.21).

The literary motif of the hero's sword, so variously employed in epic and romance literature, is mythologised in *The Wallace*. While swords such as Arthur's Excalibur or the Cid's Tizona were used as literary elements which highlighted the *proeza* of their owners, the importance of Wallace's newly acquired weapon operates both morally/politically and spiritually. It is the instrument of quasi-sacred justice to liberate Scotland.

Subsequently, Saint Andrew leads Wallace to a mountain, which is symbolically connected with the "knawledge [...] off wrang [and] [...] rycht" (VII. 126). Again the biblical reference to *Revelations* 21 is present. Saint John writes that "he carried me away in the spirit to a great and high mountain, and showed me a great city, the holy Jerusalem, descending out of heaven from God" (*Rev.* 21.20). In *The Wallace*, the hero sees events from past and present Scotland. He progresses to the next stage of the allegorical dream. The patron saint of Scotland conducts the hero to the Virgin Mary, who will be Wallace's guide:

"Welcum," scho said. "I cheis the as my luff.
Thow art grantyt be the gret god abuff
Till help pepill that sufferis mekill wrang". (VII. 95–97)

The image of Wallace as a Christ-like figure takes on further import as the Virgin Mary explicitly asserts his divine designation. The saintly authority contradicts human dictates, which are by definition imperfect. Her words attest the incorrectness of the Anglo-Scottish peace, while the *true* Scots are enduring English tyranny.

While the intervention of Saint Andrew synthesised political reality and allegorical significance, Mary elevates Wallace's *avanture* to the realm of anagogy. As a Christological incarnation, his mission will typologically bring to the audience's mind Jesus Christ's death to save humankind. Mary's subsequent oration will accentuate this anagogical simile:

This rycht regioun thow mon redeme it all.
Thi last reward in erd sall be bot small.
Let nocht tharfor tak redres off this mys,
To thi reward thou sall haiff lestand blys". (VII. 101–4)

In a new reminder of his duty, Hary deploys the verb "redeme" instead of "liberate" or "fight". The specific use of this word is deliberate: in Older Scots, it can either mean "to recover or regain by force" or "to return (to grace)" (Craigie et al ed. 1931–2002: VII. 165–66). The religious connotations of the term reinforce the almost hallowed enterprise of the hero and evoke Jesus Christ's redemption of the world through death. Constant suffering and painful torture as a consequence of carrying out his *avanture* will be recompensed in heaven with *beatitudo*. The dream vision evolves from moral and ethical issues about Scotland to spiritual and anagogical revelations, which re-codify the liberation of the nation within the parameters of divinity.

The death of the hero follows the patterning of saints' legends and the passion of Christ. When Wallace returns to Scotland in Book XII, the arch Scottish traitor Sir John Menteth, like Judas, sells him to the English. Hary refuses to relate the knight's torture:

Bot Wallace end in warld was displesans,
Tharoff I ces and puttis it nocht in rym. (XII. 1230–31)

Hary's refusal to elaborate on this is explained in terms of moral abhorrence at English cruelty rather than historical ignorance or rhetorical inadequacy. The dramatic effect is poignant: silence will move the audience to feel sympathy and pity for Wallace. They are left to imagine the viciousness of their foes' actions. This rhetorical device is employed on other occasions. According to Goldstein, Hary opts not to depict violence when the Scots are the victims. This "inability" topos spares the audience unnecessary sorrow (Goldstein 1993: 227–28). Despite his image of the hero as saint, Hary decides not to describe one of the essential elements of a typical saint's *vita*; that of the torture of the saint. His saintly construction will be accomplished by other means.

The narrative continues with an assurance that the sense of bewilderment and defeat will not last much longer:

Scotland may thank the blyssyt, happy tym
At he was born, be prynsuall poyntis two.
This is the first, or that we forthyr go,
Scotland he fred and brocht it off thrillage;
And now in hewin he has his heretage,
As It prewyt be gud experians. (XII. 1232–37)

Wallace's sufferings and death are turned into joyful praise of his achievements. National freedom and anagogy interlace at the ultimate moment of victory over momentary earthly defeat. This is a recurrent structural pattern in saints' lives, in which the saint's sorrow occasioned by torture and death is immediately followed by his real *victory* in the realm of the sacred.

In the Middle Scots version of the life of Saint Lawrence, when the Romans are roasting the martyr, he utters the following words:

"now þu ma se
þat þi fel fyre refreschis me,
and to þe ay-lestand payne
It sal mynistere, nocht to layne;
fore god wat I nyt hyme nocht,
accusit in word na in thocht,
& now one þe rost-yrne layd
I ȝeld hyme thank". ("Laurentius", ll.471–78)

Even during his terrible punishment, Lawrence's faith in God prevents him from extreme suffering. God's intervention signifies the superior value of the Christian creed in diametric contraposition to the false Roman gods. The definitive victory of the saint comes with death:

"lord Ihesu, ay lowyt mot þu be,
fore I ame worthy to haf entre
with þe ȝatis of þi blyse,"
& ȝauld þe spryt sayand þus. (ll.493–96)

This structural parallelism testifies that Hary designed Wallace's final stage of his life according to a saint's life, which, at the same time, was typologically based on that of Christ. Wallace incarnates the perfect representation of an agon, a saint who is defeated physically, but triumphs spiritually. As Jack remarks, the work comes to an end with the anagogical death of Wallace, pointing to mysteries of divine truth. It also projects "an image of [...] absolute harmony which reconciles contingent discords within the harmony of spheres" (Jack 2001: 51).

Another vision, in which a dead priest is waiting to enter paradise because Wallace is given priority over him, confirms the knight's entrance into heaven. The priest has to explain to his brother and, by implication, to the audience of the poem, why such "a gret slaar of men" (XII. 1278) precedes a pious member of the clergy:

"He is Wallace, defendour off Scotland,
For rychtwys wer that he tuk apon hand.
Thar rychtwysnes is lowyt our the lawe,
Tharfor in hewyn he sall that honour hawe". (XII. 1285–88)

As in the knight's conversation with Mary, the imperfection of human
law is accentuated. Scotland's right to freedom justifies the divinely
designated Wallace and his slaughter. The mysterious paradigms of
divinity are inseparable from the nation's priorities in Hary's ideological disposition of the romance.

The divine patterning of *The Wallace* also functions through the
thematic opposition between bodily desires and spirit, which was a
typical theme developed in the literature of the late Middle Ages. By
the loss of his terrestrial body, Wallace also gets rid of his human
appetites. He leaves earthly life behind and embraces spiritual truth.
The ending corroborates this definitive progression from the mutable
human world to God's *beatitudo*:

I will nocht tell how he dewydyt was
In v parties and ordand for to pas.
Bot thus his spreyt be liklynes was weill. (XII. 1407–9)

Similarly, in the case of Saint Lawrence (1.496), as a paradigmatic
example of a *vita*, the "spryt / spreyt", as the purest substance of a
pious being, ascends into heaven. Hary concludes with the typology
which he has maintained all through the poem with Wallace as a
Christ-like or saint-like figure.

The King's penitence and redemption in *The Bruce*

Barbour finishes his romance with unmistakable allegorical correspondences between the sovereign's and Christ's deaths within pious
parameters. Although *The Bruce* focuses on martial action, Barbour's
rearrangement of historical events in the first half of the poem also
entails deeper levels of interpretation. Within Bruce's maturation
process to become the kind monarch required to "rwle and lede" his
nation, the painful process to the crown can be viewed as his obliga-
tory atonement for the killing of Comyn in the Greyfriars' church. The
unavoidable historical context of the romance does not allow Barbour

to represent Bruce participating in a fight against the heathen, as it was the King of Scots' intention to do. Alternatively, Bruce's pilgrimage may be interpreted as an allegorical atonement before he can be regarded as the legitimate King of Scots. While such a reading of *The Bruce* after the killing of Comyn might not be obvious at first sight, I shall argue that the author, as a clergyman, cannot permit Bruce to become the King of Scots without being punished and redeemed. Barbour must negotiate between the representations of Bruce as the national Scottish leader and the perfect Christian monarch.

The makar's university education reveals something about his philosophical and theological background. The University of Paris was famous for its strongly Aristotelian teaching. As Jack suggests, while Barbour structures his work within the Aristotelian-Christian tradition, its framework should be "typologically patterned in order to highlight the clear signing system which translates mystery into history" (Jack 2000: 32–33). Similarly, Snell was probably the first scholar to suggest a possible interpretation of those passages in *The Bruce*, in which John of Lorne incessantly and distressingly chases the hero, as an allegorical punishment for killing Comyn (Snell 1899: 57). The hardships Bruce must confront may be interpreted as a Christian penitence which will help him to become a better person, in general, and a better monarch, in particular.

Just after Comyn's death at the altar, the makar hastens to tell (and acknowledge) that:

Nocht-for-yi ȝeit sum men sayis
At yat debat fell oyer-ways,
Bot quhat-sa-euyr maid ye debate
Yar-throuch he [Comyn] deyt weill I wat
He mysdyd yar gretly but wer
Yat gave no gyrth to ye awter,
Yarfor sa hard myscheiff him fell
Yat ik herd neuer in romanys tell
Off man sa hard frayit as wes he
Yat efterwart com to sic bounte. (II. 39–48)

Barbour severely condemns Bruce's action. This attitude is difficult to find in any other romance of the time. The author refuses to make use of an idealised portrayal of the romance hero, accusing him of a terrible sin. Neither does he make any concession to any other version of the story which may exonerate the hero or, at least, soften his guilt.

"The rhythm of the whole might be described as a wheel of fortune, a favorite paradigm in the Middle Ages. The hero begins from the lowest point, having murdered Comyn" (Kliman 1977: 112). It is plausible to assume that Barbour, Archdeacon of Aberdeen, equates the "hard myscheiff" (here, "hard myscheiff" must be interpreted as "evil" with all its chivalric and religious connotations) with the tortuous path which Bruce must follow towards penitence and redemption. Lois Ebin claims that "the idea of a hard struggle before success as a result of Bruce's sin is reiterated throughout the first section of the narrative becoming almost a leit-motif to the action" (Ebin 1971–72: 231). In spite of this statement, she does not treat these incidents allegorically however, but just as a way in which to "rationalise the action". Notwithstanding the hardness of Barbour's accusation, the author from his pro-Brucean and Stewart discourse cannot help foretelling Bruce's final success by concluding that he finally "com to sic bounte". As well as the obvious chivalric meaning of "bounte", the makar seems to imply Bruce's redemption.

After Barbour's severe criticism of the King of Scots, the following books relate the hero's sufferings and exile. The constructions of these episodes give the reader certain clues to be interpreted as Robert I's penance. At a rhetorical level, Kliman defines this rearrangement of events as "the rhythm of incidents", describing "the relationship between incidents that occur not through cause and effect, but through poetic logic" (Kliman 1977: 109). The author selects and reorganises historical events in a way in which a possible allegorical interpretation is bestowed on them. This is the first such instance:

And so feile fayis about him wer
Yat all ye countre yaim werrayit.
So hard anoy yaim yan assayit
Off hunger could with schowris snell
Yat nane yat levys can weill it tell.
Ye king saw how his folk wes stad
And quhat anoyis yat yai had,
And saw wynter wes cummand ner,
And yat he mycht on na maner
Dre in ye hillys ye cauld lying
Na ye land nychtis waking. (III. 374–84)

At the literal and historical level, the author gives a clear, descriptive account of King Robert's defeat at Methven and its consequences.

Kliman claims that Barbour does not explain Bruce's defeat as a consequence of the killing of Comyn (Kliman 1973: 506). Nonetheless, should the trained medieval audience notice the makar's harsh condemnation of Comyn's death, they would expect some kind of punishment and regeneration of Bruce. The newly crowned monarch is chased by his enemies, facing hunger, rain and the cold Scottish winter. Like his men, he cannot sleep at night and is not safe on the hills, which can be interpreted as the first stage of his penitence.

Similarly, the construction of Bruce and his party's exile to the island is reminiscent of both classical and Christian tropes:

Ye schippys our ye wawys slayd
For wynd at poynt blawand yai had,
Bot nocht-for-yi quha had yar bene
A gret stertling he mycht haiff seyne
Off schippys, for quhilum sum wald be
Rycht on ye wawys as on mounte,
And sum wald slyd fra heycht to law
Rycht as yai doune till hell wald draw,
Syne on ye waw stert sodanly,
And oyer schippys yat war yarby
Deliuerly drew to ye depe. (III. 701–11)

At a purely literal level, it is easy to understand that sailors may have tremendous difficulties in piloting a boat at sea in Northern Scotland. Barbour may have also had Virgil's *Aeneid* in mind in the composition of this passage, in which Aeneas's voyages are frequently accompanied by terrible storms. In his journey to Thrace, for instance:

[Palinurus] Turned away first to port, the bows of his vessel creaking;
Then the whole convoy, with oars and sails, clawed off to port.
We were tossed up high on an arching surge, then down we went
In the trough as the wave fell away, down the very pit.
Thrice roared aloud the reefs and the caverns of rock beneath us,
Thrice we beheld the sky through a spattering flounce of spindrift. (83)

Aeneas's fulfilment of his destiny is subjected to the gods' will. Their manipulation of the weather conditions takes Aeneas to their intended places. The possible adaption of this scene to *The Bruce* confers on the narrative and Bruce himself an epic dimension. If Aeneas's *avanture* is found to be the future site of the Roman Empire, Bruce's is to establish a new free and prosperous Scotland.

When this epic motif is *translated* into Christian terms, first an intertextual reference to the Bible can be observed. In Psalm 107, a psalm of thanksgiving for being saved from dangerous situations, there is an allusion to God lifting and calming the waves, whose allegorical meaning and description have inescapable correspondences to this passage in *The Bruce*.[1] These lines also remind the audience of the frailty of human existence and the mutability of this world.

Although Bruce is certainly not set adrift, the action being set on the sea suggests a recurrent topos in medieval, allegorical literature, that of God's judgement by elements:

Persons were often set adrift for one of the three reasons: when guilt could not be conclusively determined by human investigation, when men wished to combine severity with some possibility of mercy, or when […] society wished to expel an unwanted person from its midst. The Christian instances assume that God is the sole arbiter of guilt and innocence, and the sea merely an instrument through which He expresses His judgement. (Kolve 1984: 326)

This manner of judging people was very popular among medieval authors particularly of pious texts: Chaucer and the Gawain-Pearl poet, both English contemporaries of Barbour, also employed this topos. The elements of earth, air, fire and water function as the allies of *Fortuna*, which is the mutable, contingent face of Divine Providence's mysterious ways. In Chaucer's *Man of Law's Tale*, for example, after the killing of all the Christians in Syria:

Custance han they take anon, foot-hoot,
And in a ship steerelees, God woot,
They han hir set, and bidde hire lerne saille
Out of Surrye agaynward to Ytaille
A certein tresor that she thider ladde,
And, sooth to seyn, vitaille greet plentee
They han hire yeven, and clothes eek she hadde,
And forth she sailleth in the salte see.

---

[1] "They that go down to the sea in ships, that do business in great waters; These see the works of the Lord, and his wonders in the deep. For he commandeth, and raiseth the stormy wind, which lifteth up the waves thereof. They mount up to the heaven, they go down again to the depths: their soul is melted because of trouble. They reel to and fro, and stagger like a drunken man, and are at their wit's end. Then they cry unto the Lord in their trouble, and he bringeth them out of their distresses. He maketh the storm calm, so that the waves thereof are still. Then are they glad because they be quiet; so He bringeth them unto their desired haven". (*Ps.* 107.23–30)

O my Custance, ful of benignitee,
O Emperoures younge doghter deere,
He that is lord of Fortune be thy steere! (ll.438–48)

Chaucer, in one of the most profoundly Christian stories of *The Canterbury Tales*, employs the topos of setting someone adrift on her/his own. In this case, the English poet's use of this device highlights both the saintly figure of Custance and her *fortitudo* (constancy is a virtue closely associated with *fortitudo* in the medieval tradition; see Kolve 1984: 304). Similarly, it is also remarkable that the narrator extols her goodness (benignitee) and immediately afterwards God is invoked to steer the boat (l.448). The Gawain-Pearl poet makes use of almost the same expression in *Cleanness* in order to explain why Noah's Ark did not sink:

Nyff oure Lorde hade ben her lodesmon, hem had lumpen harde. (l.424)

After Bruce's exile in the islands, he and his followers return to the mainland when the former's penitence has been almost completed. The beginning of Book V is introduced with an idealised representation of spring, in which "ye nychtyngale / Begouth rycht sariely to syng / Swete notis and sownys ser" / [...] / "And ye treis begouth to ma / Burgeans and brycht blomys alsua" (V.1–13). As Duncan reminds us, in romances the harmonising singing of birds in a spring-like *locus amoenus* serves to indicate "an abrupt change of action" (Duncan ed. 1997: 190). The use of this topos in *The Bruce* denotes that the king's fate is about to change, now that he is coming back to the mainland. While it cannot be conclusively claimed that the sovereign's growth in maturity will finally mean that he is absolved for the murder at Greyfriars' Church, it does imply that he is at a later stage of his penitence and sufferings.

Indeed, it is not until Book IX that Robert Bruce's penitence can be said to finish allegorically:

And yar him [Bruce] tuk sik a seknes
Yat put him to full hard distres.
He forbar bath drink & mete,
His men ne medicyne couth get
Yat euer mycht to ye king awaile,
Hys force gan him halyly faile
Yat he mycht noyer rid na ga. (IX.35–41)

The terrible sickness affecting the king may suggest a figurative interpretation. That he had to stop both drinking and eating (IX.38) is an
obvious symbol of atonement, an allegory of what monks and clergymen, in general, literally did as penitence. After this illness, Bruce
finally awakes to his *vita nuova* as the king that Scotland needs, a
short time before the decisive battle of Bannockburn. After his long,
painful learning process and redemption, Robert Bruce evolves from
the impulsive young king to the mature monarch who will govern
Scotland with a perfect balance of justice and mercy.

The death of the main character conveys an allegorical parallel
reading of the action, leading to his salvation after a warrior's life.
Prior to death, however, because of the political milieu into which the
work is integrated, the already ill hero must ensure the accomplishment of his regal duties, which rounds out his image completely. In
Book XX, King Robert finally signs a peace with England:

Quhen men yir thingis for-spokyn had
And with selis and athis maid
Festnyng off frendschip and of pes
Yat neuer for na chaunc suld ces. (XX.55–58)

At last, historically, the enemy recognises Robert I's royalty and
Scottish national freedom: Bruce's victory is definitive. Allegorically,
the harmony among the spheres is finally recovered through "pes"; the
reader is symbolically brought back to the idealised times of
Alexander III, mentioned at the beginning of work. This represents the
perfection of a circular structure. Alexander III's idealised reign intimately connected with good leadership and kingship is regained
through Bruce and his successors: "Qwhen Alexander ye king wes
deid / Yat Scotland haid to steyr & leid" (I. 37–38). The marriage and
coronation of Bruce's son follow which, within the allegorical framework and limits of the poem, secure the continuation of an ideal state
of things after Bruce's death (although historically this was not so).

This is an archetypal death for monarchs or rulers in chronicles
and historical literature of the late Middle Ages. In French literature,
for example, in Joinville's *Vie de Saint Louis*, when Louis IX senses
that death is approaching, the first thing he does is to settle his succession. He calls his son and gives him advice on good kingship:

"Biau filz, la premiere chose que je t'enseigne si est que tu mettes ton cuer en amer Dieu. Car sanz ce, nulz ne peut estre sauvé. [...] Se Dieu t'envoie perversité, si le reçoif en patience et en rent graces a Nostre Seigneur, et pense que tu l'as deservi, et que il te tournera tout a preu". (ch. 740–41)

["Good son, the first thing I teach you is to give your heart to love God. Because without this, no-one can be saved. [...] If God sends you adversities, accept them patiently and thank our Lord. Think that you deserve them, and He will chanel this into your own benefit."]

Significantly, as in the case of Amytans's lesson to Arthur in *Lancelot of the Laik*, the counselling commences not with an allusion to political tactics or policies but to the humility and devotion owed to God. Only through being a good Christian can someone become a good monarch. As an old wise man who has learnt from experience, the king's second piece of advice parallels the teachings of Lady Philosophy in Boethius' *De Consolatione*. Without explicitly referring to fortune and Divine Providence, Louis instructs his son on how to act in adverse situations from a Christian perspective. In the *Vie*, then, the lines before the hero's death extol the narrative's main theme, the sanctity of Louis IX.

As a Christian knight, one of the protagonist's main goals would be to go on a crusade to defend the faith and recover the Holy Sepulchre. Nevertheless, the King of Scots could never go on a crusade. Although he intended to do so, his war against the English forced him to stay in Scotland during his lifetime (Schwend 1986: 208). Bruce's way to paradise is delineated in the shape of his symbolic participation in the Crusades after his death. Interestingly, this scene, more characteristic of a romance than of reality, seems to be historically supported:

In the early years of the nineteenth century, when the Abbey Church of Dunfermline was being restored, the workmen came upon the remains of a splendid tomb in the spot which tradition assigned to the grave of Bruce. Within, amid the fragments of cloth of gold, lay the skeleton of a tall man, and the fact that the breastbone had been sawn through confirmed the poet's account of the removal of the king's heart. (Eyre-Todd trans. 1996: 358n)

As a Christological figure, by symbolically rising from the dead, the King of Scots consummates the holy enterprise of confronting the heathen. This intervention in the crusade, as well as guaranteeing him a place in heaven, parallels Edward's desertion of holy war in Book I.

This follows the structural parameters of divinity: "the temporality and devilish 'sleness' of the English king are thus counterpointed against the holy death and resurrective journey of his Scottish counterpart, when Douglas carries his heart on crusade" (Jack 2000: 34). Bruce accomplishes an allegorical return to origins in accordance with the mythological origins of Scotland. If it was Edward Bruce who first returned to Ireland, now it is Bruce's heart and Douglas which close the perfect circular narrative structure by going on a crusade to Spain. This mythical journey is highlighted by Jack and Rozendaal:

> The Maccabees were the chosen biblical race. By linking the Scottish people with them, Barbour introduces the line of mythic history which traces back Scotland's history via a journey from the Holy Land, by way of Spain and Ireland, to their intended homeland. Fordun makes the same comparison. (Jack and Rozendaal ed. 1997: 12n)

Intervention in a crusade is the best way in which a knight can serve God according to the mythological origins of chivalry:

> In the tyme that cheritee, leautee, justice, and veritee was failit in the warld, than began crueltee, unlautee, injure and falsete: and than was errour and distrublaunce in the warld; in the quhilk warld God had maid man to duell to trowe in him, serve him, honore him, love him, and dout him. Bot first quhen despising of justice come in the warld, and than was syk mysreugle and misgovernaunce in the warld amang the peple for fault of justice, that for to ger the reugle of gude governaunce cum agayn with force and drede of awe, the peple gert chese a man amang a thousand, the quhilk was maist wise, maist stark and sturdy, and best of governaunce, maist godlyke, and full of grete leautee, and of maist noblesse, maist curageus, and best techit in vertues. (Haye 1901–14: II. 11)

Thus, the Order of Chivalry was ideally founded to defend God and his teachings in the middle of chaos. Bruce wins his most important battle, unifying knightly and religious responsibilities even after his death.

Golagros and Gawane: Arthur's spiritual and political need for regeneration

The Arthurian romance, *Golagros and Gawane*, begins with Arthur going on a pilgrimage, which suggests that the King may undergo some kind of spiritual process of regeneration. As Jack affirms, Arthur's adventure is redefined in the context of a spiritual, and not simply chivalric, pilgrimage (Jack 1974–75: 5):

In the tyme of Arthur, as trew men me tald,
The King turnit on ane tyde towart Tuskane,
Hym to seik ovr the sey, that saiklese was sald,
The syre that sendis all seill, suthly to sane. (ll.1–4)

The need for a *peregrinatio* re-codifies the subtext of the literal journey. In *Golagros and Gawane* the pilgrimage motif, which is absent from the original, becomes an important narrative axis to the detriment of the chivalric and courtly concerns of the French source. It also generates a series of expectations in the audience, who will look for signs building on an allegorical structure.

The fabulous retinue of the king with "Cumly kingis with croune / Of gold that was cleir" (ll.12–13) and shining armour (ll.20–22) can be interpreted in contrary ways. The most obvious one is the chivalric topos of a glorious army advancing in full array – its image being that of invincible power. Yet, in the more Christian framework of a *peregrinatio*, distinct spiritual questions are implied contextually: is there any reason why the display of riches and weapons is needed in an *a priori* pacific journey to a holy seat? In the context of a spiritual interpretation, Arthur and his court are made obscure by pride, the origin of all sins. The author ironically transfers the implicit pride of the *Chastel Orgueilleux* in the French original to the Arthurian world. Therefore, the attire and general attitude of Arthur and his retinue determine that the pilgrimage will only be completed as a physical journey. Spiritual blindness prevents the court from realising the true significance of their enterprise.

Hollowness is reaffirmed when Arthur wishes to conquer Golagros's lands without any justifiable reason. Arthur's intentions and methods do not correspond to any chivalric feat of arms but, as Jack claims, to his thirst for earthly power since he has perverted the concept of fealty to subserve his own ambitions (Jack 1974–75: 12). As argued in Chapter 1, in the *First Continuation* the imprisonment of Gyflet fils Do justifies Arthur's attack on the Riche Soudoyer, a fact absent from *Golagros and Gawane*. Golagros's castle excels in magnificence:

Syne war thai war of ane wane, wrocht with ane wal,
Reirdit on ane riche roche, beside ane riveir,
With doubill dykis bedene drawin ovr all;
Micht nane thame note with invy, nor nygh thame to neir.
The land wes likand in large and lufsum to call;
Propir schene schane the son, seymly and feir. (ll.237–42)

The perfection of the spot functions as an adaptation of the *locus
amoenus* of classical and medieval literature to the seigniorial stronghold of chivalric romances. Furthermore, its sudden appearance in the
middle of the forest suggests an element of the Other World. Both the
locus amoenus and the supernatural conventionally imply that the
romance hero will have to undergo a test or a series of tests. Arthur's
thirst for power will be challenged not in the physical pilgrimage but
in Golagros's territories.

The journey to the Holy Land loses all its significance for
Arthur:

The Roy rial raid withoutin resting,
And socht to the cieté of Criste, ovr the salt flude
With mekil honour in erd he maid his offering,
Syne buskit hame the samyne way that he before yude. (ll.301–4)

The main objective of the travel and, by implication, its meaning, is
displaced. Jerusalem becomes a place Arthur merely passes through
before invading Golagros's lands. The "honour" he displays in his
offering can only be contextualised as an empty act in which the
manners and ritualistic proceedings of devotion have replaced the
religious significance of penance and repentance. Moreover, the
earthly ("in erd") nature of such "honour" shows Arthur's incapaticity
to see beyond the materiality of this world, even in a pilgrimage. If
Arthur's political righteousness is put into question through his
menace to Golagros, so is his Christian piety in the Holy Land. The
monarch and his concept of *pax arturica* will have to be regenerated
both in the political and spiritual arenas. Arthur's military intervention
is by no means just since, according to Aquinas, in such cases warfare
would be vindicated only if "on the part of those making the war there
is a right intention, to achieve some good or avoid some evil" (*Summa
Theologiae* II–II, Qu. 40).

The reworking of the meaning of the *First Continuation* affects
not only the plot, but the representation of characters, too. Spynagros,

one of Arthur's knights, acting as a mediator's voice between the audience and the poet, takes it upon himself to tell Arthur's retinue (and by implication the audience) about Golagros's attributes. Rhiannon Purdie suggests that Spynagros's name probably derives from Latin *spina* (thorn or prick) which was used as a metaphor for conscience. If so, he could be seen as the voice of Arthur's conscience in the romance (Purdie 2005: 103). Spynagros's *encomium* of Golagros first centres on his *proeza* and handsomeness. More important than his courtly and knightly virtues, however, is the following remark: "He [Golagros] is ane lord riale, / Ane seymly soverane in sale" (ll.359–60), whom his subjects love.

Arthur's spiritual evolution is discussed in connection with sovereignty and undermines the Arthurian dream of conquest. The King must redress his actions and understand the real range and limitations of his royal privileges. Jack notes that, owing to the evolution of the battle, Arthur is forced to cast doubt on his earlier pride (Jack 1974–75: 14). The series of combats between Arthur's and Golagros's men lacks the ornamented language of chivalry of the French original. If this serves to challenge the nature of warfare and undermine its presupposed heroism and chivalric worth, within the King of Britain's regeneration process the meaningless displays of violence also operate as the progressive development of spiritual awareness.

From the first joust between Gaudifeir and Galiot (ll.545–83), there is a gradual escalation of bloodshed and desolation, which the monarch cannot fail to see. Spynagros's warning is confirmed, as "Mony ledis salbe loissit, and liffis forlorne" (l.277). As in most Scottish romances, it is through an adverse situation of profound crisis (in this case, the disastrous development of the confrontation) that the king will begin his learning process. Only through several blows to the Arthurian order will Arthur start questioning the correctness of his policies and actions owing to a progressive spiritual awareness.

While the first fight ends with Gaudifeir taking Galiot prisoner, subsequent confrontations cause the death of Sir Regal, Sir Ranald and Sir Edmond. Prisoners are taken on both sides, too. No band seems to have gained a clear advantage over the opponent. Apparently, the audience's only conclusion is the uselessness of Arthur's unjust attack on Golagros's territory. Arthur, however, will take longer to understand this. The King is not prepared to abandon his desire for conquest:

The King grantit the gait to Schir Gawane,
And prayt to the grete God to grant him his grace,
Him to save and to salf, that is our soverane,
As he is the makar of man, and alkyn myght haise. (ll.791–94)

Although Arthur's first address to God acknowledges the superiority of His mysterious ways over the British King's own will and plans, the only reason why he reverts to Him is that the one who is going to combat Golagros is Gawain, his nephew, whom he holds in high esteem. As well as being his favourite knight and one of his own kin, Gawain is the King's sole hope to perpetuate his dream, insofar as he does not have a rightful heir with his wife Guenevere. The familial and hierarchical position at this stage results in a formal rather than in a heartfelt submission to God. Indeed his previous assumption that God is on his side demonstrates his complete blindness and misunderstanding of what is occurring. The first approach to the Almighty proves to be as hollow and meaningless as his conception of *pax arturica* and his strictly physical peregrination to Jerusalem. The only positive feature about the monarch is that, at least, he shows some kind of humane attitude, which he had not expressed before the battle when he menacingly claimed that "mony wedou / Ful wraithly sal weip" (ll.297–98).

   Not until he sees Gawain in real peril, does he behave in a more profoundly pious manner: he prays with tears streaming down his face "[f]or Gawyne the gude" (l.953–59). For the first time, the king is primarily concerned with his nephew's fate rather than with his own conquests. Nevertheless, the sovereign does not yet consider the wrongfulness of overstepping his authority. A more radical change in the Wheel of Fortune is needed before he redresses his attitude towards the good administration of justice. Hence, Gawain's fake defeat works on two main levels of interpretation: first, it helps Arthur to realise that the foundations of the *pax arturica* are not always synonymous with a just cause; and second, he finally comprehends the temporality of earthly power and possessions:

"The flour of knighthede is caught throu his cruelté!
Now is the Round Tabil rebutit, richest of rent,

Quhen wourschipfull Wawane, the wit of our were,
Is led to ane presoune;
Now failyeis gude fortoune!" (ll.1135–39)

In the defeat of Gawain, he discerns the catastrophic end of the Round
Table and its ideals, which he has not respected by waging war on
Golagros.

Still blind, Arthur puts the blame on *Fortuna* in the same way as
Boethius does in *De Consolatione Philosophiae*:

Else why does slippery Fortune range,
Encompassing such violent change?
Harsh pains, owed villainy as its due
Instead the innocent pursue.
With wicked ways ensconced on high,
We blameless souls unjustly lie,
Our necks pressed down by guilty men;
Virtue's bright sheen is hidden then
In blind darkness. Probity
Endures crushing iniquity
Sworn lies and specious deceit
Attract no danger or defeat; (Book I. 5)

At this stage, neither Arthur nor the Boethius persona can perceive
God's divine patterning of the world; they are still too attached to
material precepts to assimilate it. As Lady Philosophy will demonstrate in *De Consolatione*, Fortune is only a tool of Divine Providence.
Late medieval commentators on Boethius's work such as Remigius of
Auxerre systematically Christianised the "questions that touched the
Christian faith. The problems of providence, free will, fate, the nature
of God and of good and evil were interpreted largely on Augustinian
lines" (Beaumont 1981: 290). In this milieu, the temporal harshness
and incomprehensibility of earthly existence conform to an anagogical
providential design whose ends are good, which leads to *beatitudo*.

The Boethian-Augustinian philosophical bedrock is not so evident in the *First Continuation*. This is shown in Arthur's reaction after
listening to the news about his nephew's joust:

Le rois ne les pot plus oïr,
Ains se vait sor un lit gesir;
De son mantel son cief covri,
Ainc hom ne vit mais si mari. (ll.6437–40)

[The king cannot listen to them any longer. He covers his face with his topcoat. He is the unhappiest man that anyone has ever seen.]

The image of Arthur is one of profound sadness, but the Boethian element is not present. The Scottish author re-elaborates the representation of the British King according to different thematic and structural principles. The Boethian background revitalises the notion of a spiritual journey. The last passages of the romance will reveal to what extent Arthur has learned his lesson.

By the end of *Golagros and Gawane*, Arthur renounces Golagros's allegiance, which at first sight seems to imply that he has learned to be a good monarch again. However, it is Golagros who emerges as the perfect representation of a lord since he prioritises his country's interests over his own. Like Arthur, the knight laments the loss of sovereignty in a manner consistent with Boethian-Aristotelian philosophical thought. This is again absent from the French original:

"Sen Fortoune cachis the cours, throu hir quentys,
I did it noght for nane dreid that I had to de,
Na for na fauting of hart, na for na fantise". (ll.1220–22)

The beginning of his complaint follows the same thematic structure as that of Arthur. Golagros does not seem to understand why everything has gone so wrong, when he did his best. At first sight, then, both characters may seem to share a similar misunderstanding of God's mysterious procedures. But unlike Arthur, Golagros did fight according to right. Further, as lines 1223–28 underline, Golagros acknowledges God's Divine Providence on which the capricious *Fortuna* depends:

"Quhare Criste cachis the cours, it rynnis quently –
May nowthir power nor pith put him to prise.
Quhan onfortone quhelmys the quheil, thair gais grace by;
Quha may his danger endure or destanye dispise,
That led men in langour ay lestand inly,
The date na langar may endure na Drightin devinis. (ll.1223–28)

His conclusion entails an acceptance of his fate and his willingness to comprehend the course of things within the limitation of human knowledge: "Ilkane be werk and be will / Is worth his rewarde" (ll.1244–45). He possesses a spiritual nobility superior to that of the British monarch. Like Boethius, he learns that

Adverse Fortune benefits people more than good, for whereas good Fortune seems to fawn on us, she invariably deceives us with the appearance of happiness, adverse Fortune is always truthful, and shows by her mutability that she is inconstant. The first deceives, the second instructs. (*De Consolatione Philosophiae*, Book II. 8)

Golagros's implied disposition to comprehend and learn rounds off his image as perfect knight and ruler. As a matter of fact, he has already seen the loyalty and love of his subjects even after defeat.

After this, Arthur is the one who should show equal magnanimity and knowledge gained. In victory, Arthur shows the *cortesia* that appertains to a king. If in the previous passages he has come to resemble Kay owing to his *vilania* and proneness to unjustified use of violence (Jack 1974–75: 10), now he behaves according to the courtly norm:

sen thi [Golagros's] lawté is lell,
That thow my kyndnes wil heill,
The mare is thi price. (ll.1308–10)

Arthur gallantly recognises Golagros's worth and has no qualms about praising a valiant enemy. Now that the war is over, he does not look for revenge but acts as a regenerated person and "[o]f Schir Gologras grant blith wes the King" (l.1328). At a personal level, then, Arthur has recovered successfully.

After enjoying Golagros's hospitality for nine days, the British King will have to prove whether he has also gained the necessary knowledge in the territory of politics. Although he implicitly realises the failure of the *pax arturica* being based on military destruction, when he allows Golagros to regain his freedom, he does so as a "reward" rather than on the basis of Golagros's right to sovereignty:

"Heir mak I the reward, as I have resoune,
Before thir senyeouris in sight, semely beside,
As tuiching thi temporalité, in toure and in toune,
In firth, forest, and fell, and woddis so wide:
I mak releisching of thin allegiance". (ll.1354–58)

Therefore, although Arthur has learned a lesson, he fails to understand the real nature of a nation's right to freedom. Like Edward I, he only sees himself as the Elect able to govern over other countries other than his own. This extra tension is most probably reminiscent of the Scottish political situation since in the *First Continuation* Arthur never renounces the Riche Soudoyer's fealty:

Leur homages prent demanois,
Ainc en un jor tant n'en cosquist,
Si con Bliobliheri dist.
Puis li orent molt grant mestier
En mains lius li bons saudoier. (ll.6550–54)

[[Arthur] accepted their homage immediately. Never had he won so many knights in a single day, as Bliobliheri corroborates. Later, the good Soudoyer helped him on many occasions.]

Arthur's conquest is represented as heroic action of the greatest magnitude. The political references which problematise the vassalage of the Riche Soudoyer/Golagros are exclusive to the Scottish romance.

According to medieval political theory, as John of Salisbury cites from the *Deuteronomy* in Book IV of his *Policraticus*, right can only be given by God:

"When thou art come," He says, into the land which the Lord thy God shall give to thee, and shalt possess it and shalt dwell therein and shalt say, "I will set over me a king such all the nations that are round about me have over them;" thou shalt appoint him king over thee whom the Lord thy God shall choose from the number of thy brethren. Thou mayst not asset over thee for thy king a man of another nation, who is not thy brother. (*Deut* XVII.14 ff. in *Policraticus* IV.iv.15)

Hence, by bestowing the privileges of kingship and freedom as a personal "reward" rather than as a right, Arthur plays a role which is reserved to God himself. As a human being, the monarch should have grasped the real nature of kingship and sovereignty as a divine gift, not as a matter on which a person can decide. Moreover, his being a foreigner disqualifies him from ruling over another people. Arthur comprehends the absurdity of his non-justifiable invasion, but he is still blind to the significance of royalty beyond earthly power. His merely partial regeneration foreshadows the future downfall of the Arthurian kingdom.

Lancelot of the Laik and the *Buik of Alexander*: **parallel learning processes**

In the Scottish *Lancelot*, Arthur's learning process is totally dependent on the conception of good kingship. In this context, the inclusion of a prophetic vision does not operate as a justification for political action as in *The Wallace* or *La Vie de Saint Louis*, but as a warning to Arthur owing to his bad administration of justice. The *Buik of Alexander* offers a parallel instructive method. Notwithstanding his peripherality to the core of the narrative, King Clarus, Alexander's enemy, is taught how he should redress his conception of kingship.

In *Lancelot of the Laik*, even before Galiot challenges Arthur's kingdom, strange nightmares disturb the king's sleep:

> Apone the ground and liging hyme besid,
> Throw wich anon out of his slep he stert,
> Abasit and adred into his hart. (ll.376–78)

Arthur's insomnia implies some kind of internal preoccupation which prevents him from sleeping peacefully. Later, the audience will learn that it is a subconscious reaction to his bad government.

Macrobius's *Commentary on the Dream of Scipio*, which became one of the most authoritative books on the interpretations of dreams in the Middle Ages (Stahl, trans. 1952: 54), analyses and catalogues the nature and meaning of dreams:

> All dreams may be classified under five main types: There is the enigmatic dream, in Greek *oneiros*, in Latin *somnium*; second, there is the prophetic vision, in Greek *horama*, in Latin *visio*; third there is the oracular dream, in Greek *chrematismos*, in Latin *oraculum*; fourth, there is the nightmare, in Greek *enypnion*, in Latin *insomnium*; and last, the apparition, in Greek *phantasma*, which Cicero, when he has occasion to use the word, calls *visum*. (Book I. iii)

Some of these dreams are mere nightmares with no hidden significance and others such as the prophetic *visio* and the *oraculum*, when interpreted correctly, reveal truths. According to this classification, that of Arthur falls into the category of *visio*, as the reader will learn when Amytans unveils its meaning (see also Lupack ed. 1994: 119).

Although the monarch's dream is taken from the French original, there are two main differences between the texts. First, the chaplain to whom Arthur first relates his dream is not present in the Middle Scots romance. Second, the Queen's replies entail a distinct attitude towards her husband. In the *Prose Lancelot*, the aforesaid chaplain dismisses Arthur's concern: "'Sire, fait il, ne vos chaut, car songes est noianz'" (261) ["Sire," he said, "do not worry too much since the dream means nothing"]. The deployment of the word "songes" is of the greatest significance in the context of prophetic dreams. In French, "songe" is used to cover both *somnium* and *insomnium*, while "vision" encapsulates the meanings of *visio* and *visum*. The chaplain's use of "songe" denies its Christian-divine origin. The impossibility of disentangling the meaning of the dream ontologically underlines the political and chivalric decline of Arthur's court.

In the *Prose Lancelot*, Guenevere simply confirms the chaplain's assertion: "Et li rois lo redit a la reine, et ele lo dit tot autretel" (261) [Then the king told the queen, and she said the same (208)]. Conversely, in the Middle Scots text, the Queen's answer is longer and far more severe:

"Shir, no record lyith to such thing;
Wharfor now, shir, I pray yow tak no kep
Nore traist into the vanyteis of slep.
For thei are thingis that askith no credens
Bot causith of sum maner influens,
Empriss of thoght, ore superfleuytee,
Or than sum othir casualytee" (ll.388–94)

In the *amplificatio* of the original, Guenevere exercises the chaplain's role. In doing so, the makar makes her deploy the authoritative language of clerks to put forward an issue about which she proves to be absolutely mistaken. But even more important than her erroneous reply is the manner in which it differs from the original prose romance. The French Guenevere seems to corroborate an idea without making any kind of judgement, whereas the Scottish Guenevere's severe reprimand accentuates the distance between the king and his spouse.

Despite his wife's opposition, Arthur wants to unveil the meaning of his nightmares. His procedures will indicate that he is no longer the idealised ruler of Britain. Conversely, insofar as the astrologers have hidden what they have discovered "for dreid of his danger" (l.444), he makes use of all his power to force them to tell him what they see in his dreams:

Than was he [Arthur] wroth into hisself and noyt
And maid his vow that thei [the astrologers] shal ben destroyt.
[…]
He bad them [his men] into secret wyss that thei
Shud do no harm but only them assey. (ll.471–72; 477–78)

The astrologers' terror expressed in line 444 is totally justified. The king employs royal authority not for the common welfare but to obtain the desired information from the soothsayers. Feigned though the execution is, this extremely cruel proceeding has nothing to do with the notion of good kingship. Although it can be argued that the future of the monarch cannot be disengaged from that of the kingdom and, therefore, the "common weal" is also at stake, the methods Arthur deploys question the abusive overstepping of authority. At the same time, the fact that the astrologers are terrified even before the threat to their lives confirms both the distance between the monarch and his subjects and the abhorrent perception that they have of him.

In Philippe de Mézières' allegorical composition *Le Songe du Vieil Pelerin* (c.1389), whose third book also deals with a king's instruction, Royne Verite stresses the importance of treating fairly all the people under young Charles' charge. She tells him:

Que tu doyes garder souverainement a ton plain pouoir les femmes de tes subgiez, les mariz, et tous leurs biens quelxconques de toute violence et de toute tyrannie, voire de ta personne royalle premierement, de ceulx de ton hostel, des poursuivans et de toutes autres personnes, par telle maniere que tu vouldroies que on feist de toy et de tes choses. (Book III. 203)

[That you must protect with all your power the women of your subjects, the married ones, and all their property devoid of any violence and of any tyranny, indeed by your royal person first, of those of your household, of plaintiffs and of all other people, in the same way as you would like someone to treat you and your possessions.]

This profoundly Christian and politically effective attitude has nothing to do with Arthur at the beginning of *Lancelot of the Laik*. He is failing both as a Christian and as a capable king. As a result, the kingdom itself is bound to collapse.

In order to discredit him even more, the undermining description of Arthur and his royal policies is quickly contrasted with those of Galiot, who possesses all the possible knightly and courtly virtues: he is "the farest knycht, / […] ful of larges and humylytee / [and] curag", a great young conqueror and is by "[…] his men so louit" (ll.601–20).

Mapstone affirms that the virtues of wisdom, manhood and courage
attached to Galiot suggest that he is a standard against which the
deteriorated image of Arthur will be compared (Mapstone 1986: 171–
72). The war is transferred to the domain of personal confrontation:
apparently, only Arthur's personal and political regeneration could
withstand Galiot's invasion. The narrative will thus focus on
instruction about exemplary kingship, reducing the learning process to
the necessary steps which Arthur must take to become a good
monarch again.

In the second part of the *Buik of Alexander*, the *Avowis of
Alexander*, King Clarus of India besieges Ephesus. His image accords
with that of a tyrant rather than a good king. His thirst for power
rather than his *mesura* dominates his acts. First, he wants to take
revenge on Alexander without any apparent provocation from the
latter (ll.1245–46). Then, he shows unwise obstinacy by refusing to
follow Marciane's advice to retire when the battle is lost (ll.1477–94).
Finally, it is Alexander himself who delivers the hardest asseveration
against Clarus:

"The King Clarus is wyse in were,
Richt stout and hardy of affere,
Bot his men him hates as the dede;
To his tynsall thay will him lede.
Sen he is hated, I warne yow this:
We sall discumfete him and his" (ll.1547–51)

Alexander's words situate the poem in the same advice to princes
tradition as *Lancelot of the Laik*, in which the instruction of Amytans,
the wise clerk, will also allude to the debilitation of a sovereign's
power should his vassals not love him. At this point in the narrative,
however, the remarks about Clarus only operate as a contrast with
Alexander, a *speculum principis* himself. Not until more than a
thousand lines later, does the author introduce the didactic account on
good kingship.

In the Middle Scots *Lancelot*, after a first battle with Galiot's
superior army, the British King will benefit from Galiot's *cortesia*,
whereas the wise clerk's advice will enable Arthur to understand his
misdeeds and find the right way again. In his learning evolution, the
personal and the political will become interdependent. The name of
the clerk itself underlines the transcendence of the passage. Although

his name is not mentioned at this stage in the *Prose Lancelot*, the author of the Scottish text took Amytans from a later scene occurring in the *Cyclic Lancelot*, in which the adviser is not just a clerk but a hermit and former chaplain. In Sommer's edition (IV.76–77), Amustans is a hermit, who had been Arthur's chaplain. He reproves Arthur for having disobeyed the Holy Church and deserted his wife in favour of the false Guenevere. This situation is parallel to that of the unnamed clerk: both clerks admonish the king to redress his wicked ways at a time when his kingdom is in danger. The Scottish makar's transmutation of the name posits his intention to provide the advice to Arthur with a spiritual aura. That the hermit's scene occurs in the *Cyclic Lancelot*, but is absent from the *Non-Cyclic*, indicates that the makar was probably working with a version of the *Cyclic* text. At this point of profound crisis, the King requires Amytans's presence and counsel. He hastens to pronounce the most severe statement possible concerning Arthur's government of his lands:

That is to say, yow art so far myswent
Of wykitness upone the urechit dans
That yow art fallyng in the storng vengans
Of Goddis wreth that shal the son devour. (ll.1320–23)

These lines reaffirm the astrologers' suppositions and allow the king to realise the extent to which his Arthurian dream has degenerated. He has offended the source of his power, God, whom, as stated in medieval treatises on kingship, he should try to imitate, being his representative on earth.

The fact that he is illegitimate intensifies Arthur's reliance on God's grace in choosing him as ruler. Amytans recalls:

For, as theselvyne wat,
It cummyth al bot only of His myght
And not of the nor of thi elderis richt
To the discending as in heritage,
For yow was not byget onto spousag. (ll.1330–34)

The clerk persists in using the same menacing tone to open Arthur's eyes. The wise man's authority contrasts with that of the astrologers who did not dare to tell the King what they saw in his dreams. But it is only under these particular circumstances, in which his material possessions are jeopardised, that he agrees to accept criticism. As with the Boethian persona in *De Consolatione*, the precariousness of earthly stability is the first cause that enables the protagonist to progress spiritually. At this stage, then, Arthur's concern is the safeguard of his territories rather than a profound spiritual commitment.

As a good orator with an excellent command of the *Modus Proferendi* (which helps to understand the ideas in the Bible and was later applied to literature in general), Amytans seeks to move Arthur so that he can be more convincingly persuaded into instruction. In *De Doctrina Christiana*, Saint Augustine recommends Cicero as the preceptor of Christian oratory. Following the latter's schema of oratorical delivery, based upon the triad *docere* (instruct), *delectare* (delight) and *movere* (move), the Bishop of Hippo devised guidelines for the Christian orator. The precept of *docere* basically deals with the subject matter, whereas *delectare* and *movere* centre on the manner in which this subject matter is to be transmitted. As well as its obvious informative objective, instruction should be pleasant and appealing to hold the attention of the audience. Amytans avoids *delectare* through his speech. By way of contrast, he threatens and disturbs Arthur to the extreme. Not only is this method appropriate to the circumstances, but it also enhances Arthur's culpability; he can do nothing but acknowledge his sins against God through the misgovernance of his subjects.

Before instruction itself, Amytans enumerates Arthur's faults, emphasising the oppression of the poor and the loss of his people's hearts. Consequently, he can only expect God to destroy him since "He is bycummyn thi [Arthur's] fo" (ll.1344–88). Amytans's oration has an immediate effect on Arthur. His speech has been successful:

"Maister," quod he, "of youre benevolens
Y yow besech that tueching myn offens
Yhe wald vichsaif your consell to me if
How I sal mend and ek hereftir leif". (ll.1389–92)

Submission to his instructor is absolute. There is a first sign of Arthur's evolution from the haughty king who menaced the astrologers to a humble apprentice who wants to redress his wrongdoings. He implicitly acknowledges his fallibility and the jeopardising of the Arthurian dream.

In the more markedly courtly elaboration of the second part of the *Buik of Alexander*, the reason for King Clarus to recognise his flaws and be keen to rectify his kingly conduct relates to his unrequited love for Fesonas. At first, his passion for her derives from her political and dynastic position; should he marry her, his claim over Ephesus would be justified in hereditary terms. When he discovers she is not interested in submitting to his advances, his first reaction is further revenge (ll.6926–45). Yet rejection brings out Clarus's more humane self:

"For thay haue left me na kin thing
To confort me in na louing!
Bot quha hes gift of lemmen deir,
And [wis] to lufe forout dangeir,
And yarning worship for to prufe,
He aucht wele to begin sic thing,
To put the body to amending!" (ll.6978–85)

For someone who is accustomed to take everything by force, this is a significant change of attitude. When he realises that, to conquer a lady's heart, a powerful position and the display of prowess on the battlefield in not enough, Clarus translates the personal, courtly incident into the public, political domain. If he cannot attain the love of a single lady because of his tyrannical exercise of authority, how can he be sure about the loyalty of his own subjects, whom he treats with even more disdain?

After Arthur is made to confess his sins in *Lancelot of the Laik*, a significant divergence from the source occurs. In the French original, although Galehot decides to stop the war against Arthur just before the wise sage's arrival (283), he does not communicate his decision to Arthur through "li Roi des Cent Chevaliers" until after the king has already learned his lesson (293). On the contrary, in the Scottish *Lancelot*, the makar places this scene a short time after his confession. By so doing, the direct intervention of God is implied, as Amytans states:

This Maister saith, "How lykith God dispone
Now may yhow se and suth is my recorde.
For by Hyme now is makith this accorde,
And by non uthir worldly providens
Sauf only grant of His benevolans,
To se if that the likyth to amend
And to provid thi cuntré to defend". (ll.1590–96)

With this rearrangement of the narrative, there is a direct causal connection between Arthur's willingness to atone for his sins, his subsequent confession and God's intrusion in the normal development of events. According to Mapstone, this re-structuring of events stresses the Christian element. Should the British King act following God's precepts, his possibilities of recovery will increase (Mapstone 1986: 177). In fact, had it not been for the truce, the battle would certainly have ended up with Arthur's defeat since both his champions, Gawain and the disguised Lancelot, were recovering from their wounds. That Amytans attributes this to Divine Providence redefines the nature of war in the realm of the sacred in a much more explicit way than in the *Prose Lancelot*. Galiot and his army are allegorically transmuted into God's weapons to chastise the Elect once the British King has misused the Almighty's gift and lost the real spirit of the *pax arturica* of chivalry and Christian order. Arthur's adverse fortune acquires spiritual resonance when redefined under the auspices of Divine Providence.

The new significance attained by Amytans's admonition transcends the merely earthly aspects of good government. Not only has Arthur failed as a monarch, but also as a Christian knight. The wise clerk deploys many rhetorical devices in the structuring of his speech with direct and clear language insofar as the main aim of an oration is clarity:

Of al thi puple the hartis ben ylost
And tynt richt throw thyne awn mysgovernans,
Of averice and of thyne errogans.
What is o prince, quhat is o governoure
Withouten fame of worschip and honour?
What is his mycht, suppos he be a lorde,
If that his folk sal nocht to hyme accorde? (ll. 1520–26)

Amytans reminds listeners of the lost hearts of a monarch's subjects once more. He counterbalances the King's vices with the necessary features he should possess. Rhetorical questions are deployed to encourage Arthur's meditation on his failure. As expounded in the representation of Balliol and Comyn in *The Bruce*, young Bruce in *The Wallace* and Arthur in *Golagros and Gawane*, the exercise of a king's *privata voluntas*, rather than acting according to the common good, is the very origin of iniquitous rule. The association of bad government with two of the deadly sins, avarice and pride, situates Arthur in an unsustainable position. It also justifies the desertion of his vassals, as he himself has failed to fulfil the feudal contract.

Arthur's image is further damaged through the reference to renown and honour, which the Round Table no longer possesses:

Nay! that shal sone his hie estat consome,
For many o knycht therby is broght ydoune
All uteraly to ther confusioune.
For oft it makith uther kingis by
To wer on them in trast of victory. (ll.1532–36)

Amytans's exposition of Arthur's "mysgouernans" is completed with the loss of his position if he fails to perform his royal duties. As a leader of his country, his behaviour should serve as a mirror. The ultimate consequence of that recalls the war against Galiot: the instablitiy derived from bad rule encourages others to overthrow his power. In this particular context, God's intervention implicitly legitimises the religious correctness of Galiot's invasion. In the Scottish context, an implicit understanding between king and nobles is preferable to a disunited country, which could be more easily invaded.

Subsequently, Amytans proceeds to instruct Arthur in the mechanisms of kingship. On the whole, Amytans's counsel closely follows the typical characteristics associated with a Christian king: he advocates *justice* and *mercy* for both "pur & rik" (ll.1611–68) as an earthly mirror of the divine administration and ordering of the world. After these typically kingly characteristics, Amytans also stresses the qualities of "larges, humilitee and manhed", citing Alexander as an example of the three (ll.1835–53). These features are more generally associated with knights as an integrative part of the courtly and knightly norms. The three virtues embrace the main attributes of a Christian king or knight. The monarch's demeanour towards others either nobles or members of the Third Estate must be governed by his *cortesia* as the reference to "larges" indicates. The more purely religious components of his behaviour are enshrined in "humilitee", whereas his way of action on the battlefield must show his "manhed". By alluding to these three attributes, Amytans summarises the entire regal and knightly conduct in the different spheres of the society.

Mapstone points out that "in *Lancelot of the Laik*, as far as it has survived, although Arthur may regain his wisdom, "manhede" is far

more a characteristic of his knights" (Mapstone 1986: 171). It is
necessary to examine the whole context of the orginal *Prose Lancelot*
including not only *The Prose Lancelot* but also *La Queste de le Sainct
Graal* and *La Morte le Roi Artu*, to encounter the British King fighting
for his lands. In fact, in the final battle against Modred, Arthur takes a
very active role not only as a military leader, but also as a warrior:

Il [Arthur] tint un glaive gros et fort, et lesse corre tant comme il pot del cheval trere;
et Modrés, qui bien connoist que li rois ne bee fors a li acirre, nel refusa pas, einz li
adesce la teste del cheval, et li rois, qui li vient de toute sa force, le firent si durement
qu'il li ront les mailles del hauberc et li met par mi le cors e fer de son glaive. (*La
Morte le Roi Artu*, 245)

[He [Arthur] takes a wide and strong lance, and gallops on his horse; and Modred,
who did not know that the king only wanted to kill him, does not avoid him, but
address his horse's head towards the king, who comes in full strength. He hits him so
fiercely that he breaks the cote de maille and sinks the spearhead in his body.]

In an opposite manner to the passive Arthur of Chrétien de Troyes's
compositions, the King of the *Vulgate* does display his "manhede" as
this last combat with Modred proves. Whereas in Chrétien's *romans*
the heart of the narrative explores the ethos of individual knights, the
more epic tone of the *Lancelot en prose*, in which the whole worth and
evolution of the Arthurian kingdom is debated, helps to reassess the
role of its leader.

One of the passages that the makar highlights is that concerning
largeza. Although the French author already places a lot of importance on a king's liberality, the Scottish poet reworks and extends the
main remarks about *largeza*. He regards this virtue as the key point in
the relationship between the monarch and his subjects no matter to
what social stratum they belong. Amytans's insistence on this, which
he labels as "the tresour of o king" (1:1766), develops two major
conceptualisations. First, its most concrete utility is not simple generosity devoid of self-interest, as expected from a knight without the
political responsibilities of a monarch. Rather it is a tool to keep the
subjects happy and secure their loyalty to the crown. Yet Amytans
does not tell Arthur to do this arbitrarily but rather according to
position and merit, an idea very different from the French original.
While it is stated that "povretez n'a mestier que d'amendement, et
richece n'a mestier que de delit" (288) [poverty requires compensation
and richness requires delight], *The Prose Lancelot* does so in the

milieu of the usefulness those things can have, something that has little to do with merit.

Secondly, the wise clerk manages to reach a consensus between this rather utilitarian interpretation of *largeza* and a more affectionate vision of it:

Bot that thow ifith, if with boith two,
That is to say, uith hart and hand atonis.
As so the wys man ay the ift disponis. (ll.1763–65)

In this understanding of good kingship as a learning process within an essentially moral and affective view of authority, to give riches for the sake of buying loyalty would not be a correct policy, but a simple tool to maintain a king's position in power. Being generous "uith hart" recaptures the original significance of *largeza*. Arthur needs to comprehend this if he wants to regain his wisdom, otherwise his acts will remain valueless at the spiritual level of regeneration. Earthly power and possessions would be prioritised, which is exactly the opposite of Amytans's intention. If loyalty can be bought, it can be short-lived, too, inasmuch as any other lord could offer more material rewards in return for the service of Arthur's subjects. Therefore, only a more profound conception of *largeza* as true generosity can gain what Amytans accused Arthur of having lost: his people's hearts. Unlike bought loyalty, love between lord and vassal coming from the sincere use of liberality can make Arthur's reign survive Galiot's attack.

In the *Buik of Alexander*, Marciane plays much the same role as Amytans. They are both figures of authority rather than authoritarian figures. The two instructors are the only ones who dare to tell the monarchs what their bad policies are. By way of contrast with Amytans, however, Marciane is not an old sage, but Clarus's nephew, which makes his ascendancy over his uncle even more interesting. Accepting the counsel of a younger member of his retinue denotes an implicit acknowledgement of his fallibility and an inner intention for reformation. Marciane's first piece of advice entirely coincides with that of Amytans:

With-haldis your friends with yow all
And honour thame, baith great and small,
And hetchis and geues thame largely!

Sa sall men lufe yow certanely,
And ay to your auancement
Sall thay haue hart, will and talent. (ll.2665–70)

The identical affective vision of *largeza*, in which generosity will not only serve to buy loyalty, but as a token of sincere adherence between lord and vassal situates the teaching and learning processes in the same advice to princes tradition as the Middle Scots *Lancelot*. The reference to the subjects' "hart" reinforces the link even more emphatically.

Porrus, although not talking directly to his father, also alludes to the same virtues as Marciane does. A good leader must behave honourably and courteously at all times so that his people can love him. More importantly, and again in complete consonance with *Lancelot of the Laik*, Porrus claims that:

Quhen a lord of hart is large and fre,
Large and courtes and hes pietie,
And he anoyit beis of his skaith,
Hardy, lele and luffand baith –
Than is ane worth vther tua,
Quhen lord has nede agane his fa. (ll.2785–90)

The inclusion of "pietie" bestows a Christian aura on the ideal behaviour of monarchs. Christian virtues distinguish tyrants from Christian rulers. As in the invasion of Galiot, the lack of love towards a lord debilitates his position of power: only a lord who is loved will be defended properly before an enemy. Both Arthur and Clarus lack their subjects' affection at this stage of the narrative. *Largeza* and loyalty make a king strong. Significantly, Porrus finishes his speech by reminding the audience that "Ane King is but ane man". Therefore, he must abide to human laws and treat other people accordingly.

The next piece of advice Marciane gives to Clarus parallels Bruce's attitude to the French prisoners in Barbour's *Bruce*. With the King of India willing to listen for the first time when he sees that the battle is lost, Marciane tells him to honour the enemy with great courtesy (ll.6285–309). The political implications of such an asseveration supersede the dominant courtly discourse of the *Avowis*. As in *The Bruce*, by behaving honourably towards noble prisoners, one helps ensure that they might become future allies once they are freed or ransomed. In a long disquisition about the nature of lord-vassal relationships, Marciane returns to the same ideas expressed by Amytans. He harshly admonishes Clarus (ll.6638–41) and enlightens him about the dangers of hatred:

"And auld hatrent, as men sais,
Beris ane new deid aluais.
[...]
Haue ye na hope throw thare helping
To haue victory na great winning,
Bot gif baith lufe and laute
In thare body assembled be!" (ll.6660–61; 6682–85)

Marciane reverts to the dichotomy between a good ruler and a tyrant. Hatred is equated with death: only love and loyalty can provide victory. The cultivation of good affiliation between lord and subject finally finds its way through to Clarus's heart. Afer he realises Fesonas does not love him and Marciane's advice is the right path to follow, he begins to act according to what a good lord should do:

"To amend wrang and velany,
And my great treasour halely
Sall delt be, with thy counsale, all,
And partit in great and small". (ll.6998–7001)

Like Arthur in *Lancelot of the Laik*, Clarus tries to redress his misbehaviour first through the display of *largeza* to recapture his subjects' hearts. Like the British monarch too, he submits to his teacher's guidance humbly and completely.

In a later stage of the narrative, Clarus's progression is palpable. Although he is not willing to stop the siege, he does feel ashamed when he is seeking revenge for its own sake (ll.7844–72). He implicitly acknowledges the wrong foundations of his invasion. This also creates a thematic parallel with the first part of the *Buik*, the *Forray of Gadderis*, in which vengeance operates as the moving force of the action. At this juncture, in a tragic vision of the villain, Clarus cannot change his fate. He has gone too far: he knows the war he caused is not fair. Although he endeavours to change, it is too late for him. As Cassamus kills him in battle (ll.9563–73), no-one mourns his death:

Pride, enuy and skarsite,
Couatyce, reif and succudry,
And that gudemen and worthy.

And than defoulit and vntrew ay,
Hes brocht the now to thyne ending day! (ll.9606–10)

Clarus does not even receive praise in death. The passage operates as a
warning to any ruler listening to the romance. The only manner in
which to govern is through the lesson Marciane taught Clarus earlier
in the narrative. Like Arthur in *Golagros and Gawane*, thirst for
earthly power and unjustified invasion of others' lands can only lead
to self-destruction and a devastation of one's country and people.

In *Lancelot of the Laik*, as also noted by Mapstone, the makar
introduces "a disquisition on the dangers of flattery" (Mapstone 1986:
174), which is absent from the *Prose Lancelot*. By including this, the
Scottish text enhances the realistic atmosphere of kingly advice that is
central to the romance. Flattery as one of the most pernicious dangers
at court is a recurrent theme in late medieval Scottish literature, with
clear reference to the court of the time. Dunbar, for example, warns
James IV about the corruption of his retinue both through comedy and
serious verse. In the satirical poem "Ane Ballat of the Fenyeit Freir of
Tungland", Dunbar deploys the real person of a courtier to extrapolate
the corruption of James IV's counsellors; whereas in the poem, "How
sould I Governe me?", the makar insinuates that courtiers' behaviour
is empty. They act according to formulated norms, implying that they
always try to please the monarch through flattery. Some years later,
Lindsay in his *Ane Satyre of the Thrie Estaitis* disguises the allegorical
character of Flatterie as Devotioun, undermining King Humantie's
court.

In *Lancelot of the Laik*, the exposition of flattery works in the
same manner. Political analogies such as the following would be
interpreted locally and immediately by the audience:

Into the realme about o king is holde
O flatterere were than is the stormys cold,
Or pestelens, and mor the realme annoyith;
For he the law and puple boith destroyith. (ll.1929–32)

Flattery destabilises the kingdom. It goes beyond simple adulation to
become the cause of the corruption of law. This together with the
destruction of the king's vassals poses two great problems to Arthur.
First, law, and by implication justice, cannot be accomplished when
the king is blinded by flatterers insofar as this brings about the

sovereign's failure of his people. If Amytans has already mentioned the necessity of recovering the "puple's harts" through the good understanding and display of *largeza*, the eradication of flattery from the realm is a necessary conditioning of that argument. Otherwise feudal interdependence and support between lord and vassal will also be unsuccessful; hence, Arthur's personal and political recovery would become impossible. Significantly, Amytans attributes the existence of flattery in the court to the king's own fault owing either to his "ignorans" (ll.1935–40), his own viciousness (ll.1941–44) or his foolishness (ll.1945–51). By placing all the responsibility on Arthur's side and not on that of the flatterers, it is clear that Arthur himself will have to get rid of all these false counsellors to wipe out his misbehaviour.

Similarly, in Mézières' *Songe*, Royne Verite makes the young sovereign responsible for the choice of either good or bad members of the royal household:

"[T]u doys eslire tes conseilliers, tes officiers, et tes serviteurs, par lesquelx a ton commandement la nef francoise soit dignement governee. Car s'ilz seront bons, Beau Filz, Fieu en sera serviz et tu en seras a repoz et auras pou a faire. Et s'il sera le contraire, tu orras souvent mainte querelle, que te doivra desplaire". (Book III. 256)

[You must choose your counsellors, your officers, and your servants, so that under your command the French boat should be lead with dignity. Because it will be good, Good Son, you will be served and will be able to rest and will have little to do. And if it were the other way around, you will often have to deal with many quarrels, which will displease you.]

Thus a good monarch must learn to discern between good and evil, not only in his actions, but in his nominations of administrators of the country. Such a statement presupposes that both the literary Arthur and historical Charles must learn or possess wisdom. The similarities between both works place the advice to Arthur is a very realistic context. In the French text, Royne Verite concludes with the maxim a king should be feared without tyranny and loved without flattery (Book III. 257).

After such a devastating outline of his misrule and misconduct, the British king humbly agrees to follow the clerk's advice:

"Maister," quod he, "me think rycht profitable
Yowr conseell is and wonder honorable

For me and good. Rycht well I have consavit
And in myne hartis inwartness resavit.
I shall fulfill and do yowr ordynans
Als far of wit as my wit I have suffisans. (ll.1999–2004)

Arthur's words reveal that he is beginning to evolve: he discerns between Christian virtues and vices. Through his humility, a sign of the acknowledgement of his fallibility, he contemplates the possibility of regeneration. He does so not only because this is the sole way in which he will avoid defeat by Galiot, but also because there is an inner disposition to spiritual reformation. He comes to terms with the idea that his reign and his life are transitory. It is only in the kingdom of heaven in the afterlife that he might be rewarded.

The conclusion of the learning process differs greatly from that of *The Wallace*. While the allegorical fabric of the historical romance focuses on the religious virtues of Wallace's victory over death, the literary mode of the chivalric romance, following traditional advice to princes, conditions a completely different outcome of the narrative. Before Amytans goes away and Arthur puts into practice his good intentions, the King still has another question for the clerk. He wants to know the real meaning of his nightmare, which the astrologers failed to explain. Unlike the advice section, which the makar amplifies, the explication of the dream is simply transformed into verse. The relevance of this passage to the text's didactic purpose explains its simple translation instead of its transformation.

The final enquiry before the wise clerk's departure concerns the outcome of the battle. Amytans's answer, however, does not clarify who the victor will be:

"What that he hecht, yow shall no forther know;
His dedis sall herefterwart hyme schaw.
Bot contrar the he shall be found no way.
No more tharof as now Y will the say". (ll.2141–44)

Although Amytans acknowledges God's power to foresee and alter the course of events, the inconclusive reply connotes that Arthur's acts and his possible regeneration will determine the outcome of the war against Galiot. The clerk advocates a human being's free will to choose either good or bad, according to the Church theology of the time:

We assert both that God knows all things before they come to pass, and that we do by our free will whatsoever we know and feel to be done by us only because we will it. [...] But it does not follow that, though there is for God a certain order of all causes, there must therefore be nothing depending in the free exercise of our own wills, for our wills themselves are included in that order of causes which is certain to God, and is embraced by his foreknowledge, for human wills are also human actions. (*City of God*, V.9)

Arthur's inner metamorphosis is in his own hands. The path taken by the British sovereign towards heightening spiritual awareness is not as detailed as Amytans's lesson. Arthur's regeneration is rather schematic. Although it is true that the French original devoted just half of one paragraph to explain Arthur's inner recovery, the author of the Scottish work does not amplify this passage. Again, this confirms that the makar concentrates his discourse on the advice to princes tradition.

The first illustration of this change of attitude towards his subjects takes place during the Lady of Melyhalt's visit, when the King repeatedly asks her to stay:

Bot yhit the King hir prayt on sich wyss
That sche remanit whill the thrid day,
Syne tuk hir leif to pasing hom hir way. (ll.2346–48)

The King's hospitality and *cortesia* are highlighted. Following Amytans's counsel, political and military dexterity must be accompanied by the exhibition of the manners of *cortesia* to recover his people's hearts. That she remained for three days confirms that the Lady of Melyhalt's sincere loyalty is recovered.

Once Arthur has demonstrated he is acting in accordance with the wise man's teachings for the first time in the romance, the last twenty-eight lines of Book II (ll.2443-2470) serve to summarise the king's policies for regenerative action:

And largly he iffith and dispent
Rewardis, boith oneto the pur and riche
And holdith fest throw al the yher eliche.
In al the warld passing gan his name;
He chargit not bot of encress and famme
And how his puples hartis to empless. (ll.2450–55)

Arthur regains all the honour and modes of action which a Christian king should always possess and deploy. Symbolically his regeneration transforms him into the people's king of world-wide fame that he used to be as a young man. As the head of the communal body, his rebirth also connotes the rebirth of his country and his subjects through the recovery of harmony and happiness. Now the king can match Galiot and the two armies can confront on equal terms. As the Elect, it is not difficult for him to provide his actions with *cortesia* and *largeza*.

At the spiritual level, Arthur has accomplished his regeneration into the ideal king. In the chivalric arena, it could be considered rather ironic that after his political and moral rebirth it will be Lancelot and not himself who is going to retain the king's lands. Yet when this is redefined in the realm of allegory, Lancelot himself could be labelled as God's envoy. In this context, such an affirmation should not be considered too daring inasmuch as the figure of Lancelot in the *Vulgate* does function as a metaphorical grail. He is the one who is most desired by the queen, giving meaning to her life through *fin'amors*. Something very similar happens with Galehot, whose admiration for Lancelot seems to go beyond knightly admiration, becoming the *jois* of *fin'amors*.

Kingly instruction in Gilbert Hay's *Buik of King Alexander the Conquerour*

Written shortly after his political and chivalric treatises, Gilbert Hay's *Buik of King Alexander the Conquerour* relies on these previous works when dealing with Alexander's learning progression. Unlike Arthur in the Arthurian romances or even the young Bruce in *The Bruce*, Alexander in Hay's text is already a good king. He is not in need of a regeneration process. As Mapstone points out, such a start-ing point permits the poet "to evoke the image of an unjust knight and negligent king without appearing directly to criticise the monarch" (Mapstone 1986: 107–8). Neither is he a *tabula rasa* like King Humanitie in Sir David Lindsay's *Ane Satyre of the Thrie Estaitis* but he nevertheless demonstrates a mature attitude and sense of the responsibility of administrating power from a young age. Although Alexander listens to his first lesson on kingship early in the romance, the bulk of teaching is placed half way through in a book that Aristotle sends to Alexander at the latter's request. The instructive text is a verse reworking of Hay's earlier *Buke of the Governaunce of Princis*.

Again Mapstone observes that the author reorders the *Secreta Secretorum* is such a way that the outcome is very much his own conceptualisation of good government (Mapstone 1986: 103).

The makar specifies Aristotle's contribution to Alexander's success very early in the narrative, just after Alexander accidentally kills Nectanabus, the master his mother assigned to him (ll.319–44), and just before the philosopher's first lesson on kingship:

Syne into morall virtue he him foundit,
And into wit and wisdome he him groundit,
And bad him, gif he thocht till haue victour,
And cum to glore, wirschip, and honour,
That euir he sett resoun befoir his deid. (ll.414–18)

Although Alexander is a conquering hero, the attributes upheld to achieve glory are confined to the intellect and morality rather than to physical and martial qualities. Therefore, military accomplishments are subordinated to tropological and intellectual concerns. Alexander's conquest of the known world becomes a morally acceptable enterprise. In this way, it is detached from the Anglo-Scottish tensions all through the late Middle Ages. Whereas the repeated English attempts to invade Scotland were clearly condemned by Scottish chroniclers and makars, Hay places Alexander's exploits on a different plane. His subjugation of other people can be celebrated in Scottish literature without contradicting national, political positionings.

The first piece of advice Aristotle gives to Alexander summarises what the philosopher expands in his later book and *Physiognomy* to the Macedonian Emperor. Christian and political ethics come together in the counsel. The precepts of honouring God and having pity for mankind open the section (ll.430–37). From these two general premises, the oration moves to governmental issues:

"He suld kirkmen and laboraris forbere,
To eild and gentryce euir mair to be freind,
And euir do wirschip to women kind". (ll.439–41)

Becoming friends with the nobility has clear political significance. In a feudal society in which the nobles exercise a great deal of power, to be on good terms with them implies having a stable government and control over the Third Estate. Aristotle's recommendation that Alexander should display *cortesia* to all women, and not only to ladies, suggests the same concerns shown in *The Bruce*, when the King of Scots halts his army in order to help a parturient laundress to give birth in suitable conditions (XVI. 270–96). The philosopher ends his speech by concluding that good deeds should be rewarded (ll.469–70). As in the other Scottish romances, *largeza* is seen as a reward not devoid of political connotations. If good service is recompensed, the beneficiaries will be more than happy to continue to help Alexander.

As in *Lancelot of the Laik*, there is a great emphasis on the importance of *largeza*. Even before the central instruction on good kingship, Aristotle, proffering words parallel to those of Amytans, gives another lesson to Alexander, in which "largis/larges" to win people's "hartis" is repeated twice in three lines (ll.7322–24). Such is the philosopher's insistence that in the subsequent ordinance of the government of the newly conquered Persia, the first thing Alexander does is to assemble all "his princis" before him and divide the land amongst them (ll.7355–60). The rapid implementation of Aristotle's counsel demonstrates the Macedonian Emperor's total confidence in and submission to the former's concept of the correct administration of power. Moreover, the narrator, far from being subtle about the connotations of Alexander's actions, states that "He [Alexander] wan þare hartis and thare seruice hale / To liff and de with him in battale", (ll.7363–64). As well as mimicking Aristotle's words to reinforce the link between the lesson and its putting into practice, the narrator high-lights the political implications of the good use of *largeza*: everlasting loyalty.

The main advice section, as in *Lancelot of the Laik*, is around half way through the romance. Although Alexander asks for the advisory book on different occasions, Aristotle – or rather Hay – delays its deliverance until this juncture. Its positioning raises two key points: first it underlines the centrality of the advice to the overall plot; second, it marks the end of the conquest of the world and the fact that now the priorities will have to move on from those of a conquering military leader to those of an accomplished ruler. Just before starting the verse version *Regiment of Princis* as such (l.9664), Aristotle intro-duces the book by reminding Alexander of the exemplary nature of a king's conduct (ll.9439–44) for not only other monarchs but for the rest of his subjects to follow, a common idea in medieval political theory which *Lancelot of the Laik* explicitly echoes.

Again as in *Lancelot of the Laik* and Hay's *Buke of the Governaunce of Princis*, Aristotle places much emphasis on *largeza*. His *Regiment* opens with praise of a king's *largeza* and the profit that such an attitude generates from both the king and the country. A sovereign should be generous to all his friends and subjects. *Largeza* is seen as a way to reward and honour people (ll.9496–99). The intelligent distribution of the king's gifts will make the country richer, as opposed to the bad king, who "spendis all in prodigaletie, / In wiketnes and waisting wantonlie" (ll.9546–47). Aristotle's conclusion is that the worst king is the avaricious one, who lacks *largeza*. It might seem strange that stress on bad kingship lies in greediness rather than bad policies or tyranny, but the bottom-line of the philosopher's argument points to the common good in a quite idealistic situation, which should serve as the basis to administer power correctly.

Aristotle then moves to the necessity for a king to have a "gud name" (l.9581). As well as *largeza*, justice is indispensable for good government; and, therefore, for renown. As in *Lancelot of the Laik*, the king should safeguard his people from oppression through justice. Otherwise, he will be exposed to God's revenge (ll.9612–25), which is precisely Arthur's trouble in the Middle Scots *Lancelot* (ll.1344–88). Aristotle moves on to exemplify why a sovereign should rule according to God's ordination through the image of the body politic, in which every part of the body needs to perform its duty for the body to function correctly. Nevertheless, this is not the typical image to be found in the *Policraticus* with the King as head of the communal body (Mapstone 1986: 122). Instead, in Hay's version, the head is spirituality, the nobles and the king are together as a part of the body and most commonly, the Third Estate are the legs (ll.9659–62). The implications of Hay's theory of the body politic highlight the spiritual and religious foundations of government. The head, ruling over the body, is not represented by the human figure of a monarch but by the Christian vision of spirituality. The king as a part of the body must submit to spirituality; that is to say, he must govern according to Christian precepts. At the same time, the king is not placed over the nobles, but together with them as the body. Consequently, the monarch must act not according to his own dictates but with the nobility's consensus and approval.

The conclusion Aristotle gives to the section accords with standard political theory of the time as put forward by Saint Augustine or John of Salisbury:

All grace and gudnes fra þe Hevin ws send is,
And, as He governis the Hevynnis in vnitie,
Sa suld in erde all thingis governit be. (ll.9676–78)

Aristotle advocates that the Christian monarch should mirror God's government of heaven on earth: *Rex imago Dei*. Otherwise, as Sally Mapstone argues, a problem of "divine-earthly symmetry" takes place (Mapstone 1986: 123). After previously referring to "spirtualitie", now the philosopher also alludes to the soul to govern a king's decisions. This highly religious approach to the administration of power has its origin in Aristotle's *Politics*, to be Christianised later by Aquinas and Augustine (Mapstone 1986: 124). The idea could also be platonic in origin. In Plato's *Phaedo* (c.360 B.C.), for instance, Socrates claims that "When the soul and the body are united, then nature orders the soul to rule and govern, and the body to obey and serve" (127). Plato also expresses a similar idea in the *Republic*, in which he states that the soul has three principles: reason (the highest of the three, associated with philosophers, knowledge and reason), spirit and desire (126–35). Both in Plato and Hay, the logical progression of the argument evolves from the soul to reason, which must be used not only for good judgement but also to control the vices/appetites, which, in the *Conquerour*, are presented as allegorical personifications (ll.9761–87).

Subsequently, Aristotle warns Alexander about the perils of war. It destroys kingdoms and cities and people die. As a result, the land is lost, bringing about avarice and vice (ll.9833–38). Such advice complies with the philosopher's previous asseveration that "It war grete folie to ane pure sembill king / To conques landis quhare war na wynying" (ll.4428–29). In a romance in which war and conquest are the axis of the narrative and the hero is a conquering king, there is a necessity to outline the consequences of war and try to outline its ethics, especially in a text written in Scotland after the Wars of Independence and later English menaces to Scottish autonomy during the late Middle Ages.

From the realm of the public, Aristotle moves to the realm of the private. Being a good ruler is not only a question of administering power, but more importantly a question of being first and foremost a good Christian. Truthfulness is seen as the mother of all virtues (l.9847). Aristotle also alerts Alexander about carnal desire:

A king suld fle all bestiall appetite,
Vnhonest and onproffitabil delite –
Off sic cumys luste and lufe carnele,
And puttis away all plesance spirituall,
And garris a man to vicis be inclynit, (ll.9877–81)

Appetites, sexual appetites above all, lead to bad government. A bad Christian cannot be a good monarch. It is the same argument that Sir David Lindsay will develop in the mid-sixteenth-century *Ane Satyre of the Thrie Estaitis*. In Act I, King Humanitie succumbs to Sensualitie; hence, he surrounds himself with bad counsellors and is unable to perform his kingly duties. It is through reason and not the appetites that a monarch should rule.

Aristotle then explains that a bad monarch should be removed from office. Although he does not describe the mechanisms of such removal, Mapstone suggests that Hay might have thought of the way in which Richard II and Henry VI were forced to abdicate in England a little before the composition of the *Conquerour* (Mapstone 1986: 113). In relation to Scotland, Hay may have also had in mind the Declaration of Arbroath, a document that contemplated the possibility of changing the king were he not to fulfil his obligations. This accentuates the Scottish reference in the text.

To avoid such a political removal, the instruction concentrates on what a ruler should do and how he should behave towards the Three Estates:

The principall point of all þi governance,
The law of God to maintaine and avance:
Honoure clergie, and found scolis of lare,
Wourschip wise men, and lufe þame euermare,
Giff þame liffing, and þi regioun defend;
Pay þi seruandis, and gif þame for to spend –
[…]
And honoure all men aftir his merite,
Thare state, þare vertew, and þare gud condit; (ll.9994–99; 10,008–9)

The foundation of schools advances ideas concerning both learning in general and the patronage of the king in the promotion and diffusion of art and knowledge. The worship of wise men, from whom the monarch should learn, anticipates one of the most important points also made in *Lancelot of the Laik* and the original *Buke of the Governaunce of Princis*: the need to choose good counsellors. The inclusion of the *Phisiognomy*, which follows the *Regiment*, deals at length with the choice of appropriate advisers (ll.10,108–438).

The advice section concludes with a summary of the most important attributes that appertain to a king. The illustration of *Rex imago Dei* is emphasised once more, while the avoidance of the oppression of the poor and the bestowing of offices on only those who deserve it remind Alexander of treating all his subjects fairly and of surrounding himself only with good counsellors. The five properties which a king should prioritise (fear of God, good conscience, prudence, law and equity) complete the advice. Mapstone points out that the whole section is "an accurate reflection of the state of government in Scotland", where there were two bodies in charge of the major legislation decisions (Mapstone 1986: 126). Therefore, despite the universal value of the advice, Hay's version of the *Secreta Secretorum* also takes into account the particularities of his contemporary Scotland.

After Aristotle's instruction, Alexander visits Paradise, in which he is told that he must return to Babylon where he will die. An angel gives him an apple. When it rots, Alexander will die soon thereafter (ll.16,299–303). While death is approaching, his faithful horse, Bucephalus (ll.17,383–90), falls ill and dies. For Alexander, its loss is indicative that the end is near. He makes arrangements for after his death:

Syne wrette he pistill till all men, fare and nere,
Quhilk ony landis had to governe or stere,
Baith of þe est and of þe west cuntre: (ll.17,439–41)

With the division of the conquered territories, Alexander implicitly acknowledges that such a vast empire will be impossible to maintain by a ruler other than himself. His death will signal the end of an age.

Finally, the apple rots (ll.17,842–45) so Alexander knows that his death is approaching. He drinks Cassandra's poison and says "I am bot dede" (ll.17,950–72):

"Quhat waillȝeis now all my governyng?
I may nocht helpe me, þocht I be a king.

Quhat waillȝeis me all my warldis glore,
No ioy na plesance þat I had before?
Quhat waillȝeis me my state of ryalltie,
Na all the welth I had in magestie?" (ll.18,056–61)

The lamentation expresses the mutability of this world in Boethian terms. Like Golagros's grieving in *Golagros and Gawane*, Alexander understands the volatility of the material world: neither riches nor power is valid when death approaches. Only a good Christian monarch will overcome death in the other world.

From the personal, he advances to the common wealth of his generals and subjects. He senses beforehand the end of his conquering vision of peace and order:

And I watt nocht quha sall eftir me be lorde,
And all my chiftanis liffand in discorde,
And leif my frendis efter me in feid,
For mony a man that we haue brocht to dede. (ll.18,088–91)

His death will also signify the end of his dream. He seems to know that no-one will be good enough to preserve his legacy. But even more interesting is his last sentence: he acknowledges that even his good intentions have caused the loss of many lives. He realises that the outcome of his conquest has not been as perfect as planned. As a sovereign facing his own end, Alexander comprehends the fallibility of his policies. He comes to terms with his own human nature. In his testament, the division of all his possessions among his men expresses a similar idea (ll.18,383–423). Although he knows it is impossible, he would like his lands to remain the same way as in his lifetime:

"And als I ordand peace and rest for ay,
With luife and iustice and guid fay,
And euirie lord to keip law in his land,
To pure and riche, to lawborer and merchand,
And evirie lord be in his lordschip fre,
And als all vþer, in toun, brughe, or citie,
And evirie man to be fre in his awin, (ll.18,424–30)

For the future Alexander advocates the image of perfect earthly harmony accomplished during his reign: peace among nations, love and justice and everyone to enjoy freedom within the limit of his or her social stratum (an idea already delineated in Barbour's *Bruce*).

When death finally comes, the narrative follows the European tradition also present in *The Bruce*, the *Histoire de Guillaume le Maréchal* or the *Vie du Prince Noir*. Once Alexander, as an ideal ruler, has arranged all earthly, political matters, he is ready to leave this world, while his entrance in heaven is secured in a grandiloquent manner:

It seimit that God and all þe hevinis had steird,
That sen the tyme of Chryistis passioun,
In hevin was neuir sic ane motioun. (ll.18,465–67)

As an extraordinary human being whose ruling mirrors that of God, his death guarantees a place of privilege for him in the other world, so much so that his demise is the most important one since that of Jesus Christ. Both deaths are typologically linked through treason: Alexander is allegorically transformed into a Christ-like figure. Like Bruce in *The Bruce*, his decease causes comprehensive lamentation in his territories (ll.18,468–515). The conclusion is that every single subject loved him owing to his good administration of justice.

After his death, however, Alexander's worst predictions come true. Olympias is killed (ll.18,860–63) and discord grows between the Macedonian Emperor's former generals (ll.18,879–81). These events mark the end of the *pax alexandrica*. Chaos replaces order, peace and justice. The personal ambitions of his successors hinder Aristotle and Alexander's idea of good government from continuing. The final message in the context of late medieval Scotland is clear: only if the interests of a country precede those of the ruler can a nation prosper and live in peace.

Conclusion

The significance of the good execution of justice and exemplary ruling of a country cannot be detached from the spiritual, moral and/or political evolution of the main characters. The specific historical context of *The Bruce* and *The Wallace*, and the relocation of the main narrative focus in *Golagros and Gawane*, illustrate this link between spiritual and ideological issues, and to a lesser extent also in *Lancelot of the Laik*. The latter, together with the Alexander romances, prefers to concentrate on mainly political issues, albeit not always detached from religious concerns, along the lines of the advice to princes tradition. To do so, the makars borrow literary motifs from genres such as dream visions, saints' lives and political treatises to transform their romances, sometimes more overtly as in the case of *The Wallace* and Hay's *The Buik of King Alexander the Conquerour* and sometimes less explicitly as in the case of *The Bruce*. In the Arthurian texts, Boethian and Aristotelian influences are more evident than in the *Prose Lancelot* and *The First Continuation*. This renders Arthur's redefining of royal duties more explicit in allegorical terms. The intimate connection between the heroes' spiritual journey and political issues regarding kingship and government is a characteristic which brings the six Older Scots romances together within a distinctive literary tradition.

Chapter Three

The Historical Romances

The historical proximity of Robert I and William Wallace imposed constraints on the representation of knighthood and chivalry in Barbour's *Bruce* and Hary's *Wallace*. Unlike the Middle English Charlemagne romances or the Middle Scots Alexander romances, in which the historically based figures of Frankish and Macedonian emperors were freely reshaped, the audience's familiarity with *The Bruce* and *The Wallace* constituted an inescapable starting point for the two makars.

Barbour had Scottish texts – now lost – which he might have employed as models (McDiarmid and Stevenson ed. 1981–85: I. 4); he was also familiar with the ancient classics as well as French and Anglo-Norman literature. As argued in Chapter 1, the makar's romance served to establish a post-Wars of Independence vernacular tradition in Scots in the manner of France and England. His reworkings of knighthood and chivalry help to elucidate the main literary characteristics that he endeavoured to establish as bases of the Scottish tradition. Barbour opts to focus on epic action rather than on more embellished depiction of jousts and tournaments. The negotiation between epic and courtly virtues is also subordinated to the historical context of Robert I's life. The topoi of romance and epic literature, such as the Nine Worthies, the *sapientia et fortitudo* topos, are not ignored or replaced but reinterpreted or subverted. Barbour's singular treatment of the Third Estate responds to his innovative conception of the romance mode. This also affects the social portrayal of courtly life and personal interactions between male and female characters. Although Barbour formally deploys the vocabulary of *cortesia*, the overall elaboration of the plot does not allow for the poetic colourfulness of earlier works such as those of Chrétien de Troyes. Such a distinctive approach generates an idiosyncratic redefinition of the chivalric code.

Analysis of the same elements in Hary's *Wallace* and Lindsay's *Historie of Squyer Meldrum* will further help to trace the evolution of the Scottish romances in the domain of historical or pseudo-historical texts. Their period of composition during the fifteenth and sixteenth centuries, the influence of a larger number of French works and the burden of the Chaucerian tradition influenced the outcome of Hary's and Lindsay's narratives. The two later makars necessarily transformed the original chivalric and knightly aspects of *The Bruce*. Lindsay's approach to chivalry and knighthood was also conditioned by his critical vision of military and political issues and his satirical treatment of the genre.

Barbour's *Bruce*: forging a tradition

The time that Barbour spent studying in Paris implies that there he may have encountered contemporary manuals of chivalry which theorised and idealised visions of knightly life. It has also been suggested that Barbour

may also have spent a year or two in the University of Orléans in the faculty of civil law (this study being palpably prohibited at Paris), a speculation that is attractive in several respects. Orléans had a tradition of respect for the Latin poets; two commentaries on Lucan's libertarian epic *De Bello Civili* had been produced there, and lines from it are remembered in the *Bruce*. (McDiarmid and Stevenson ed. 1981–85: I. 5)

Although his concrete knowledge of authors such as Geoffroi de Charny and Ramon Llull cannot be categorically stated, he would have been familiar, if not with these texts themselves, at least with very similar ones. Gilbert Hay's translation of Llull's *Llibre de l'orde de cavalleria* into Middle Scots from an intermediary French source, the *Buke of the Ordre of Knychthede*, will be employed to illustrate standard views of chivalry in the late Middle Ages.

In *The Bruce*, however, festive chivalric activities such as tourneys are excluded from the narrative owing to the urgency of the Wars of Independence. As Goldstein claims, the makar's chivalry is at the service of the political discourse (Goldstein 1993: 152). Although jousting was sometimes condemned as a meaningless activity in the socio-political context of Barbour's times, leading only to vainglory (Keen 1984: 235–36), there are records of jousts and tournaments celebrated in Scotland during the late Middle Ages:

Most of the documented information about duels and jousting [in Scotland] comes from chronicle sources or royal accounts of expenditure. Both of these sources are problematic. Chroniclers usually report only the names of the participants, the length of the tournament, and who won. Royal accounts detail payments to armourers, bowyers and the other workers, with very few details. However, there is one source which may describe the details of jousting and structure of tournament although this too is enigmatic. A manuscript entitled "The Order of Combats for Life in Scotland", apparently dating from James I's reign. (Stevenson 2006: 65–66)

These events are not present in *The Bruce*, nor are they present in most medieval Scottish romances. What coincides between these records about tournaments and the romances is the few references to female characters: "Women are mostly absent from the records of Scottish tournaments. [...] Most records of tournaments are financial and carry little information about the proceedings, so it is perhaps unsurprising that we find no reference to women" (Stevenson 2006: 92). It is not a characteristic of Scottish romances to spend much time on descriptions of courtly entertainments, not even in Arthurian narratives, in which the authors may feel freer to make use of as many literary elements as they wish. *Clariodus* (c.1550) is the only Scottish romance depicting elaborate portrayals of tournaments in detail. Barbour's hero's early steps are already marked by warfare – there is no time for training games such as tournaments and jousts – but only for education in war itself.

In *The Bruce*, not only does Barbour redefine the chivalric termi-nology (McDiarmid and Stevenson ed. 1981–85: I. 45) but he also adapts the archetypal topoi of epic and romance to the requirements of his composition. Barbour employs the *loci communes* of the Nine Worthies (typical of romances) and of *sapientia et fortitudo* (typical of epics) to extol the hero's virtues and shape him as the national leader Scotland requires. Bruce is conveniently associated with the Nine Worthies on several occasions. Among the most frequently repeated allusions, the most interesting, in literary terms, is the one connecting Balliol's treason to the classical betrayals of antiquity and the Nine Worthies. First, Barbour refers to Troy (I. 521–26); then, to "Alexander ye conqueroure", who was "dystroyit throw pwsoune" (I. 529–35); followed by Julius Caesar (I. 537–48) and Arthur (I. 549–60). The makar accomplishes two objectives at the same time. First, he matches Bruce's *proeza* with that of the heroes mentioned, marking him as the Tenth Worthy. In the same way as the heroes of the Matter of Rome, France and Britain, Bruce – symbolically the Tenth Worthy – becomes the central hero of the newly created Matter of Scotland (contemporary French and English writers have their own national contenders to become the Tenth Worthy). Indeed, it is not unusual for Scottish writers of the period to portray Robert Bruce as the Tenth Worthy. In the late medieval poem *Ane Ballat of the Nine Nobles*, the author, after devoting nine stanzas to each of the Worthies, concludes in this way:

Robert the Brois throu hard feichtyng
With few venkust the mychthy Kyng
Off Ingland, Edward, twyse in fycht,
At occupit his realme but rycht
At sum tyme wes set so hard,
At hat nocht sax till hym toward.
ʒe gude men that thir balletis redis,
Deme quha dochtyast was in dedis. (Laing ed. 1895: I. 303)

As Goldstein suggests, such comparisons place Bruce in "the larger discursive space" of European literary traditions (Goldstein 1993: 146). In addition, the writer's similes place Balliol's treason on the same level as the classical exemplars as a result of Bruce's worth (Ebin 1971–72: 231). The makar also assumes that Balliol's betrayal of Bruce is a betrayal of Scotland. Bruce is symbolically transformed into the emblem of free Scotland. The romance hero, whose main individual concern is his integration into the feudal world, is replaced by the King of Scots, whose collective enterprise is national.

At first, in accordance with the knightly code, Robert Bruce tries to wage war on his enemies in a pitched battle at Methven. But the English use of non-chivalric cunning catches them unawares by night (II. 260–300): a massacre ensues in which few can escape death. In consistency with his ideological premises, Barbour does not overtly condemn the English for their unchivalric behaviour, as he is going to portray his main hero performing similar actions when clearly outnumbered. Thus, the makar's employment of these literary strategies justifies the fact that, from then on, the Scots will wage a guerrilla war until they recruit the number of soldiers needed to combat the English in open field.

After Methven, the Lord of Lorne and his army pursue the king. When Bruce realises that fighting the English openly, and in accordance with the chivalric code, would be suicidal, he tells his soldiers:

"lordyngis foly it war
Tyll ws for till assembill mar,
For yai fele off our hors has slayn,
And gyff yhe fecht with yaim agayn
We sall tyne off our small mengȝe
And our selff sall in perill be.
Yarfor me thynk maist awenand
To withdraw ws ws defendand
Till we cum owt off yar daunger,
For owr strenth at our hand is ner". (III. 35–44)

Kliman asserts that Bruce is a leader is so far as he can drive his troops to chivalric deed because he is "a master of war" (*fortitudo*) and also because he commands "the art of rhetoric (*sapientia*)" (Kliman 1975: 156). Although I agree with Kliman's affirmation as a whole, it would be helpful to redefine the two concepts within late medieval literature. *Sapientia*, as well as referring to "the art of rhetoric", also includes the military capacity to lead an army, whereas *fortitudo* can be regarded as strength on both the physical and moral/spiritual levels. The appearance of this topos of Homeric literature should not be taken at face value in *The Bruce*. Virgil incorporated the virtue of *pietas* to the dichotomy of *fortitudo* and *sapientia* (Curtius 1990: 173). A text composed during the late Middle Ages in Western Europe such as Barbour's would obviously reflect *pietas* not from a Virgilian point of view, but from a late medieval Christian perspective. Nonetheless, medieval literature rarely celebrates this topos. In the twelfth-century French adaptation of the *Aeneid*, the *Roman d'Enéas*, what Virgil presents as *sapientia* – obedience to the gods – is seen as a source of shame for the hero. It is quite likely that Barbour borrowed and reshaped this motif from the *Aeneid* itself with which he was familiar. Therefore, Barbour's construction of his Bruce emanates from both medieval and classical traditions. The makar endeavours to create not only a unique hero distinct from other medieval warriors but also a new and distinctive way of composing heroic literature in the vernacular. By conflating both traditions, the imaginary but historicised construction of Bruce becomes the standard against which the future romance protagonists in Scotland will be measured.

At the same time, after Methven, Bruce begins to learn how and when he should confront the English. As in numerous late medieval romances, the hero must experience a process of learning before becoming the best knight (or king, in his case). Indeed, it is absolutely indispensable for Bruce to obtain new awareness from experience, if he wants to vanquish a superior enemy. In the passage quoted above, the use of the word "foly" (the negative knightly counterpart of *temperance*) re-codifies the meaning of the military vanquishing. Instead of showing Bruce as a weak monarch who refuses to face the enemy, Barbour structures the king's speech in a way in which his *temperance* and *prudence* are stressed. As Hay claims in his *Buke of the Ordre of Knychthede*:

all knycht or he tak ordre suld knaw all the vii vertues, and thair branchis; that is to say, the four vertues cardinale, and the thre vertues theological. The thre theological is faith, good hope, and cheretee, as we have before touchit. The four cardinale vertues ar justice, temperance, fors, and prudence. (Haye 1901–14: II. 52)

In fact, the narrative voice concludes that "Yen yai withdrew yaim halely, / Bot yat wes nocht full cowartly" (III. 45–46). Later manuals of chivalry such as Gilbert Hay's *Buke of the Law of Armys*, a translation from Honoré Bonet's (or Bouvet) *Arbre des Bataille*, state that, when a knight is outnumbered, it is wise to leave the battlefield (Haye 1901–14: I. 84–86). As well as unveiling his epic *sapientia* and *fortitudo*, Bruce's speeches also enlighten his romance *temperance* and *prudence*. These three attributes together with his necessary commitment to *justice* define Robert Bruce as possessing the four Cardinal Virtues. As a result, he is the best knight and king to defend Scotland's interests in accordance with chivalric standards. Barbour manipulates a historical defeat at Methven to transform it into a learning stage in the creation of Bruce as the Elect. Bruce is constructed as a dynamic monarch who has the capacity of gaining knowledge through experience.

Bruce's non-chivalric attitude, however, does not please Randolph, who energetically complains about it to his uncle, Robert Bruce. When he is re-captured by the Scots, Bruce gently asks him to join his men and cause (IX.741–45). Randolph's response is particularly harsh:

"ʒe chasty me, bot ʒe
Aucht bettre chastyt for to be,
For sene ʒe werrayit ye king
Off Ingland, in playne fechting
ʒe suld pres to derenʒhe rycht
And nocht with cowardy na with slycht". (IX.747–52)

By urging Bruce to defend his right in "playne fechting", and not by cowardice and trickery, Randolph does not challenge his uncle's right to the Scottish Crown but rather the non-chivalric means he is using to attain his objective. In short, as a knight, he is wholly opposed to Scottish guerrilla warfare since it does not comply with the way in which a nobleman should fight. At this point, the earl of Moray, who, after being captured at Methven, has been fighting on the English side, does not understand the Scottish position. Finally, he comes to realise that this is the only way in which his people can defeat the powerful and much more numerous English army. In the siege of Edinburgh, Randolph himself makes use of stratagems to take the castle. By representing the change of mind of the king's nephew, the narrator implicitly validates the use of guerrilla tactics before his courtly audience. Randolph plays a mediating role between the makar and the audience. Barbour uses him to persuade the courtly listeners to think that the national liberty of Scotland is much more important than the way of action. In so far as the poet deals with harsh reality, idealised descriptions may require background placing. Kliman suggest that this "practical chivalry" was a model that Barbour's audience, the king and his nobles, could follow (Kliman 1973: 507). The dialogic interaction between Barbour's Scotland and his writing is manifest once again. Barbour shapes the appropriate attitude of the Scottish nobility, and his poem becomes a distinctive creation of late fourteenth-century Scotland.

Like Randolph, as soon as he embraces the King of Scots' cause, James Douglas is represented as a faithful knight to Robert Bruce. According to McKim, Douglas, the second most important hero in *The Bruce*, is associated with martial skills rather than with courtly virtues. In this sense, Douglas's heroism is closer to that of the *chanson de geste* rather than of that of French chivalric romances in which the protagonist's knightly and courtly virtues must be in equilibrium (McKim 1981: 172–74). McKim seems to imply that, although the romance heroes of the thirteenth and fourteenth centuries are also praised for their physical *fortitudo*, Douglas's courtly attributes are not extensively developed. Although McKim focuses mainly on physical virtues, it would be appropriate to note that Barbour's emphasis is not solely confined to them. Even the portrayal of James Douglas (the toughest, strongest knight on the field) does not neglect his spiritual

side. In Seville, Douglas politely refuses all the riches that King
Alfonso offers to him on the grounds that:

he tuk yat waiage
To pas in-till pilgrimage
On Goddis fayis, yat his trawaill
Mycht till his saule hele awaill, (XX.353–56)

By the end of the romance, the most ferocious warrior against the
English advances to a more profound understanding of knighthood in
his defence of the faith against the heathen. As Hay claims in his *Buke
of the Ordre of Knychthede*:

rycht sa is thare othir proprieteis pertenand to the saule; as justice, force, prudence,
and temperaunce, charitee and veritee, lautee and humilitee, faith, esperaunce,
subtilitee, agilitee, and with all othir vertues touchand to wisedome, appertenis till
him, as to the saule. (Haye 1901–1914: II. 23)

It is necessary to maintain a balance between bodily and spiritual
attributes to be a good knight. The exclusive reliance on physical
qualities would make a ruthless warrior but never a complete Christian
knight. Therefore, just as in the case of Bruce, the makar projects an
image of Douglas in which epic and romance traits define the hero.
The amalgamation of both traditions serves a paramount objective: the
chivalric deeds of arms are no longer exclusively at the service of
personal fulfilment and promotion but must contribute to the epic (and
national) enterprise.

Barbour redefines other romance motifs to relocate the narrative
in the field of the national discourse: the knightly rivalry between two
knights and the opposition between *foudatz* and *mesura* operate as
signs of the historicity and political ethics of *The Bruce*. The typical
sportive competition between Douglas and Randolph to be the best
knight serving Bruce is a good illustration of this:

Yis tyme yat ye gud erle Thomas
Assegyt as ye lettre sayis
Edinburgh, Iames off Douglas
Set all his wit for to purchas
How Roxburch throw sutelte
Or ony craft mycht wonnyn be, (X.357–62)

Barbour counterbalances Moray's and Douglas's actions following epic and romance motifs. Once again, the major difference from chivalric romances lies in the fact that their deeds of arms go far beyond personal *pretz* since they decisively help with his king's main goal: the liberation of Scotland.

Consistent with this idea, the technique of balancing opposites through the contrast between *mesura* and *foudatz* concerns the realm of political ethics and not simply that of knightly behaviour. Edward Bruce is the selected figure to stand out against his more poised brother. Before Bannockburn, however, Edward Bruce's conduct is exemplary. In Book V, for instance, when the king returns to the mainland from Arran, he is told that Lord Percy, one of his enemies, is in a castle nearby with three hundred men at least. The king hesitates whether to attack his foe (V.1–63). Edward then asserts:

"I say ʒow sekyrly
Yar sall na perell yat may be
Dryve me eftsonys to ye se.
Myne auentur her tak will I
Quheyir it be esfull or angry". (V.66–70)[1]

Thanks to Edward's daring suggestion, the Scots vanquish Lord Percy and his men. Edward can only be fêted in so far as his decision contributes to the Scottish enterprise.

Afterwards, however, his excessive chivalrous determination dangerously increases until his death. Structurally and thematically, Barbour anticipates his downfall from favour just after Bannockburn where Edward begins to seek personal glory at the expence of a more collective objective. Therefore, he starts to condemn his extreme audacity. *Foudatz* rather than *sapientia* guides his acts. In Book XVIII, Edward Bruce, leader of the Scots in Ireland, decides to fight a much larger Anglo-Irish army, instead of waiting for imminent reinforcements, which are about to come. His impatience causes both his death and the failure of Scottish aspirations to conquer or liberate

---

[1] These words of the hero facing his *auenture* (fate, destiny) are very typical of epic poetry. In book IV of the *Aeneid*, for instance, in his departure, Aeneas assumes his fate: "[…] Sed nullis ille mouetur / fletibus aut uoces ullas tractabilis audit; / fata obstant placidasque uiri dues obstruit auris" (*Aeneid* IV.438–40). In Lonsdale and Lee's translation: "He is not melted by lamentations, nor listens compliantly to any address; fate stands in the way, and heaven stops the unmoved ears of the hero".

the neighbouring island. At a chivalric level, Edward lacks the *temperance* and *sapientia* which his brother possesses. Gilbert Hay resolves this conflict in the following way:

> And thus is it, that sen the ordre is reuglit be witt and wisdome, than suld all gude knychtis pres theme to be wys, and sett tharon all thair hert and mynde; the quhilk makis knycht sa curageus, that he doubtis nocht the dede, in regarde of honoure and his rychtwis caus, that he may lufe and honour his ordre, to sauf bathe saule and honour, in the contrair of foly and ingnoraunce. (Haye 1901–14: II. 26–27)

Barbour overtly censures Edward Bruce when his way of action is no longer productive for the national struggle. The dichotomy of *sapientia* and foolhardiness is also a *locus communis* of epic poetry which Barbour adapted to the historical context of *The Bruce*. This situation permits the makar to justify those instances where patriotic pragmatism drives the Scots into unchivalric behaviour. The poet anticipates a possible negative response on the audience's part and, at the same time, manipulates their reaction. Barbour hopes to persuade them that if they had confronted the English in the same way as Edward faced them in Ireland, they would have been vanquished in the same way as Edward was. Thus, the authorial control of the narrative creates a thematic parallelism which elevates Bruce's accomplishment of his national goal through the employment of guerrilla warfare above chivalric action.

Although the members of the Third Estate are by definition excluded from knightly deeds and ideals, they play a much larger part in *The Bruce* than either social or literary convention normally permitted. Even if the validity of the medieval division of labour may be questioned owing to its excessive rigidity, it seems legitimate to maintain this theoretical standpoint in regard to literature, inasmuch as serious literature in the late Middle Ages tended to portray an idealised vision of society, however critical that might be. Accordingly, everyone in society had his/her own role to fulfil; romances, as a mirror of a hierarchically structured world, portrayed and problematised this. From romances to dream visions, late medieval European literature complied with such a vision of society. As expressed by Duby, "What matters is to seek, in the disorderly jumble of sublunary world, the proper bases for the harmonious and reasonable construction which would appear to reflect the intentions of the Creator" (Duby 1980: 2).

Yet in Scotland, notwithstanding the burden of such a wide-spread convention, Barbour opted to construct a more flexible picture of society which would facilitate the transmission of his ideological purposes. Although commoners never played central roles in serious *romans courtois*, in *The Bruce* Barbour subverts literary convention by attaching importance to their actions. From the beginning, the author equates the suffering of the common folk with that of knights and lords, which is markedly innovative in contemporary compositions of romances. All the people of Scotland must stand together in the defence of their country to attain freedom. In Book II, when the commoners do not follow Bruce, Barbour does not criticise them. He just states the fact that they desert him "for he / Yaim fro yar fais mycht nocht warand" (II. 503–510). The text suggests that this is a valid way of action since Bruce cannot now fulfil the duty to his subjects. The vassals exercise their right as their lord cannot fulfil his duty:

Whatever the inequalities between the obligations of the respective parties, those obligations were none the less mutual: the obedience of the vassal was conditional upon the scrupulous fulfilment of his engagements by the lord. The reciprocity in un-equal obligations, which was Emphasised by Fulbert de Chartres as early as the eleventh century and which was very strongly felt to the end, was the really distinctive feature of European vassalage. (Bloch 1962: 228)

In the same way, when the king comes back to mainland in Book V, the people fear the English so much that they do not collaborate with Bruce who "fand litill tendyrnes" (V.123–32). Again Barbour excuses the commoners' behaviour. Not until Bruce's victory in the first real pitched battle after Methven, Loudoun Hill, does a considerable number of Scots join the monarch (VIII. 506–11). In spite of his generally practical representation of chivalry, the makar conceptually resorts to the chivalric code (Bruce has to prove his *proeza* in a *proper* pitched battle to be recognised as the leader of Scotland among his countrymen).

Only the English underestimate the Scottish Third Estate: at the battle of Bannockburn, Edward II feels offended when a knight suggests that they should withdraw before the attack of the Scottish army on foot:

"I will nocht," said ye king, "perfay
Do sa, for yar sall no man say

Yat I sall eschew ye bataill
Na withdraw me for sic rangaile". (XII. 473–76)

The intervention of this "rangaile" at Bannockburn is vital. Crucially, in the middle of the battle, the commons take the initiative: "ʒoman, swanys, and pitaill", minding the victuals, decide to enter the battle. Goldstein sees their intervention on the battle as an imitation of class privilege, concluding that peasants in *The Bruce* "are not revolutionary" at all (Goldstein 193: 189–90). Although it is true that, as far as they support their monarch, the peasants cannot be catalogued as revolutionary in the same sense as Wat Tyler, John Ball, Jack Straw and their followers during the Peasants' Revolt in 1381, they are certainly going beyond class imitation. By doing what the upper classes are exclusively legitimised to do, they are assuming and exercising the same power and authority as their lords. Their military manoeuvre serves to win the Wars of Independence (XIII. 225–264) inasmuch as the English cannot distinguish whether they are knights or common folk. Ironically, now Edward II must "eschew ye bataill" and "withdraw" if he does not want to be captured. This instance is revealing: in the climax of the romance Barbour destabilises the chivalric code by this displacement of roles.

But even before Bannockburn, the text repeatedly subverts the knightly standards to highlight the role of the commoners. This same "rangaile" led by Bruce had already defeated Sir Aymer (VIII. 355–70). As a knight, Sir Aymer feels ashamed after having been vanquished by commoners that he swears he will never come back to Scotland again. At first sight, it might be arguable that Barbour intends to discredit the English leader, since it is uncharacteristic of the genre to see a knight defeated by (or simply fighting) members of the lower classes. Indeed, these interclass confrontations, while abundantly present in comic or carnivalesque fiction, are absent from the vast majority of the serious literature in the Middle Ages. Nevertheless, in the context of his shame, the poet praises him: "[Sir Aymer] yat war renonyt off gret bounte" (VIII. 370). Sir Aymer's general portrayal as a bold knight generates an even more powerful image of the Scottish Third Estate's contribution to victory.

Subversion goes even further: as well as praising them as a group, Barbour also describes the common folk as individuals performing feats of arms, just as knights would (Kliman 1973–74: 109). The Scottish leaders have no qualms about working together with those, whose local knowledge of the country (as opposed to the knightly *sapientia* of the king, ornamented with numerous rhetorical tropes, the commoners' knowledge is based on their own life experience and the use of cunning) and willing collaboration is decisive in the taking of strongholds. For example, in the taking of Edinburgh Castle, Randolph, who had previously opposed guerrilla warfare, asks:

Giff ony man mycht fundyn be
yat couth fynd ony iuperty
To clymb ye wallis preuely
And he suld hace his warysoun, (X.528–31)

Unlike in most romances, the knight is disposed to follow an inferior's advice, thereby ignoring class distinction. Indeed, had it not been for William Francis's knowledge of a secret way to climb the walls, Edinburgh would not have been taken.

There are many other illustrations in which the commoners act in a heroic manner, either advising or leading their own *troop*. Such passages displace the roles traditionally associated with knights exclusively. By showing this, Barbour stresses the importance of every single Scot, regardless of their social status. Likewise, in the English party, Sir Ingram de Umphraville also praises the courage of the Scottish peasantry at war: "ilk ʒowman is sa wicht / Off his yat he is worth a knyght" (XIX.165–66), he tells the king. Umphraville elevates the military significance of the common folk to that of knightly warriors. He attaches the same worth both to knights and the Third Estate in the defence and liberation of Scotland, again challenging the most elemental chivalric conventions.

If Barbour's project re-codifies traditional components of knightly representation, the martially centred narrative alters the conceptualisation of *cortesia* and chivalry even more profoundly. *Largeza*, disinterested generosity, and *fin'amors* are also modified and re-adapted to the structural, stylistic and thematic methodologies of the text. Courtly scenes are scanty and sporadic because the nominal presence of female characters prevents a further development of courtly action. Hence, as demonstrated earlier, the hero's virtues are mainly defined in martial terms, while their courtly attributes only feature when the male characters are accompanied by a woman.

The urgency of warfare does not leave room for many actions driven by an unselfish sense of *largeza* but the concept is adapted to the Scottish political circumstances in realistic terms. The rewarding of individuals who have excelled in particular knightly feats is common practice. Robert Bruce generously rewards his men who are either nobles, such as Moray in book IX, or commoners, like Philip the forester in book VIII, when they perform a valiant chivalric deed, contributing to the emancipation of the realm. Thus, the hero's *largeza* stems from its practical application in a warrior's daily life. In the vast majority of cases, *largeza* is understood as a reward for good service which at the same time will symbolically renew the subjects' vow of loyalty and secure future adherence to Bruce's cause. This practice was customary in late medieval Europe where the greater lord offered rewards in return for good services. The lesser lords or knights could profit from material generosity such as money, lands or arms; a good marriage or legal measures could bestow extra security on their territorial domains. (Keen 1984: 29)

The few courtly scenes in which Bruce is involved also disseminate a functional view of chivalry. Barbour reshapes the characterisation lady helpers from chivalric romances to construct the numerous women who assist the King of Scots. Indeed, the dialogues between these female characters and the king maintain the courtly rhetoric typical of the *roman courtois* tradition:

> "Dame," said ye king, "wald yow me wis
> To yat place quhar yar repair is
> I sall reward ye but lessing,
> For yai ar all off my duelling
> And I rycht blythly wald yaim se
> And swa trow I yat yai wald me."
> "Yhis," said scho, "Schir I will blythly
> Ga with ȝow and ȝour cumpany
> Till yat I schaw ȝow yar repair."
> "Yat is inewch my sister fayr,
> Now ga we forth-wart," said ye king. (IV.478–88)

The language employed also corresponds to the realm of courtly life. The lady's offer to accompany Bruce reminds the reader of the *roman courtois* conventions. These few chivalrous scenes operate as the complementary courtly qualities a romance hero must possess according to tradition. They develop the representation of the knights fully both on the battlefield and in the company of noblewomen. But the makar does not forget reality as he negotiates between Bruce's *cortesia* and the harsh reality of the Wars of Independence. Bruce offers a reward to the lady in return for information. Here again, through figures of rhetoric, Barbour resolves the tension between realistic exposition of events and courtly ideal by portraying potentially historical based scenes in a manner in which they still show some of those sophisticated aspects characteristic of their predecessors. This schematic portrayal of *cortesia* is also characteristic of most Anglo-Norman and English romances, with only a few but remarkable exceptions such as Thomas of Britain's *Tristan*, the Anglo-Norman *Ipomedon* and its English translation and the romances of the Ricardian England. The defence of the baronial interest and the perceived decadence of French Arthurian romance were the two main reasons why English texts were primarily centred on epic action. At any rate, some of them show a more playful, if sporadic, game with established courtly romance standards, demonstrating more flexibility than *The Bruce*. Even the *Histoire de Guillaume le Maréchal* exhibits a couple of scenes in which this sophisticated courtly ambience can be perceived. Firstly, a lady cures the young Guillaume's wounds after a tourney (ll.1760–88); and, secondly, the most courteous scene takes place. The Anglo-Norman warrior, still as a young man and always described in close connection with warfare, sings a song:

Li Marischa[l]s qui bien chantout
E qui de riens ne se vantout
Lors commensa une chansun,(ll.3477–79)

[The Marshal, who sang well and did not boast about anything, then started singing a song]

The representation of female commoners also challenges the conventions of Barbour's time as he strikingly adapts the concept of courtesy. The scene (XVI. 270–96), in which a king stops his armies' advance to help a poor pregnant laundress bear the baby in suitable conditions, would rarely occur in chivalric romances. Such acts of *cortesia* were only expected to take place between knights and ladies as a social exchange between the upper classes: never with an inferior. *The Bruce* is a very exceptional case in which this concept is transferred to an inter-class exchange between King Robert and a commoner. Instead of cataloguing Bruce's conduct as a simple act of mercy towards a member of the Third Estate, the makar emphasises Bruce's *cortesia*: "Yis wes a full gret curtasy" (XVI. 293). The author could easily have ignored this deed, or even converted the laundress into a helpless courtly lady. Barbour's deployment of this narrative strategy undermines the convention and characterises Bruce as a people's king with an egalitarian attitude towards all Scots.

   One of the central themes of the *roman courtois* is the evocation of *fin'amors* which very often functions as a moving force and the goal of the knight's *avanture* in itself. Either a married lady or a single heiress may become an emblematic figure of financial security; this process is disguised by the idealisation of love at the same time that the landless knight will offer protection in exchange. In *The Bruce*, the personal quest for love and social status is redefined into the collective quest for national freedom and identity. For this reason, not only are the scenes involving love affairs either extramarital or within the bond of matrimony scarce but, when referred to, are schematically depicted too. In the makar's representation of his heroes, love relationships either historical or fictional are marginalised. At most, the reader can only find a few hints of the *historical* Bruce's well-known predilection for enjoying the company of mistresses, who bore him several illegitimate children. The author admits that en passant:

& mony tyme as I herd say
Throw wemen yat he wyth wald play
Yat wald tell all yat yai mycht her,
& swa mycht happyn yat it fell her, (V.543–46)

This is the clearest instance which touches on Bruce's extramarital relationships; but these references are always vague (Kliman 1973: 80) and also lack rhetorical embellishment. Furthermore, the textual composition of the passage favours a practical reading of these "wemen's" role by cataloguing them as informers, which diminishes a more courtly or amorous interpretation. Apart from the author's dismissal of courtly conventions, there is another reason why Barbour might not say anything else relating the hero's multiple affairs. According to Llull: "E si justícia e lutxúria son [*sic*] contraris, e cavayleria és per mantenir justícia, doncs cavayler lutxuriós e cavayleria són contraris."[2] (Llull 1988: 187). The fact that a knight (and more concretely a *Christian* one) could have several mistresses would also contradict the conception of perfect Christian chivalry, implying his lack of *temperance* – here understood in Aristotelian terms as "a virtue, through which men are disposed as the law enjoins towards the pleasures of the body" (Aristotle's *Rhetoric* I.ix.9). As a result, a knight lacking *temperance* could not be a completely ideal knight. It is noteworthy that this moralistic and profoundly Christian vision of chivalry is typical of the Scottish romances. The fact that Gilbert Hay translated Llull's *Llibre* into Scots reaffirms the Scottish interest for this kind spiritual chivalry. Other romances of the fifteenth century offer a more ironic and less moral approach to the subject. In Antoine de la Sale's *Jehan de Saintré*, for example, lust and chivalry are perfectly compatible:

À lire *Saintré*, on a l'impression d'une contre-épreuve burlesque d'un roman courtois traditionnel, d'une illustration inversée de certaines valeurs que l'auteur chercherait à miner, à travestir, tant les situations développées dans le récit sont peu courtoises [...]dans un univers de luxure et de débauche où l'on exalte de la fête des sens et la virilité du moine! (Blanchard ed. 1995: 8)

[When reading *Saintré*, one has the impression of a burlesque cross-check of a traditional courtly romance, a reversed illustration of certain values which the author would try to undermine, to subvert, since the situations developed in the plot are not very courteous [...] in a world of lust and dissoluteness where the indulgence of senses and the virility of the monk are celebrated!]

Further, the author is not interested in describing *fin'amors* within the morally correct Christian institution of matrimony. Although love and marriage were not traditionally compatible in the poetry of the troubadours, in early French romances the notion of *fin'amors* began to be developed beyond the limits of the poetry of the troubadours. The narrative length of the *romans* imposed a redefinition of the notion. Unlike a short lyric poem (*canso*), in which an illicit relation was imagined, narrative action was necessary. For this reason, they evolved to the extent that the final attainment of

---

[2] Here I quote Llull's original since Hay's, being a Scots translation mediated through a French translation, does not always correspond to the original Catalan. In this particular instance, Hay reads as: "bresing and othir disordinate lechery discordis with justice [...]." (Haye 1901–1914: 32). My translation of the last sentence follows: "therefore, a lecherous knight and chivalry are opposites."

fin'amors (sometimes as the goal of the knight's *avanture* itself) culminated with the marriage of the *fins amants*. One of the earliest examples of this shift is Chrétien de Troyes' *Erec et Enide* (composed around 1170), in which the love relation between Erec (a knight) and Enide (a single lady) evolved into their marriage. Even in Chandos Herald's historicised *Vie du Prince Noir*, for instance, the Black Prince addresses his wife in terms of *fin'amors* just before departing for the Spanish campaign (ll.2048–101).

As mentioned earlier, Barbour possessed a very good knowledge of French literature. Had he wished to describe the affection between King Robert and his kidnapped wife, Elizabeth, along the lines of chivalric marital love, thematically he could have structured the plot around the *amor de lonh* tradition (literally, "love from afar"), this lyric subgenre deals with the sufferings of the lover when he is apart from his beloved. Conversely, the affection between Bruce and his wife is never described. Indeed, from the moment she is captured (IV.39) until she is liberated (XIII. 693–97), she is not mentioned at all. Being aware of the fact that the presence of *fin'amors* (either marital or extramarital) would not contribute to his main literary and ideological purposes, the poet does not mind suppressing it completely. According to Janet M. Smith, this is typical of early Scottish romances, in which action is preferred to "l'élégance sociale" (Smith 1934: 18).

The only courtly affair following the ideals of *fin'amors* is displaced to the English side. In Book VIII, Douglas manages to trick the garrison guarding the Scottish knight's former castle, "And yai [the Scots] so angryly yaim socht / Yat off thaim all [the English] eschapyt nane" (VIII. 486–87). Among the slain Englishmen, a letter is discovered in the purse of Sir John Webton:

A lettyr yat him send a lady
Yat he luffyt per drouery,
Yat said quhen he had ȝemyt a ȝer
In wer as a gud bachiller
Ye awenturis castell of Douglas
Yat to kepe sa peralus was
Yan mycht he weile ask a lady
Hyr amowris and hyr drouery. (VIII. 491–98)

Traditionally, in the *roman courtois* the motif of chivalric love service duly rewarded is associated with the hero. Barbour shifts the love motif to the English party and mentions the unsuccessful outcome of the enterprise. The makar questions and destabilises the validity of idealised but rashly heroic actions in real warfare. He subverts the *locus communis* of feats of arms rewarded with love. Another of the topoi commonly appearing in courtly romances, that of *militia et amor*, is implicitly undermined, too. There is no place for "amowris" and "drouery" (sex) in Barbour's literary world.

When composing *The Bruce*, Barbour was endeavouring to establish a new literary tradition in Scots after the Wars of Independence. He succeeded in creating a new way of composing romances, which not only transformed topoi from existing European traditions but more originally challenged conventions and offered an innovative, revitalising Scottish conception of the genre or mode. Barbour provided the audience with a vision of knighthood in which the epic elements, subservient to the national, dynastic and collective ideology, are at the core of the narrative. The makar destabilises some of the basic chivalric principles by portraying the common folk performing valiant feats of arms in war. Similarly, he has no qualms about describing the king himself showing courtesy towards a laundress. In such an understanding of romance, there is little space for long disquisitions on the manners of *cortesia* or the psychology of *fin'amors*.

Hary's *Wallace*: prevalence and evolution

Hary's *Wallace* inevitably invites comparison to Barbour's *Bruce*. Indeed, as mentioned in the first chapter, Hary's indebtedness to Barbour is unanimously recognised by scholars. Nevertheless, the composition of *The Wallace* about one hundred years after *The Bruce* situates the romance in a totally different literary and socio-historical context. Barbour was not Hary's only influence:

He [Hary] was a diligent student of histories, both vernacular, Latin and French. Barbour, Wyntoun, Bower, Froissart are only the certainly identified chroniclers that he consulted. He read the more popular didactic or informative writings of his day, such as Boethius's *De Consolatione Philosophiae*, the pseudo-Aristotle's *Secrees*, *The Travels of Sir John Mandeville*, saints' Legends, perhaps some treatises of astrology, [...] Chaucer's *Troilus and Criseyde* and *Canterbury Tales* and minor poems – that very clever astrological conceit, *The Compleynt of Mars*, seems to have been particularly admired – were closely studied by him. (MacDiarmid ed. 1968: I.xxxvii–xxxviii)

Although some of his readings such as *De Consolatione* or saints' legends coincide with those of Barbour, it is evident that Hary's range of literary influences differs very much from that of the Archdeacon. The sole mention of Chaucer and his impact on the fifteenth- and early sixteenth-century makars presupposes a distinct approach to literature from that of Barbour. Although Chaucer's first works, such as *The Book of the Duchess*, are slightly prior or contemporary to *The Bruce*, it is obvious that, at such an early stage of his career, Chaucer's reputation was not as widespread in Scotland as in the fifteenth and sixteenth centuries:

> Chaucer influenced immediately and profoundly the English tradition, so that the bulk of the more pretentious fifteenth-century English verse was Chaucerian; his influence on Scottish verse was slower and less overwhelming, so the pre-Chaucerian ways of writing were still fashionable in Scotland in the fifteenth century. (Fox 1966: 166)

It will therefore be necessary to examine the manner in which the distinctive elements deployed by Barbour prevail and are transformed in Hary's portrayal of knighthood, chivalry and *cortesia*. The makar's construction of the hero's *proeza*, his approach to the Third Estate, and the treatment of female characters will serve to provide evidence for this.

Although themes such as *cortesia* and *fin'amors* do not lie at the core of the narrative, *The Wallace* offers a more elaborate approach to them than *The Bruce*. Rhetorically, Hary conceives a narrative in which the treatment of female characters differs from his predecessor's, helping to project the image of the protagonist fully (Goldstein 1993: 253). While his concern with the national struggle is still central, the knight's stubborn unforgiving demeanour is softened to suit the requirement of *cortesia*. In Book IV, for instance, his affair with a woman (her social status is not revealed) is discovered. The English tempt her to betray Wallace in return for a reward:

> "Giff thou will help to bring ȝon rebell doun
> We sall the mak a lady off renoun."
> Thai gaiff till hyr baith gold and siluir brycht
> And said scho suld be weddyt with ane knycht. (IV.723–26)

She cannot resist temptation and sells her lover. However, she repents and confesses this betrayal to Wallace that "I haiff ȝou sald [...]" (IV.760). Up to this juncture, the reader/listener has learned about the hero's attitude towards foes and traitors: pitiless revenge was the norm. The only traitor he forgives is Bruce himself only because he is aware of the future King of Scots' *avanture*.

Notwithstanding his previous action, Wallace demonstrates his *cortesia* for the first time:

"Will god I sall eschape this tresoune fals.
I the forgyff with-outyn wordis mair."
He kissyt hir, syne tuk his leiff to fayr. (IV.770–72)

The courtly portrayal suggests not only Wallace's representation as a romance hero but also his dissociation between the world of war and the world of *amors* and court. He understands that, when dealing with women, courtly language and manners must replace the manly and vengeful deeds on the battlefield. His forgiveness accompanied by a kiss reveals a side of Wallace which the author will deploy as a recurrent pattern of behaviour in the few scenes where there is interaction between male and female characters.

If, in *The Bruce*, the main character's marriage is secondary to the action, in *The Wallace* Hary elaborates that of the hero along the lines of *fin'amors* as adapted to epic poetry. The introductory portrait of Wallace's future wife combines the archetypal qualities of the courtly damsel – youth, high birth and *gentilesse*:

In Lanryk duelt a gentill woman thar,
A madyn myld, as my buk will declar,
Off xviii ȝeris ald or litill mor off age.
Als born scho was till part off heretage.
Hyr fadyr was of worschipe and renounce. (V.579–83)

The lady's description is supplemented by a summary of traditional female courtly attributes: she is humble, virtuous, sweet, discreet in speech and praiseworthy (V.597–603). The makar adopts a middle ground position between the succinctness of Barbour's courtliness and the ornamented courtly elaboration of Chaucer. For example, the sophistication of Emily's first appearance in the "Knight's Tale" goes far beyond that of Wallace's beloved:

That Emelye, that fairer was to sene
Than is the lylie upon his stalke grene,
And fressher than the May with floures newe –

For with the rose colour stroof hire hewe,
I noot which was the fyner of hem two –
[…]
Yclothed was she fressh, for to devyse:
Hir yelow heer was broyded in a tresse
Bihynde hir bak, a yerde long, I gesse.
And in the gardyn, at the sonne upriste,
She walketh up and doun, and as hire liste
She gadereth floures, party white and rede,
To make a subtil gerland for hire hede;
And as an aungel hevenysshly she soong. (ll.1035–39; 1048–55)

Hary could have easily taken inspiration from Chaucer as he does in other passages. Yet there is no *locus amoenus*, flowery imagery, long braided blonde hair or elegant attire such as the depiction of Emily in "The Knight's Tale" (ll.1033–61). The reason for the writer's less elaborate portrayal is explained straight away when he tells us that the English have killed both her father and her brother. Not only does the courtly scene merge with the national cause but it becomes subservient to the ideological framework of the romance.

Faced by this lady, Wallace falls in love immediately:

Apon a day to the kyrk as scho went
Wallace hyr saw as he his eyne can cast.
The prent off luff him punʒeit at the last
So asprely, throuch bewte off that brycht,
With gret wnes in presence bid he mycht.
He knew full weyll hyr kynrent and hyr blud. (V.604–09)

Despite its brevity, the passage is not as conventional as it may seem at first. The fact that he sees her for the first time at church, and not at court, should not be overlooked. Instead of the more sensual and suggestive garden of earthly pleasures, the church entails a distinct sets of implications: the sensual is replaced by the sacred, the human by the divine. God approves of Wallace's love. Politically, the replacement of the common meeting place for knights and ladies accords with Hary's ideological project. As argued in the first and second chapters, the notion of King and Church, so imbedded in early Scottish conceptions of nation, is equated to Nation and God in *The Wallace*. Apart from her "bewte", there are other aspects of the young woman which attract the hero. Although the reference to "hyr kynrent" and "hyr blud" is a *locus communis* of both epic and romance adaptations of *fin'amors*, the political overtones of the national struggle reappear once again in what was theoretically a courtly and stereotypical scene. Thus their first meeting in a holy venue and the lady's origin contribute to Hary's portrayal of Wallace's spiritual nationalism.

The makar introduces a conflict typical of epic poetry when Wallace thinks about marrying her. The hero cannot reconcile his *avanture* with his love as, for example, happens in the *Aeneid*, where Aeneas must choose between his love for Dido and his duty. Nevertheless, the tension between his knightly obligations and his feelings is also re-codified within the national parameters of *The Wallace*. The hero seeks advice about his "lusty baille" in Kerle (V.617). At this juncture, however, there is no profound philosophical debate along Boethian lines about the instability of love and the fickleness of fortune; instead, Wallace's speech is much more pragmatic than the reader might expect from a romance lover:

"To mary thus I can nocht ʒeit attend.
I wald of wer fyrst se a finaill end.
I will no mor allayne to my luff gang.
Tak tent to me or dreid we suffer wrang.
To proffer luff thus sone I wald nocht preffe.
Mycht I leyff off, in wer I lik to leyff". (V.625–30)

His single-minded objective gives him a clarity of thought rarely found in knight-lovers such as Lancelot, Troilus or Tristan. Hary does not allow for any kind of emotional paroxysm; the protagonist's suffering is schematically condensed in no more than a couple of lines, staying away from Chaucerian models: "On othir thing he maid his witt to walk, / Prefand giff he mycht off that languor slalk" (V.655–56). Wallace's pragmatism posits the dilemma between his feelings and his service to the country. His words and state of mind have little to do with the Petrarchan *Canticus Troili* in Book I. 400–34 of *Troilus and Criseyde*, whose first lines already denote a more psychological approach to *fin'amors*:

"If no love is, O Gold, what fele I so?
And if love is, what thing and which is he?
If love be good, from whennes cometh my woo?
If it be wikke, a wonder thynketh me,
When every torment and adversite

That cometh of hym may to me savory thinke;
For ay thurst I, the more that ich it drynke". (I. 400–06)

Even when Wallace confesses his love for her, her reply (although expressed in terms of courtly refinement) cannot escape the nationalistic nuances of the whole romance. She will willingly submit to Wallace's advances, not like a lover, but as a wife. She wants to preserve her virtue which has been repeatedly threatened by Englishmen (V.690–91). Temporarily, Wallace renounces love in favour of his duty to liberate Scotland. After defeating the English, Wallace meets his beloved again at the beginning of Book VI in which the European tradition probably mediated by Chaucer is evident:

In Aperill, quhen cleithit is but weyne
The abill ground be wyrking off natur,
And woddis has won thar worthy weid off greyne;
Quhen Nympheus, in beldyn off his bour
Wyth oyle and balm fullfillit off suet odour,
Faunis maceris, as thai war wount to gang,
Walkyn thar cours in euiry casuall hour
To glaid the huntar with thar merye sang – (VI. 9–16)

Although this cannot be categorically claimed, some references may point to the Chaucerian influence: the allusion to "Aperill" can be easily connected to the opening lines of the *Canterbury Tales*: "Whan that Aprill with his shoures soote, / the droughte of March hath perced to the roote" (ll.1–2).[3] Even if these lines might seem too conventional to propose a source, the topos of the renewal of nature in a pseudo-classical setting suggests that Hary was borrowing from either Chaucer's *Book of the Duchess* (ll.291–324) or from Machaut or Froissart directly.[4] In these moments of high emotion, Hary employed the sophisticated elements of a broader European courtly tradition. As Jack claims, this stanzaic shift to the French octave serves to

---

[3] Chaucer appears to be the most likely source for Hary since, in the fourteenth-century French tradition, authors such as Guillaume de Machaut or Froissart normally refer to May or spring in general. One of the few exceptions it is precisely the opening lines of Machaut's *Le Dit dou Vergier*, in which he alludes to "avril" (l.8).

[4] The connection of the renewal of nature with love is typical of the poetry of the troubadours. Yet, during the fourteenth century, Machaut and Froissart incorporated a pseudo-classical setting within the topos. In Machaut's *Fonteinne Amoureuse*, for instance, the narrator-protagonist is conducted to the *locus amoenus* of the fountain in which he can see classical figures, thus lending a pseudo-mythical aura to the setting.

emphasise this moment of *jois* expressed by the *fins amants* in their reunion (Jack 2001: 45).

At this point, Wallace is still doubtful and upset:

"Qwhat is this luff? It is bot gret mischance,
That me wald bring fra armes wtterly.
I will nocht los my worschip for pleasance.
I wer I think my tyme till occupy.
ʒeit hyr to luff I will nocht lat forthy". (VI. 33–37)

Wallace's dilemma is presented in chivalric terms: his own personal preferences and human impulses clash with his knightly worth. Yet, in the particular case of Wallace, *proeza* is not at the service of his individual *pretz* but at that of the liberation of his nation. By implication, his sufferings and those of Scotland are equated once more. He cannot enjoy the "plesance" of love until his country is freed. Goldstein defines the warrior's anxiety as the irruption of the feminine other into his aggressive masculine world (Goldstein 1993: 256). At this point, Wallace finally endures Boethian tribulations about the nature of fortune. Highly conventional though it is, McDiarmid convincingly associates this passage with the lament of Chaucer's Troilus for Criseyde (IV.296), in which the mutability of this world as represented by fortune stands out against the truth of heaven (McDiarmid ed. 1968: II. 184 n. 1.88). Only after the philosophical disquisition, probably the most profound one in the martially centred romance, Wallace decides to marry his beloved: "He thinkis als luff did him hye awance, / So ewynly held be fauour the ballance" (VI. 52–53). The makar reverts to a typical romance motif in which the knight needs to find the balance between *fin'amors* and chivalric deeds of arms. Should he accomplish this, love will help him to fight better and his lady will love him even more thanks to his knightly dexterity and *fame*. Nonetheless, the employment of the eight line stanza, which Chaucer's Monk uses in his tragic discourses, anticipates the future dreadful ending of their love (Jack 2001: 45; McKim ed. 2003: 407). As a tragic hero, the Scottish leader's marriage and *jois* cannot last long. He cannot escape his *fatum*: death itself destroys Wallace's matrimony. The English kill his wife: Wallace will not find peace until his entrance in heaven as a martyr. Further personal revenge is required: not only does Wallace avenge himself, but he also expels the English from Lanark. The courtly discourse intermingles with, and depends upon, the national discourse once again. Hary represents the tragedy of the lover as a useful means for the liberation of the country. Even the most overtly courtly scenes are integrated within the national and ideological project.

The best example of the hero's display of *cortesia* is his conversation with the Queen of England when she is sent as an ambassador to negotiate peace with the Scottish knight. The Queen herself is the one who suggests seeking a truce with Wallace. Her love for the Scottish leader seems to be her main motivation: "Sum off thaim said the queyn luffyt Wallace" (VIII. 1137). The meeting takes place in St Albans. Again, the bloodthirsty characterisation of Wallace at war is redefined in the context of courtly behaviour:

In armys sone he caucht this queyn with croun
And kyssyt hyr with-outyn wordis mor.
Sa dyd he neuir to na Sotheron befor.
"Madem," he said, "rycht welcum mot ʒe be.
How plesis ʒow our ostyng for to se?" (VIII. 1234–38)

Even the body language of this scene presents a very different Wallace from the one who hates the English. His embracing and kissing of her denote an absolute turn from the prevailing vocabulary and epic action to portrayal of the exquisiteness of the life at court. Such an attitude elucidates Wallace as a man highly versed in the art of *cortesia*. His act of welcome also deploys the words expected from a refined conversation among the upper classes. These polite manners, however, do not make him forget his main enterprise. He conflates the languages of *cortesia* and war when the Queen demands peace by appealing to Wallace's Christianity:

"Quhen ʒour fals king had Scotland gryppyt haill,
For nakyn thing that he befor him fand
He wald nocht thoill the rycht blud in our land,
Bot reft thar rent, syne put thaim selff to ded". (VIII. 1296–99)

With his wife, with the English Queen and even in courtly interchanges with ladies, Wallace understands what his priorities and those of his nation are. Even when the Queen confesses her love, the hero's reply still captures all the sophistication of courtly language:

"Syn plesand wordis off ʒou and ladyis fair,

As quha suld dryff the byrdis till a swar
With the small pype, for it most fresche will call.
Madem, as ʒit ʒe ma nocht tempt ws all". (VIII. 1421–24)

The metaphor of the entrapped bird reinforces the rejection; but, at the same time, it softens the effect and crudeness of a more direct "no". It also expresses his absolute commitment to the Scottish cause through the firm refusal of any material or sentimental English offer. His command of rhetoric projects Wallace's image as an educated man, who possesses not only knightly attributes, but also courtly virtues. Both of them elevate him to the category of the perfect romance hero.

Similar to the depiction of Robert I in Barbour's *Bruce*, Wallace's *proeza* is also weighed against its relevance to the national cause. As mentioned in the Chapter 1, the prime motivation for fighting is personal revenge, a thematic element traditionally associated with *chansons de geste* rather than with *romans courtois*:

Than Wallace said, "Her was my fadir slayne,
My brothir als, quhilk dois me mekill payne;
So sall my selff, or wengit be but dreid.
The traytour is her, causer was off that deid."
Than hecht thai all to bide with hartlye will.
Be that the power was takand Lowdoun hill. (III. 111–16)

The integration of the original personal vendetta of the hero within the liberation of Scotland is an essential feature of Hary's narrative. The voice of Wallace himself reinforces the ideological discourse. Such bloodthirsty vengeance is appropriately articulated through the terminology of medieval epics. In the battle of "Lowdoun Hill", for instance, the language of the *chansons de geste* characterises the general tone and thematic style of the confrontation:

The knycht Fenweik that cruell was and keyne,
He had at dede off Wallace fadyr beyne
And his brodyr that douchty was and der.
Quhen Wallace saw that fals knycht was so ner
His corage grew in Ire as a lyoune. (III. 169–73)

The deep-rooted desire for revenge enhances the knight's attributes as a warrior. His "corage" benefits from such a situation, allowing him not only to perform more chivalric feats but also to avenge himself of the crimes committed towards his family. Interestingly, his being governed by "Ire" is seen a positive way of action. This is not an isolated example, but Hary refers to Wallace's "Ire" in many different occasions in the narrative. Traditionally, in courtly romances, wrath, as one of the Seven Deadly Sins, would not be the ideal state of mind of a Christian knight. It would also denote lack of *mesura*. For instance, Gilbert Hay emphasises the sinful nature of anger in his *Buik of the Ordre of Knychthede*: "jre is a stroublance of curage and of gude mynde and of gude will and disturnis a mannis curage to vengeaunce" (Haye 1901–14: 47). Only epic heroes such as Roland in the *Chanson de Roland* are ruled by anger. In *The Wallace*, all faults and excessive violence for which the hero might be responsible are justified in so far as his fight is allegorically seconded by God himself.

Although both Bruce and Wallace fuse their personal enterprise with the country's interests, the narrative fabric of the two historical romances involves a very different development of this common feature. While Bruce's revenge is a first step in his career in the leadership of the country, that of Wallace is the leitmotif of the whole story. In religious terms, Bruce's is framed within a sinful act which will stay with the hero until his final expiatory crusade after death, whereas Wallace's is directly supported by the Virgin Mary, a fact which elevates his vengeance to the realm of the sacred. In this milieu, the bloodthirsty story line of *The Wallace* evokes a tension between the ethical validity of such a cruel revenge and the pseudo-divine *avanture* of the hero. As shown in Chapter 2, this thematic opposition is negotiated through the formulation of the allegorical interpretative methods applied to late medieval literature. On the basis that a text can have different allegorical perspectives, this evaluative hierarchy places the anagogical/divine level on a superior level to the tropological/ethical. Thus, the cruelty of the vendetta, unethical though it might be, appears as the means through which a more sacred aim can be attained. Bloodshed is justified in anagogical terms.

It is noteworthy that in a historicised work such as *The Wallace*, in which the leader of the national cause is not a member of the high nobility but a knight, the Third Estate's role is not so important and elaborate as in *The Bruce*. Hary articulates his discourse in more conventional terms as far as the lower classes are concerned. His most subversive character is the hero himself: a knight who acts as if he were the sovereign of Scotland. The commoners, though present as supporters of the main hero, do not take an active part in heroic action as individual figures:

A hundreth dede in field was lewyt thar,
And iii ȝemen that Wallace menyde fer mar;
Twa was of Kyle, and the one of Conyngayme
With Robert Boide, to Wallace com fra hayme. (III. 205–08)

While the yeomen are placed alongside the main hero and his best companions, as Goldstein remarks, Hary does not attach much importance to the members of the Third Estate who supported Wallace. The romance mainly concentrates on the queens, kings, the nobility and the clergy, following the conventions of the genre (Goldstein 1993: 236). The presence of commoners has a patent purpose. As a people's hero, Wallace must be backed by the Third Estate. In this way, Hary offers an image of Wallace supported by those whose commitment to the national emancipation of Scotland is not mediated by the political and economic concerns of the nobility. If in some instances of *The Bruce*, they are named as individuals and perform valiant feats, in *The Wallace* Hary sticks to tradition as far as the commoners are integrated in the national fight within the hierarchical late medieval order. They participate in the struggle, but under the commands of the upper classes, who are those permitted to perform chivalric deeds of arms. Therefore, Hary's construction of the Third Estate follows established conventions, conforming to John of Salisbury's analogy of the commonwealth with the human body:

The husbandmen correspond to the feet, which always cleave to the soil, and need more specially the care of the head since, while they walk upon the earth doing service with their bodies, they are more likely than others to stumble over stones and therefore deserve aid and protection all the more justly since it is they who raise, sustain, and move forward the weight of the entire body. (*Policraticus* V.ii.65)

Wallace, then, is represented as a very strong and powerful knight on the battlefield with a single-minded objective: the liberation of Scotland. This portrayal accords with (and is probably much indebted to) that of Robert Bruce in Barbour's poem in which any personal aspiration is subservient to the national cause. Nevertheless, the courtly elements either directly borrowed for the French tradition or mediated by Chaucer are more prominent than in Barbour's text. The courtly scenes in *The Wallace*, though also scarce, are more fully developed than in its predecessor: the Scottish knight behaves as a very courteous nobleman in his interactions with women. By way of contrast, as opposed to *The Bruce*, Wallace's knighthood is much bloodier and crueller than that of the King of Scots. Stylistically, Hary's negotiation between the influences of Barbour's work, and those of French and especially Chaucerian models, results in a quite distinctive work of art. Therefore, despite its particular traits along the lines of the Scottish poetry of the late fifteenth and early sixteenth century, the literary composition of *The Wallace* reveals the prevalence and evolution of the same Scottish tradition as codified by Barbour in *The Bruce*.

Sir David Lindsay's *Squyer Meldrum* and the historical limits of courtliness

Sir David Lindsay's only romance *The Historie of Squyer Meldrum* plays with, and undermines, the conventions of the genre. Like those of Barbour and Hary, Lindsay's representations of knighthood and chivalry are heavily politicised. At the same time, *Squyer Meldrum* shares rhetorical and compositional features with other satirical texts by Lindsay such as *Ane Satyre of the Thrie Estaitis* and *The Dreme*, in which social critique is abundant. The probable date of the romance's composition, some time in the early 1550s, also entails a different set of socio-political and intellectual contexts from Barbour's or Hary's works.

Lindsay's portrayal of knighthood accords with the orthodox rules and procedures of knightly confrontations. At the same time, however, the author explores the cruelties of real warfare instead of depicting battles and jousting along the lines of idealised courtly scenes. Realism is also present in the heralds' supervision of a single combat between Meldrum and the English champion, Master Talbart, being reminiscent of Lindsay's heraldic career (Edington 1994: 29). The combat's narrative outline is written according to the same narrative strategy as the violent encounters between knights in the Middle Scots *Golagros and Gawane*. The poem's vocabulary, topoi and ritualistic, chivalric norms conflate with the highly politicised framework of a historically-based romance. Meldrum's bold acceptance of the English champion's challenge is entirely conventional:

Than, said he [Meldrum], it weer greit schame,
Without battell ʒe suld pas hame.
Thairfoir, to God I mak ane vow,
The morne my self sall fecht with ʒow,
Outher on Horsbak or on fute:
ʒour crakkis I count thame not ane cute. (ll.289–94)

Meldrum, the young squire dares to confront Talbart, the renowned
knight. Yet, when contextualised, it is not just the squire's customary
response which suggests that he seeks a place in the knightly society,
but acquires another political dimension within the Anglo-Scottish
tensions of the first half of the sixteenth century. Even when the figure
of Talbart is evocative of the archetypal villain of *romans courtois*, the
ideological overtones are inescapable:

Of Scottis & Frenche quhilk [Talbart] spak disdane;
And, on his Bonnet, vsit to beir
Of Siluer fine takinnis of weir:
[…]
Bot Talbart maid at him [Meldrum] bot Scorne,
Lychtlyand him with wordis of pryde;
Syne, hamewart to his Oist culd ryde.
And shew the Brethren of his Land,
How ane ʒoung Scot had tane on hand
To fecht with him beside Montruill; (ll.272–74; 328–33)

Lindsay constructs Talbart's characterisation following that of the
Haughty Knight with his disdain for the Scots and the French and the
particularly scornful attitude towards Meldrum. His attire, full of
golden and silver ornaments, denotes his vanity, too. Meldrum
compares himself with "ʒoung David" confronting "Golias" (ll.311–
12). The typology can be easily transferred to the military conflicts
between England and Scotland about 40 years after Flodden. Just
before the combat with Talbart, Lindsay hastens to highlight that
Meldrum is not fighting for individual glory, but for "the honour of
Scotland" (l.351). Just like the heroes of *The Bruce* and *The Wallace*,
personal heroics are at the service of the national cause.

In the arrangement for the battle, Lindsay reverts to the pomp
and paraphernalia of the chivalric world again. Meldrum can choose
between 100 horses (l.360), his armour is succinctly described (ll.369–
76), 100 men at arms escort him (ll.380–83) and the "sound of Trum-
pet and Clarioun" announces the fight (l.388). This idealistic depiction

creates an unreal scenario for the two adversaries. Yet the two men's behaviour is very human. They joust, get tired and rest for a while until Talbart is seriously hurt:

Sir Talbart to the earth dang doun.
That straik was with sic micht and fors,
That on the ground lay man and hors;
And throw the brydell hand him bair,
And in the breist ane span and mair,
Throw curras and throw gluifis of plait,
That Talbart micht mak na debait:
The trencheour of the Squyeris spear
Stak still into Sir Talbartis Geir. (ll.532–40)

Talbart's terrible state after the fight undermines the previous idealistic atmosphere, which disguised the cruelties of fierce military encounters. The narrative voice's disapproval of warlike life was already expressed earlier through Meldrum's words, telling the Lady of Craigfergus not to travel by sea because of the people she might come across, especially "Men of weir".

In a later sea battle, the realities of war also play a central part. Meldrum corners the English captain, who implores mercy:

[…] O gentill Capitane,
Thoill me not for to be slane.
My lyfe to ȝow salbe mair pryse
Nor sall my deith, ane thowsand syse:
For ȝe may get, as I suppois,
Thrie thowsand Nobillis of the Rois
Of me and of my companie:
Thairfoir, I cry ȝow loud mercie.
Except my lyfe, nothing I craif:
Tak ȝow the schip and all the laif. (ll.785–94)

The tone switches from the first four lines, in which the language of knighthood is displayed ("gentill Capitane") to the realistic language of warfare, in which powerful nobles were taken prisoners, being released only in exchange for great sums of money. The polysemous nature of late medieval literature allows for a multiplicity of interpretations: "Except my lyfe, nothing I craif" (l.793) can be regarded as the English captain's desperate supplication to save his life, dramatising the cruel rather than chivalric realities of war. Alternatively, it can also be explained in a more satirical light: the enemy, far from heroic, is willing to humiliate himself to avoid death. The stronger, aggressive and more powerful foe as represented by the English captain has to withdraw in front of the representative of heroic Scotland, Meldrum. Satire and nationalistic discourse merge together. Either way, death is detached from any kind of epic glorification. Like in *Golagros and Gawane*, warfare is not only about valiant deeds of arms, but it also exposes the less glamorous brutality of military action. Thus, in the representation of the English Lindsay problematises the use of romance and epic motifs within a historicised narrative. Anglo-Scottish tensions are mediated through the language of literary convention.

Lindsay's characterisation of courtly norm and behaviour is intentionally ambiguous. After a clear allusion to the functionality of the text as a mirror for knightly demeanour (ll.1–20), the makar refers to Chaucer's *Troilus and Criseyde* (l.24) and the story of Lancelot of the Lake (l.48). The references to the latter suggest that Lindsay is exemplifying Lancelot and Guenevere's love affair as a whole rather than concentrating on any Lancelot romance in particular; and certainly not the Middle Scots *Lancelot of the Laik*, in which the adulterous relationship between the two protagonists is not developed at all. Nevertheless, Lindsay does not affirm that he will take the two romances as models. The case of Chaucer might be misleading for the reader or listener. Although there is no explicit connection between the *Troilus* and *Squyer Meldrum*, Lindsay's first mention of his hero is placed just after that of Chaucer. The narrator also claims that:

With the help of Cleo, I intend,
Sa Minerue wald me Sapience send,
A Nobill Squyer to discryfe, (ll.27–29)

The allusions to the *Troilus* and the classical deities appear to anticipate a highly sophisticated treatment of courtliness. Yet the actual friendship between Lindsay and Meldrum, to which the text alludes (ll.29–34), connotes a very different approach to established romance heroes such as Troilus.

The tension between romance and biographical account reappears in the reference to Lancelot and Guenevere. The typical comparison between a romance hero and other (more famous) romance figures operates on a moralistic and satiric level more than on a knightly one. If Meldrum is superior to Lancelot it is because the

Arthurian hero's love was adulterous; hence, "Of sic amour culd cum na gude" (l.64); whilst Meldrum's lover had no other husband or lover (l.59). Lindsay denounces Lancelot and Guenevere's "sordid adulterous liaison" (Edington 1994: 123). Thus it is not so much that Meldrum's knighthood is eulogised as Lancelot's morality is questioned. The opening lines offer a patent warning that the makar will deal with love and *cortesia* in a detached and ironic manner. As Riddy suggests, as a late romance (even by Scottish standards), Lindsay could no longer seriously approach romance as a genre. (Riddy 1974: 26)

Regarding Meldrum's attitude either on the battlefield or at court, the narrator makes explicit what is implicit in Hary's *Wallace*:

Becaus he was so courageous,
Ladies of him wes amorous.
He was ane Munʒeoun for a Dame,
Meik, in chalmer, lyk a lame;
Bot, in the Field, ane Champioun,
Rampand lyke ane wyld lyoun. (ll.231–36)

As a romance hero, Meldrum understands the difference between the masculine world of warfare and the feminine world of gallant exchanges with ladies. At the same time, the epic and the courtly realms are bound together by the *amor et militia* topos: his dexterity on the battlefield is conventionally rewarded with the admiration of ladies.

The first example of this is Meldrum's intervention in Craigfergus when the Scottish army ravages the land and behaves cruelly to the people. The protagonist saves the lives of women, priests and friars (ll.102–03). Among them is an Irish lady, whose elegant attire reveals her high social status (ll.121–27). She is so impressed with Meldrum that she asks him to marry her when he is about to leave (ll.175–80). Conveniently, she is a rich heiress. Yet Meldrum wants to pursue his career as a soldier before marrying her. According to convention, the hero needs to prove his worth as a warrior before settling down. At any rate, he promises her that "ʒe sall haue lufe for lufe again / Trewlie, vnto my Lifis end" (ll.208–09). At this juncture, Meldrum seems to be making use of the language and practices of *cortesia* within the courtly game rather than committing to long-lasting love for the lady.

The lady of Craigfergus is not mentioned again until the "Testament" which follows the romance. Meldrum blames his "ʒouth and insolence" (1.224) for rejecting her. Nonetheless, the overall comic tone of the mock testament posits the question of how seriously Meldrum's remark should be taken. He unashamedly conflates marriage, sex and material commodities in the same stanza: "ʒe suld haue been my spous and paramour, / With Rent and riches for my recompence" (ll.222–23). There is no space for the subtleties of courtly diction and elegant expressivity of *fin'amors*. Through the hero's voice, Lindsay straightforwardly recapitulates the episodes of Meldrum's life. The outcome is a satirical approach, not so much to Meldrum's achievements, as to the conventions of courtly poetry and romance. In a text that claims to narrate real events in the life of a Scottish squire in the first half of the sixteenth century, the blatantly inappropriate classical allusions enhance the satiric tone of the "Testament". Meldrum leaves his body to Mars, his tongue to Mercury and his heart to Venus (ll.76–88). The unsuitability of elements drawn from classical epics intensifies the detachment and mocking character of the "Testament", which emphasises the limits of epic and romance motifs to portray potentially realistic events.

The gap between reality and courtly standards becomes more dramatically evident when Meldrum returns to Scotland after fighting in France. The hero falls in love with a lady who has recently been widowed; her name is never mentioned. In this instance, Lindsay seems to be reverting to a courtly motif, extending back to the poetry of the troubadours. Although her name is not transformed into the traditional *senhal* or nickname to preserve her identity safe, the makar does not reveal that she is the Lady of Gleneagles, just referring to her as a "lady". Lindsay, like many troubadours addressing their lyrics to married women, had powerful reasons to conceal her name insofar as she finally remarried someone other than Meldrum, whose immediate surrender to the Lady of Gleneagles is described as follows:

[Meldrum turned] To Fair Venus makand his mane,
Sayand: Ladie, quhat may this mene?
I was ane fre man lait ʒistrene,
And now ane catiue bound and thrall
For ane that I think the Flour of all. (ll.906–10)

There nothing unconventional about his entering in the service of love. Now a renowned hero, Meldrum seems to have found the perfect partner, with lands and possessions, to marry. The love and the financial interests seem to conflate as in many other romances. Yet once again Lindsay will challenge the reader's expectations. Meldrum and the lady do not live in a vaguely located place of the Arthurian world but in Scotland. They must conform to the laws of country. The lady needs a dispensation to be able to remarry. The reference to Aeneas and Dido (ll.875–78), even if designed to laud the lovers' passion at first, subtly anticipates the impossibility of their *fin'amors*.

The dispensation never arrives, leaving the lovers in a rather precarious situation:

In that meine time, this ladie fair
Ane douchter to the Squyer bair:
Nane fund wes fairer of visage. (ll.1161–63)

Reality shakes the foundations of courtly idealisation once again. As Edington points out, ideals of love and chivalry are not viable in the real world (Edington 1994: 124). Meldrum and the Lady of Gleneagles will have to deal not only with the fact of their love and the impossibility of marriage but also with the bastard daughter which their relationship has brought about. Lindsay's ironic detachment could not be more manifest. His words as a narrator summarised his vision of *fin'amors*: "For I am not in lufe expart / And neuer studyit in that art" (ll.1157–58).

Notwithstanding obvious compositional divergences between Barbour's *Bruce*, Hary's *Wallace* and Lindsay *Squyer Meldrum*, there are also remarkable similarities in Lindsay's treatment of knighthood and *cortesia*. The three narratives favour martial action to elaborated pictures of courtly etiquette. The main characters' heroism is at the service of the collective good, understood as the national struggle against the "Auld Enemy". In Lindsay's *Squyer Meldrum*, the representation of *cortesia* and *fin'amors* is as secondary as in the other two texts but Lindsay infuses his story with substantial irony which questions and destabilises the basis of *cortesia* in the late medieval and early modern world.

Chapter Four

The Arthurian Romances

While the historical romances deal with Scottish material, the chivalric romances are derived from the French literary tradition. The Arthurian narratives are based on selected passages from French sources. One might expect that the primary sources impose constraints on the artistic design and scope of these works from which *The Bruce* and *The Wallace* were free. However, the existence of a French source for each text facilitates the study and understanding of the ways in which the makars either follow tradition or manipulate and adapt it to their own purposes. The fact that these Arthurian romances are contemporaneous with Hary's composition arguably implies the existence of a wider cultural milieu than in Barbour's period. French *romans courtois* such as those by Chrétien de Troyes, and the original texts, the *First Continuation of Perceval* and the *Prose Lancelot*, will be used in this chapter to contextualise the Scottish tradition within a broader field in which the influence – and sometimes rejection – of French themes and forms shows the particular construction of knightly and courtly values in the Scottish romance tradition.

Lancelot of the Laik and the *Prose Lancelot*: Lancelot reinvented, *fin'amors* displaced

In the historical romances, the idiosyncratic representation of knighthood, chivalry and *cortesia* is conditioned by their national and nationalistic subject matter. Similarly the chivalric romances generate analogous images of these concepts. This appears to be a consequence of the specific evolution of the genre in Scotland. A comparative study of these notions in *Lancelot of the Laik* and the Old French *Prose Lancelot* will help us to trace the Scottish tradition through Barbour up to the end of the Middle Ages. The study of the original will elucidate the manner in which some of the most important elements in the description of Lancelot and *fin'amors* are not present in the Middle Scots text. The adaptation of the French *Prose Lancelot* to

Scottish standards results in a series of distinctive features which often alter and displace the meaning and focus of the narrative.

In the *Prose Lancelot*, the author envisages the hero's condition as outsider much more emphatically than does either Chrétien de Troyes in his *Chevalier de la Charrette* or the anonymous author of *Lancelot of the Laik*. The prose text forces the knight into the world of the feminine throughout the rejection of father figures and his education in the magical and feminine world of the Lady of the Lake and her fairies. Although the *rejection* of Ban, his real father, is not intentional, the reasons which cause his death might be understood as the first instance leading Lancelot to a more conscientious future rejection of male figures. After the seneschal's treason, the world of Lancelot's father is destroyed:

Li rois Bans voit son chastel ardoir qu'il amoit plus que nul chastel qu'il eüst, car par ce seul chastel estoit s'esperance de recovrer tote sa terre. (13)

[King Ban saw his castle burning, the castle which he loved more than any other, for it was his comfort, and his only hope of recovering all his land. (18)]

The aggressive masculine world of warriors and knights deprives Ban and, implicitly, Lancelot, of their "terre". The ultimate loss of "esperance" is an unequivocal sign of Ban's renunciation of life. The accident from which he dies is just anecdotal. The real cause of his death is the loss of his realm. The king without a kingdom prefers to perish. Therefore, Lancelot's first rejection of the father and the masculine is doubly significant. As William Calin points out, "from birth, the hero of love is associated with women and men are prominent by their absence" (Calin 1994: 146). The masculine knightly world of war kills Ban and forces Lancelot, still a baby, into the realm of the feminine. The hero's fate is bound to the feminine at the same time as father figures will be confronted and repudiated.

In the Scottish *Lancelot*, the reference to Ban is completely different in context and intention. He is simply mentioned as Lancelot's father:

Quharfor thareone I wil me not depend
How he was borne, nore how his fader deid
And ek his moder. (ll.214–16)

The allusion en passant does not help the creation of Lancelot's image as an outsider. This can only be guessed on the basis of the reader/listener's knowledge of the French original.[1] Even his mother's life is ignored: there is no reference to her becoming a nun. She seems to have died at the same time as her husband. The makar methodically deploys the rhetorical figure of *reductio* in the scenes which are not central to his literary and ideological tenets.

In the *Prose Lancelot*, again, when Lancelot is taken by a damsel to the lake (15), which Laurence Harf claims that can also be interpreted as a second birth (Harf 1984: 27), the image of the hero as a stranger to Arthur's chivalric rules begins taking shape. If the father figure is excluded, the mother figure is displaced: the real mother of the feudal/chivalric world is replaced by the Lady of the Lake and the world of magic. The hero is dissociated from both the knightly realm of the father and the presence of the mother to be transported to the kingdom of the *unreal* and magical. Crucially,

[w]hat distinguishes the land lying beneath the appearance of a lake from other lands in the *PL* is not anything strange about the land itself or its inhabitants, but the fact that its lies outside the network of feudal relationships and is free from conflict between rival lords (Kennedy 1986: 117).

This will explain Lancelot's inability to conform to the feudal laws in Arthur's court. Its isolation and links with white magic also confer a mythical character on this mysterious place. The mythical and nonfeudal traits transform the Lake into another womb in which Lancelot's early education will take place. Notwithstanding the Lady of the Lake's willingness to introduce Lancelot to the art of knighthood with the hiring of a master, Lancelot rejects yet another father figure because he does not understand the hero's disinterested sense of *largeza* (45–46). The tension between magic/femininity/

---

[1] Although Lancelot's story was probably known to the audience, the familiarity with the original might not have been so homogeneous. Those who were familiar with the *Prose Lancelot* would have an intertextual reference of the hero as an outsider bereft of patriarchal links, whereas the rest of the listeners would have *read* the story in a different manner. As Joanna Martin remarks, owing to the numerous Scots in France in the fifteenth century, it is quite possible that a printed copy of the *Prose Lancelot* was taken to Scotland or that the author of *Lancelot of the Laik* acquired his own copy in France. (Martin 2002: 171 and 2008: 57–58)

otherness and knighthood/masculinity/centrality will be a recurrent feature in the narrative.

The Scottish text underplays the influence of the Lady of the Lake. The makar insists on not relating how Lancelot "was tak / And nwrist with the Lady of the Lak" (ll.219–20). He relies on the listener's intertextual knowledge once more. As a matter of fact, the only textual evidence of his position as an outsider at Arthur's court is in his name's allusion to the "Laik". Neither is there any reference to the hero's tutor, who is completely ignored.

At this juncture in the French work, Lancelot returns to the maternal womb. He retreats from the masculine realm of knighthood to the Lady of the Lake again. She decides that she will be his instructor in the art of chivalry which presupposes a particular understanding of the matter. Consequently, as pointed out by Elspeth Kennedy, the Lady of the Lake gives her own interpretation of chivalry (142–46): on the one hand, there is the typical emphasis of the knight as the champion of justice and defender of those in need; on the other, the Lady of the Lake does not allude to the relationship between a knight and his lord (Kennedy 1986: 119). Crucially, one of the basic pillars of the feudal society is obviated, anticipating Lancelot's *treason* towards Arthur. The former's role as an alien to Arthur's world is consistently represented. The Lady of the Lake also exhorts the defence of the Church as a knight's main duty. This *locus communis* in medieval manuals of chivalry is of special importance in this context owing to the origin of the Lady of the Lake herself. As a fairy, she would be associated with the pagan world and detached from Christian orthodoxy. Yet, thanks to this affirmation, she joins the Christian faith at the same time as she confirms her attachment to goodness and white magic.

The last rejection of a father figure is that of Arthur, an occurence which is intimately related to the main love interest of the romance. Because Arthur is Lancelot's lord, the betrayal is particularly difficult to handle for the author. He deploys series of narrative strategies to create a very sophisticated plot with situations and characters absent from Chrétien's *Chevalier de la Charrette*. Lancelot becomes Guenevere's knight rather than the King's both as a *fin amant* and according to the rules of knighthood. Hence, the sword used to dub Lancelot as a knight is not that of Arthur but Guenevere's:

"Or les menez, fait li vallez [Lancelot], a la cort monseignor lo roi Artu, si dites a madame la reine que li vallez qui va por lo secors a la dame de Nohaut les li envoie. Et li dites que ge li ment que, por moi gaaigner a tozjorz, que ele me face chevalier, si m'envoit une espee com a celui qui ses chevaliers sera". (174)

["Then, take them", the youth (Lancelot) said, "to the court of my lord king Arthur and tell my lady the queen that the youth who has gone to the Lady of Nohaut sends them to her. Tell her also that I send her word that, to win me to her for ever, she should make me a knight, and send me a sword so that I may be her knight". (92)]

It is Lancelot's initiative to become the Queen's and not the King's knight. The hero's attitude can be interpreted at different allegorical levels. At a political and ethical level, the feudal relationship between lord and vassal will be doubly accomplished in purely contractual terms: he owes vassalage only to his *lord* (it is worth noting that the troubadours' term to refer to the beloved lady, *midons*, originally meant "my lord"). In the world of *fin'amors*, the lord/vassal relation-ship of *fins amants* is axiomatic – the lady plays the role of the feudal lord, whereas the knight is the vassal of both the lady and *Amor*. At the allegorical level, however, Lancelot is not only rejecting Arthur as a father but trying to realise "an oedipal wish-fulfilment fantasy" (Calin 1994: 147), in which he will replace the father figure. It is not only a fantasy of sexual consummation disguised by the idealisation of *fin'amors*, but a dream of power and possession: the landless knight aims to replace the rich king. As Tom Scott defines it,

[*fin'amors*] is a huge elaborate dream of eternal youth in pursuit of the unattainable, a materialist parody of religious life, and at the bottom is the longing of landless adolescent squires and suchlike to possess the power and castles of their overlords. (Scott 1966: 29)

Lancelot, unknowingly, is symbolically claiming what was snatched from him. Arthur's indifference to Ban's request for help deprived Lancelot of land and mother. At another level of interpretation, this rejection of Arthur further develops the image of Lancelot as an outsider. Once again, he disrupts masculine knighthood in favour of his own interpretation of it: his master and initiator in the art of chivalry was the Lady of the Lake, his only *lord* is going to be Guenevere. Lancelot challenges the knights' world and replaces it with the feminine. In *Lancelot of the Laik*, the more schematic adaptation of the relationships between Lancelot and Arthur, and between Lancelot and Guenevere, does not highlight the betrayal so thoroughly. In fact, there is no scene in which Lancelot appears with either the king or the queen. The hero's treason against Arthur can be assumed only in the fact that Lancelot loves the Queen. But the absence of direct interactions between these characters forces the audience to fill the gaps.

If the Middle Scots romance had followed its source closely, it would have concentrated on the hero-lover's progression both as the best knight and as a *fin amant*. The Prologue contains a full range of conventional courtly elements and apparently anticipates the centrality of the love plot. A.C. Spearing comments on the influence of the *Prologue* to *The Legend of Good Women* on this opening. The beginning recreates the typical atmosphere of medieval love poetry:

> The soft morow ande the lustee Aperill,
> The wynter set, the stormys in exill,
> Quhen that the brycht and fresch illumynare
> Uprisith arly in his fyré chare
> His hot courss into the orient,
> And frome his spere his goldine stremis sent
> Wpone the grond, in maner off mesag
> One every thing, to ualkyne thar curage,
> That natur haith set wnder hire mycht,
> Boith gyrss and flour and every lusty uicht,
> And namly thame that felith the assay
> Of lufe, to schew the kandelis of May,
> Throw birdis songe with opine vox one hy
> That sessit not one lufaris for to cry,
> Lest thai forghet, throw slewth of ignorans,
> The old wsage of Lovis observans. (ll.1–16)

The conventional spring setting with the renewal of nature provides the perfect scenario for a presentation and debate on love. The author ingeniously links the regenerative force of nature with "every lusty uicht", who is prone to love. This image is completed by the singing birds, which are central figures in the lyrics of the late Middle Ages. Not only do they stand as messengers of *Amor* but their singing symbolically brings harmony to the poem: "a multidimensional and enclosed space, a *hortus conclusus* of the *chant*, that is the harmony constrained by the harmony called love, of which the bird and the flower are the emblem" (Zumthor 1992: 192). The long introduction to the poem also lays stress on what was supposed to be its main theme: the dichotomy between the pleasures and the sufferings of love (l.14). They will be enunciated in accordance with the conventions of the time: "the old wsage of Lovis observans" (l.16).

This is followed by the narrator's exposition of his sorrowful love until the intervention of a bird, here as an agent of love as personified by the "King of Love" (l.93), reprimands him for his passive and querulous attitude:

> "Ful," quod the bird, "lat be thi nyss dispare,
> For in this erith no lady is so fare,
> So hie estat, nore of so gret empriss
> That in hireself haith uisdome ore gentrice,
> Yf that o wicht, that worthy is to be
> Of Lovis court schew til hir that he
> Servith hire in lovis hartly wyss
> That schall tharfor hyme hating or dispiss.
> The god of Love thus chargit the, at schort,
> That to thi lady yhoue thi wo report". (ll.127–36)

The bird's language situates the poem within the courtly lyric tradition. The attributes bestowed on the lady and her failure to understand the narrator's feelings derive from the late medieval *lai* tradition of Machaut and Froissart, probably mediated by Chaucer. In Machaut's *Remede de Fortune*, for instance, a similar situation takes place. Like the narrator of *Lancelot of the Laik*, the "I" persona of the *Remede* wants to let his beloved know about his love through his literary compositions:

> Et tous les chans que je ditoie,
> A sa loange les faisoie
> En pensant que, s'il avenist
> Que mes chans devant li venist,
> Qu'elle porroit savoir comment
> Je l'aim et sui en son comment.
> Et mes cuers moult s'y deduisoit,
> Quant ma dame a ce me duisoit
> Qu'a sa loange et a s'onnour
> Me faisoit chanter pour s'amour. (ll.413–22)

[And all the songs I sing I wrote them to praise her, thinking that if it happens that she comes across my songs, she may know how much I love her and am her love thrall. And my heart was so full of joy when the lady directed me to do this that her praise and her honour made me sing for her love.]

A lady's demeanour must be dictated by *taciturnitas*, which implies not only the minimum and precise use of speech but also the occultation of her real feelings. All these features transford the lady into an object of mystery and adoration. Nevertheless, it also provokes the customary desperation of the lover (in so far as it was also a literary figure), who is suffering in this situation.

As expressed in the poetry of the troubadours, the lover is at the earliest stage of the way to *fin'amors*: as the *fenhedor*, he is still too timid to show his feelings to his *domna*. Hence, the bird's intervention is crucial in encouraging him to express his love in an artful manner:

"Sum trety schall yhoue for thi lady sak,
That wnkouth is, als tak one hand and mak
Of love ore armys or sum othir thing
That may hir oneto thi remembryng brynge". (ll.145–48)

The passage highlights the narrative axis of the romance: the tension between "love" and "armys". The subject matter and the parts of the French original selected would certainly support this presumption. Yet, the protagonist and narrator of the main story also seems to take on board the final words of the same line "or sum othir thing" as the thematic leitmotif of his poem. As the reader will soon begin to suspect, the *amor et militia* topos will become secondary to something else. This "sum othir thing" is Amytans's instructive lesson on good kingship to Arthur.

Despite the author's insistence on his story being based on "love and armys" (l.200), several elements in the Prologue indicate otherwise. One of these indications, as Walter Scheps remarks, is the fact that the lover-narrator proffers what must be the longest *occupatio* in the medieval literature of the British Isles. For eighty-four lines (215–98), he enumerates all the episodes from the *Prose Lancelot* which he is going to exclude from his narration (Scheps 1967–68: 168). Significantly, one of the episodes the author omits is:

how that he was tak
By love and was iwondit to the stak
And throuch and throuch persit to the hart
That al his tyme he couth it not astart;
For thare of Love he enterit in service
Of Wanore throuch the beuté and franchis, (ll.225–30)

The exclusion of Lancelot falling in love and entering its service relocates the focus of the love story: Lancelot is already a knight in love. The *fin amant's* progression from chivalric deeds to attain the Queen's heart in the *Prose Lancelot* is absent, or rather simply reduced to the war against Galiot. Although at first sight the Scottish delineation of the plot might remind the reader of Chretien's *Le Chevalier de la Charrette*, in which Lancelot's affection for Guenevere is already present in his first appearance, the context of the Scottish Lancelot is arguably different. In the Middle Scots text, the knight has already started his maturing and learning process. At any rate, this progression is assumed rather than described. His feelings are also established and do not evolve: *fin'amors* is present but static.

Furthermore, the French verse *roman* is markedly courtly with the developing love story at the core of its narrative, whilst *Lancelot of the Laik* attaches much more importance to the national/regal components. This instigates a very significant shift from Lancelot's personal enterprise to Arthur's defence of his kingdom. Hence, for most of the narrative it is the British King who becomes the main character of a romance whose title is *Lancelot of the Laik*. In Chrétien's romance, the knight's love not only evolves until consummation, but even after that, the relationship between Lancelot and Guenevere seems more solid and Lancelot much more secure in their love. This is manifest in the way in which he interacts with other women. In an early scene a lady offers shelter to Lancelot in return for his *amors* (ll.940–45), which he courteously but firmly declines leaving no room for courtly games (1.950–53). After the night of love with the Queen passed, he is more inclined to play with the language of *cortesia* even if he has no intention of submitting to another woman. When Maleagant's sister liberates him from prison and provides him with beautiful clothes, he does not hesitate to reply:

"Amie, fet il, seulemant
A Deu et a vos rant merciz
De ce que sains sui et gariz.
Par vos sui de prison estors.
Por ce poez mon cuer, mon cors
Et mon servise et mon avoir
Quant vos pleira prandre et avoir. (ll.6680–86)

["My dear friend, to God and to you alone I give thanks for being healed and healthy. Because you have made possible my escape, I give you my heart, my body, my service, and my possessions to take and keep whenever you wish. (289)][2]

Both Lancelot and the lady know that these are only words of gratitude within the game of *cortesia*. While Lancelot was previously unable to dissociate the language of *fin'amors* from that of *cortesia*, as a mature knight and lover, he can be playfully courteous without being unfaithful to his beloved. The essentially courtly context in which the love plot develops is systematically reduced in the Scottish text. Its reliance on the *Prose Lancelot*, which emphasises military action, already envisaged a more epic milieu. Unlike in Chrétien's text, in the composition of the prose romance, Arthur's defence of his kingdom plays an important role.

In both the *Prose Lancelot* and *Lancelot of the Laik*, the fate of Arthur's kingdom is dependent upon the display of the hero's *proeza* and its interrelation with love. Nevertheless, the disposition of the Scottish romance prevents the love component from becoming central. Even Lancelot's most amorous speeches, such as this one before fighting Galiot's army, connote an interpretation different from that of the original text:

"Bot, hart, sen at yow knaiwth she is here
That of thi lyve and of thi deith is stere,
Now is thi tyme, now help thiself at neid
And the devod of every point of dred
That cowardy be none into the senn;
Fore and yow do, yow knowis thi peyne, I weyn.
Yow art wnable ever to attane
To hir mercy or cum be ony mayne.
Tharfor Y red hir thonk at yow disserve
Or in hir presens lyk o knycht to sterf". (ll.1019–28)

While the *locus communis* of *amor et militia* is taken from the French *Prose Lancelot*, the contextualisation of the Scottish narrative allows for a different set of implications; one in which the epic discourse forces the courtly discourse into the background. Although on a rhetorical level Lancelot's reference to his "hart" presupposes the subordination of the military action to love, the makar transforms the more markedly chivalric milieu of the French text into a new (but

---

[2] I am using William W. Kibler's translation in *Arthurian Romances*.

typically Scottish) re-interpretation. Lancelot's *proeza* and knighthood
are at the service of the liberation of Arthur's realm. There are no
personal knightly *avantures* to glorify the hero's worth on the
battlefield, but, as in the other Older Scots historical and Arthurian
romances, individual ambitions are integrated into a national or
collective enterprise. Within the boundaries of the romance, this will
be the one and only touchstone of Lancelot's recognition as the best
knight and his last step towards Guenevere's heart. The absence of
previous encounters between the two *fins amants* concentrates the
entire love story on this one epic adventure. As the thematic axis of
romance lies in good kingship, the narrative framework minimises the
paramount importance of chivalry and courtesy and makes them
subservient to Arthur's preservation of his kingdom. The result of the
situation could not be more ironic inasmuch as Arthur's victory over
Galiot can occur only if Lancelot intervenes. But the successful
intervention of Lancelot will mean Guenevere's subsequent surrender
to his advances. Consequently, whatever the outcome of the battle
may be, the monarch is going to lose either his kingdom or his wife's
fidelity.

   The evolution of *fin'amors* in the *Prose Lancelot* is strikingly
different from that in *Lancelot of the Laik*. The examination of love in
the French text will help to illuminate the singularity of its treatment
in the Scottish romance. In the French, the hero's devotion to
Guenevere is obvious from the very first instant he sees her:

Maintenant aparçoit bien la reine qu'il est esbahiz et trespansez, mais ele n'osse pas
cuidier que ce soit por li; et neporquant ele lo sospece un po, si an laisse la parole
ester attant. Et por ce qu'ele nel velt en greignor folie metre, ele se lieve de la place.
(158)

[The queen saw that he was troubled and thoughtful, but she did not dare think it was
because of her; none the less she rather suspected it, and said no more for the moment.
And since she did not want to encourage his foolishness, she got up from the couch,
(71)]

Although the scene takes place in the presence of Arthur's courtiers,
none of them is able to interpret the signs, code and careful choice of
the words of *fin'amors*. These people are part of the masculine world
of Arthur's knights. The hero's inability to speak properly is a clear
sign of his falling in love. The only one who does realise is Guinevere.
Her understanding of the symptoms of love functions at two different

levels: symbolically, she is prepared to experience the vicissitudes of *fin'amors*; pragmatically, she proves to be worthy of Lancelot's admiration. She endeavours to divert attention so as not to be discovered. This is another unequivocal sign that she is aware of the conventions; secrecy, following the troubadours' tradition, is vital between the two lovers because of the illicit nature of their relationship:

The poet would often express himself in a deliberately enigmatic style, either because he wished to convey a private message without improperty or fear of scandal […], or because he wished to provide the connoisseur with the pleasure of exegesis. Words in common usage thus acquired a specialised meaning within the context of the troubadour tradition. (Boase 1977: 104)

In their next meeting, Lancelot manages to be more articulate. All his words are of the greatest significance for the love theme:

"Ha! Dame, fait il [Lancelot] en sospirant, vos me pardonroiz avant la folie que ge ai faite."
"Quel folie, fait ele [Guinevere], feïstes vos?"
"Dame, fait il, de ce que ge m'en issi de ceianz sanz prandre congié a vos."
"Biax dolz amis, fait la reine, vos iestes si juenes hom que l'an vos doit bien pardoner un tel mesfait, et gel vos pardoign mout volentiers."
"Dame, fait il, vostre merci. Dame, fait il, se vos plaisoit, ge me tandroie en quel que leu que ge alasse por vostre chevalier."
"Certes, fait ele, ce voil ge mout."
"Dame, fait il, des or m'en irai a vostre congié."
"A Deu, fait ele, biax douz amis."
Et il respont entre ses danz:
"Granz merciz, dame, qant il vos plaist que ge lo soie". (165)

["Ah, my lady," he (Lancelot) said, with a sigh, "first you must forgive me the foolish thing I have done."
"What foolish thing is that?" she (Guenevere) asked.
"My lady," he said, "I left here without taking leave of you."
"My dear friend," said the queen, "you are so young that you should certainly be forgiven such a misdemeanour, and I forgive you gladly."
"My lady," he said, "I thank you. My lady," he went on, "if you please I should like to consider myself your knight, wherever I may be."
"Certainly," she said, "I should like that very much."
"Then, my lady," he said, "I shall go, by your leave."
"Go with God," she said, "dear friend."
He replied under his breath:
"I thank you, my lady, since you are pleased to call me that". (81)]

The polyvalence and ambiguity of language between Lancelot and Guenevere construct a conversation with different levels of meaning in which knighthood, *cortesia* and *fin'amors* intermingle. The author merges the concepts of *chevalier* and *ami* in the hero at the same time as the Queen's *cortesia* reveals her predisposition towards him. Although Lancelot asks to be her knight (which could be understood only in literal terms), her use of "biax dolz amiz" (twice) recalls the language of *fin'amors*, in which the lover is called *ami*. Again, Guenevere's employment of the word "jeunes" is full of courtly reminiscences, going far beyond the fact that he is actually young. The Occitan term *joven* does not exclusively refers to young age, but rather to an inner quality of spontaneous generosity in love. His being *joven* is exculpatory of his self-confessed "folie". In this context, "folie" or *foudatz* in the language of the troubadours functions as an unmistakable allusion to a lover's process of falling in love, in which joy and sadness come together without the *amant* being able to control them. As expressed in this *canso* by Marcabru (c.1130–49):

Amors es mout de mal avi:
mil homes a mortz ses glavi,
Dieus no fetz tant fort gramavi,
 – Escoutatz! –
que tot nesci del plus savi
non fa, si.l ten al latz. ("Dirai vos senes duptansa", ll.37–42)

[Love has terrible forbearers: he has killed one thousand men with his spear. God did not make a more persuasive rhetorician, – Listen! – he transforms the wisest men into a fool, if he traps him with his knot.]

Marcabru expounds the *foudatz* of love for seventy-two lines. He composes his poem by employing a series of similes to show how deceitful the personified *Amors* is and why the *amants* behave in such an insane manner while under the influence of love.

   This anxious state on Lancelot's part is present in both romances: in the *Prose Lancelot*, "the fear associated with great love can be just as important a motive force towards great deeds as is the *grant seürté* which also stems from love" (Kennedy 1986: 54). This distressful state is repeated several times during the narrative when Lancelot is physically separated from the Queen. Following the original, in the Middle Scots text, the author depicts the knight's sorrow with the same idea in mind:

This woful knyght that felith not bot peine
So prekith hyme the smert of loves sore
And every day encressith more and more.
And with this lady takine is also
And kepit whar he may nowhare go
To haunt knychthed, the wich he most desirit. (ll.720–25)

The knight, being so deeply absorbed by his sad love thoughts, is unable to perform any feat of arms at all. Therefore, although the symbiosis between *amor et militia* is perfectly incarnated in the figure of Lancelot, there are some instances in which the balance is lost and the *foudatz* of the *fin amant* reappears. *Foudatz* sporadically keeps him from his duties as a knight.

After many fights and battles, Lancelot must save Arthur's kingdom from Galehot/Galiot – the section on which the Scottish version focuses. The main plot of the romance is linked to Arthur's preservation of his territories both politically and militarily. The courtly dialectics will determine the outcome of the epic plot on which Arthur's victory is totally dependent. Previously Amytans had made clear that the king had to change his policy if he wanted to keep his lands. Indeed the military outcome of the conflict seemed to be subject to Arthur's political skills as put into practice through *cortesia* and *largeza*. Ironically, however, it will be Lancelot's presence rather than Arthur's regenerated policies that will dictate the future of the realm. At this juncture, epic and courtly scenarios must conflate again. The source of Lancelot's *proeza* does not stem from his well-known dexterity as a warrior but from his love for Guenevere:

The Blak Knycht saw the danger of the feld
And al his doingis knowith quho beheld
And ek remembrith into his entent
Of the mesag that sche haith to hyme sent.
Than curag, strenth encresing with manhed,
Ful lyk o knycht oneto the feld he raid,
Thinking to do his ladice love to have,
Or than his deth befor hir to resave. (ll.3165–72)

Lancelot's main reason for fighting has nothing to do with Arthur's cause. As in the first battle, the possibility of attaining Guenevere's love through heroic action is the moving force which feeds his desire to perform chivalric deeds of arms. After the makar has amplified the political components from the French original, the final resolution of the poem places Arthur in a rather vulnerable position in so far as *his* champion regards this battle only as a means to conquer his beloved's heart. In this particular context, then, the romance topos of *amor et militia* functions as a bridge between the epic and the courtly discourses, making the former totally dependent on the latter.

Unfortunately, the last folios of thc Scottish manuscript are lost just before one of the most important scenes in the romance takes place: Galehot/Galiot arranges a meeting between the Queen and Lancelot. According to the narrator's long *occupatio*, we can presume that this scene was the conclusion to the Scottish romance:

And how that Venus, siting hie abuf,
Reuardith hyme of travell into love
And makith hyme his ladice grace to have,
And thankfully his service can resave:
This is the mater quhich I think to tell. (ll.309–13)

In the French prose romance, the first part of the conversation between Lancelot and Guenevere is about revelation, first of *proeza*, then, of *amors*. The feats of the anonymous Red and Black knights are finally attributed to Lancelot in the presence of the queen. Now he is arguably the best knight in the world; consequently, he is in a position to request the favour of the best lady on earth. The second confession, then, will bring together these two themes:

"Or me dites, totes les chevaleries que vos avez faites, por cui les feïstes vos?"
"Dame, fait il, por vos."
"Commant? fait ele, amez me vos tant?"
"Dame, fait il, ge n'ain tant ne moi ne autrui."
"Et des qant, fait ele, m'amez vos tant?"
"Dame, fait il, des lo jor que ge sui apelez chevaliers et si ne l'estoie mie". (345)

["Now, tell me, all the knightly deeds you have done, for whom did you do them?"
"For you, my lad," he said.
"What?" she said, "do you love me so much?"
"My lady," he said, "I do not love myself or anyone else so much."
"And since when," she said, "have you love me so?"
"My lady," he aid, "since the day I was called a knight, but was not one". (317)]

Lancelot's confession renders sublime the *locus communis* of *amor et militia*. According to Franklin P. Sweetser, love is an ennobling emotion which leads the hero to accomplish his glorious destiny (Sweetser

1989: 29). Nevertheless, the knight's declaration does not culminate with Guenevere's straightforward acceptance of Lancelot's love. In what would appear to be at first a playful courtly game, she doubts Lancelot's constancy and fidelity in love. When this last test causes Lancelot to faint, Galehot intervenes in his favour. Although this works against his personal interests, Galehot's attitude is crucial for the two *fins amants* to come together. Galehot's feelings for Lancelot are far beyond simple friendship. He is also in love with Lancelot (Sweetser 1989: 27). Nonetheless, Galehot is not as successful as Guenevere. Owing to Lancelot, he renounces the possibility of con-quering Arthur's kingdom. He finally loses everything and dies. If Guenevere's is the love of fulfilment, that of Galehot is the love of renunciation. At this juncture, the Queen's kiss certifies Lancelot's acceptance in the service of love as a vassal would enter the service of a lord:

"Biaus douz anmis, fait ele au chevalier, ge suis vostre, tant avez fait; et mout an ai grant joie". (348)

["Dear friend," she said to the knight, "I am yours because of what you have done, I am overjoyed about it". (322)]

This would presumably be the end to the Scottish text. In the *Prose Lancelot*, the ultimate *jois* between lovers will occur later after another heroic feat of the greatest magnitude. Lancelot defeats the Saxons who were about to conquer Arthur's territory (544). After that, the Queen and the knight consummate their passion.

The scene, which could (or even should) have been a central epi-sode in the realisation of *fin'amors*, is hardly developed. Although the author sets the meeting of the lovers in a garden, the *locus amoenus* is not described at all. This does not accord with late medieval literary conventions: as Spearing states,   .

the *locus amoenus* or "beautiful place", which became the heavenly landscape of lit-erary visions and dreams, is basically a Mediterranean landscape, an ideal originating in Greece, Italy, and Palestine. It is typically set in bright southern sunlight (perhaps augmented by or transformed into jewelled brilliance of the Apocalypse), but it also provides shade against the sun, and is therefore furnished with a tree or trees, often fruit-trees. The trees will be in a flowery meadow, which will provide fragrance as well as bright colours, and there will probably be birds singing in them. (Spearing 1976: 17)

In the *Prose Lancelot*, consummation lacks the imaginative narrative of Chrétien's version of the night of love in *Le Chevalier de la Charrette*:

Quant li dui [Lancelot and Galehot] furent desarmé, si furent mené en deus chanbres et jut chascuns avoc s'amie, que mout s'antramoient, et orent totes joies que amant puent avoir. (547)

[When the two knights (Lancelot and Galehot) were disarmed, they were led into two chambers, and each lay with his ladylove, for they love one another dearly, and they had all the joys that lovers can have. (380)]

The scene underplays consummation. Even more striking is the exclusion of any courtly conversation between the lovers. The narrator seems to imply that the hero's adulterous relationship with the Queen may have worked against his image as the best Christian knight. His being driven by passion towards a married woman could be interpreted as lack of *mesura* led by sexual desire (*amor mixtus* or *luxuria*). As a member of the Round Table, he also appears to break one of the pillars of the knightly code, the personal pledge of loyalty to Arthur and the fellowship with all the members, a reproachable act of *desfi*. For these two reasons, the author endeavours to construct a narrative which minimises the moral and social impact of both transgressions.

Although Lancelot is always characterised as the perfect knight whose feelings for Guenevere are guided by *franchise*, his sin against the holy sacrament of marriage is lessened by Arthur's image as a bad husband. The author strategically places the King's meeting with the Saxon lady just before the lovers' consummation. The Saxon lady betrays him and Arthur ends up in prison (546). He lacks an important courtly/knightly virtue, that of *conoissensa*, "the power of discrimination, specially the ability of distinguishing the good from the bad, the true from false, the real from the illusory" (Topsfield 1981: 314). This idea will be reinforced when the king is willing to accept the false Guenevere and wants to crown her:

"Certes, fait il, il [Arthur] est en Camelide entre lui et madame la reine [the false one], et si vos [Gawain] mande, per la foi que vos li devez qui ses hom liges iestes et ses niés, que vos veigniez a lui et que vos li menez toz les barons del reiaume de Logres, car il portera corone a cest Noel en la terre ma dame et tandra cort mout efforciee". (594–95)

["Certainly, he said, Arthur is with the queen (the false one) in Camelide, and if it is your (Gawain's) wish, for your loyalty towards him as his liegeman and nephew, you came for him and you can lead all the barons of the kingdom of Logres, since he will make my lady queen of the land this Christmas and will have a very important court."]

Although under the influence of a potion, Arthur's symbolic blindness as a husband is implied in all these instances. Lancelot as a true lover deserves Guenevere's love. The other great problem of the relationship between the two *fins amants* is Lancelot's hypothetical breaking of the knightly code by betraying his lord. Yet, as mentioned earlier in this section, this is more or less satisfactorily solved by making Lancelot the Queen's and not the King's knight.

    Notwithstanding all this, the author does not seem to feel comfortable when developing the consummation scene. Interestingly, the author confronts a similar moral problem vis-à-vis the sacredness of matrimony to that faced by Chrétien in his *Chevalier de la Charrette*. Martí de Riquer claims that:

Chrétien, gran defensor tostemps del vincle matrimonial, com palesen els conflictes entre les parelles Erec-Enida i Ivany-Laudina, i que havia lluitat amb totes les forces contra el *Tristany*, on el sacrament era sollat, ara es veu obligat per la seva senyora a escriure una novel·la el tema principal de la qual són els amors adulterins d'un cavaller, Lancelot, amb la reina Ginebra, esposa del rei Artús. (Riquer ed. 1990: 16)

[Chrétien had always been a great defender of the matrimonial bond as shown by the conflicts between the couples Erec-Enida and Ivan-Laudina. He had also fought against *Tristan*. But now he was forced by his lady to write a romance in which the main theme was the adulterous love between a knight, Lancelot, and Queen Guenevere, King Arthur's wife.]

Chrétien, however, resolves the moral tension is a very sophisticated and artful manner. If the reader considers that as soon as Lancelot accepts to get into the cart, as this is the only way to discover where Guenevere might be, the narrative line becomes polysemous, the culmination of Lancelot and Guenevere's *fin'amors* acquires significance far beyond the sexual union. Lancelot becomes a particular Christ-like figure as Chrétien narrates Christ's story backwards from resurrection to annunciation. In this way, through the adulterous relationship of Lancelot of Guenevere, the author is criticising Lancelot's sacrilegious idolatry of the Queen (Robertson 1963: 451–52). Chrétien appears to challenge the troubadour's claims that the ultimate consummation of *fin'amors* beyond orgasm is a mystical and spiritual fulfilment; that is, *lo miels*, "the ultimate happiness; the furthest limit of *jois*" (Topsfield 1984: 315). Yet, owing to the rich symbolism of Chrétien's narrative, other scholars such as C.S. Lewis have argued that the religious images in the consummation scene highlight Lancelot's true devotion and perfect obedience to Guevenere (Lewis 1988: 29).

Lancelot of the Laik reduces the love plot and the characterisation of Lancelot himself. Following the literary elements shared with most Scottish romances, the makar opts to concentrate on the martial aspects of knighthood and expresses his concern with good kingship (as seen in previous chapters) rather than to elaborate on a predominantly courtly story. As opposed to Chrétien and the *Prose Lancelot*, some of the most important scenes of the *fin'amors* plot are briefly alluded to or not even mentioned. *Fin'amors* is not an evolving journey to the perfection of *amors* (perfection should be understood here as the final communion of spiritual and physical desire for the lover in the context of *fin'amors*, not as religious *caritas*), but a static state of the soul. The makar assumes the extradiegetic knowledge of the story in the audience to fill the missing gaps. For the rest of the listeners, *Lancelot of the Laik* will have a meaning of its own. As a result, the author composes a very distinct romance: while the relationship between Lancelot and Guenevere is enormously reduced, the didactic lesson of Amytans to Arthur is underlined. Arthur, whose appreciation of good government develops and changes, becomes the main character.

Golagros and Gawane and *The First Continuation*: knighthood questioned, Gawain regenerated

Golagros and Gawane thoroughly revises knighthood both as a practical concept and as an ideal. This is especially noticeable when compared to its source, the *First Continuation* of Chrétien de Troyes' *Perceval*. Through a disenchanted representation of knightly practices, the makar questions the validity of a knight's life and code when placed at the service of dubious enterprises. He also redefines Gawain's role: while the contrast between Kay's *vilania* and Gawain's *cortesia* is maintained and accentuated, the passages where Gawain's seductive charms might be questionable are simply obliterated from the narrative.

As soon as Arthur and his knights return to Golagros's domains, the British king's imperialistic ambitions lead to martial conflict. The narration of these single or small group combats reveals the cruellest and most realistic side of war. As Paul Ketrick points out, although in medieval epic and romance there was a tendency to merge the celebration of tournaments and actual warfare, in *Golagros and Gawane* the author's intention to revert to realistic battle scenes is apparent (Ketrick 1931: 108). This *realism* imposes a definite meaning on the text. Arthur and his knights are no longer representing chivalric aspirations in which the audience should find a mirror of behaviour. On the contrary, the narrator constructs a powerful set of scenes where he mistrusts the gratuitous use of violence, whose consequences can only bring about death and destruction:

Thus thai faught upone fold, with ane fel fair,
Quhill athir berne in that breth bokit in blude.
Thus thai mellit on mold, ane myle way and maire,
Wraithly wroht, as thei war witlese and wode. (ll.570–73)

Arthur forces his knights into the devastating effects of fighting. The makar places emphasis on the cruelty of the confrontation. The knights, valiant though they are ("slithly thai stude", ll.574), are represented as engaging in a fatal duel. Chivalric ideals are absent from these scenes. Jousting is not a celebration of courtly refinement as in the *First Continuation*, but the obnoxious result of the monarch's thirst for more earthly power and glory. The chivalric idealism of order and heroism is replaced by chaos and woe. It is not the archetypal fight between good and evil, heroes and villains; there are only winners and losers.

This becomes even more obvious when the original *First Continuation* and the Middle Scots romance are closely compared. As Ketrick notes, in the French, the jousts between Arthur's and the Riche Soudoyer's knights conducted in accordance according to the laws of chivalry (Ketrick 1931: 108–109); whereas in *Golagros and Gawane*, these passages are either devoid of any chivalric flair or just removed from the narrative. In the original, courtly conventions after violent but sportive confrontation peremptorily deny any disapprobation of knightly customs. After Bran de Lis defeats his opponent,

En grant joie sunt puis le jour.
Quant vint le soir vers la froidour,
Si alerent trestout jouer.
Molt par faisoit bel escouter
Les gaites des tors qui cornoient,
En pluisors sens se deduisoient.
Ainc Dex cel estrument ne fist
C'a mestier de gaite avenist,
Que laiens n'oïsiés souner.
Lors oïsiés les uns hüer,
Et li autre s'entredisoient
De bon gas, car trop en savoient. (ll.5665–76)

[It was very cheerful for the rest of the day. When the cold evening came, they all went to have some rest. It was very agreeable to listen to the watchmen blowing the horn on the towers, having a nice time in many different manners. All the instruments useful to the watchman, which God created, blared in the castle. It was easy to understand why some people laugh, and others exchange good jokes, because they knew them quite well.]

Victory at the lists is rewarded with joy and feasting. Music and the different ways in which the knights celebrate Bran de Lis's success compensate for the harshness of real battle. This dialectic makes the reader forget about the violence of the fight. The chivalric ideal is underlined; and, therefore, the glory of military enterprise is magnified. The end justifies and minimises any previous sufferings. The moral concern of the Scottish romance, which is absent from these jousting passages, shows the different focus of the two narratives. The *First Continuation*, then, would be framed within "the literature which retailed these traditional stories [and] underpinned the values of chivalry by providing them with a faultlessly antique and highly evocative pedigree" (Keen 1984: 102).

Similarly, the *First Continuation* embellishes the jousting with all the paraphernalia and stereotyped canons of the courtly norm. Although Arthur and his men are aware of the seriousness of *avanture* (they headed for the *Chastel Orgueilleux* to set Gyflet Fils Do free), the emphasis on pleasure and enjoyment gives it the quality more of a courtly excursion than of a military campaign:

Molt par fu la vile estormie.
Cil qui avoit la signorie
Vint parmi les rues pognant,
Aprés lui i vient de gent tant

Que bien les oïrent movoir
Cil del pavellon sans veoir.
Tresc'a la porte le convoient,
Ne sonent mot cil quil convoient.
Covert entresc'a l'esperon
De samit et de siglaton,
Grant aleüre s'en ist fors,
Le rice gonfanon destors.
Lors veïsiés as murs monter
Si grant puple por esgarder,
Par tot le castel environ,
Que n'estoit se mervelle non. (ll.6207–22)

[Great bustle reigns in the city. The lord of the place goes along the streets, spurring on his saddle. He was followed by such crowd that those in the pavilion understood he was passing by, even if they could not see anything. The people accompany him up to the gate without saying a single word. Covered with two rich silk cloths up to his spurs, he leaves the city at top speed, with the gonfanon unfolded. You should have seen the multitude climbing the walls all around the castle to have a good look. It was wonderful.]

The confrontation between Gawain and the Riche Soudoyer is recreated against a social backdrop, following the ritualistic proceedings of chivalry. Many people have gone there for enjoyment only. Their tension and expectation enhance the social as much as the festive nature of jousting. The narrator also takes pleasure in informing the audience about the richness of the Riche Soudoyer's attire. The fight itself becomes the central happening in a series of idealised descriptions designed as a perfect projection of chivalric behaviour.

By way of contrast, in *Golagros and Gawane*, the makar suppresses the colourfulness of his source. The result is a completely different narrative, the dialectics of which challenge the knightly practices epitomised in the *First Continuation* as exemplified in the fight between Sir Ranald and Sir Regal of Rone:

Thus thai faucht on fute, on the fair feild.
The blude famyt thame fra, on feild quhare thai found;
All the bernys on the bent about that beheild,
For pure sorow of that sight thai sighit unsound.
Schire teris schot fra schalkis, schene undir scheild,
Quhen thai foundrit and fel fey to the grund;
Baith thair hartis can brist braithly, but beild.
Thair wes na stalwart unstonait, so sterne wes the stound!
Schir Rannaldis body wes broght to the bright tent;

Syne to the castel of stone
Thai had Schir Regal of Rone;
With mekil murnyng and mone
Away with him went. (ll.635–47)

Heroism and the pomp of chivalry have nothing to do with these two knights' ineffectual deaths. Even if the beginning of the confrontation still captures the dignifying aspects of knighthood – "Thai lufly ledis belife lightit on the land, / And laught out swerdis, lufly and lang" (ll.622–23) – the author emphasises the realism of warfare rather than the artificiality of knightly language. This deliberate alteration subverts the idealism of the *First Continuation* and cast doubt on the legitimacy of violence in late medieval Europe. While the public of the original stands to witness a joust according to the established codes, the spectators in the Scottish version are the other warriors in the field. The makar defamiliarises the gaming and sociability of feigned battling. Dissociation is central to the text's discourse of anti-imperialistic denunciation. The constant references to blood (in the fight between Gaudifier and Galiot, the same atmosphere of terror devoid of chivalry prevails: "Thus thai faught upone fold, with ane fel fair, / Quhill athir berne in that breth bokit in blude" (ll.570–71)) and the inglorious death of both adversaries undermine the very principles of chivalry and heroic death.

Although this disenchanted portrayal of knightly life is not present in the parallel passage of the *First Continuation*, Chrétien's masterfulness in integrating heteroglossic discourses in his text reveals a similar approach to some forms of chivalry. In the *Conte du Graal*, Chrétien writes:

Percevax, ce conte l'estoire,
A si perdue la memoire
Que de Deu ne li sovient mais.
.V. foiz passa avris et mais,
Ce sunt .V. anz trestuit antier,
Ainz que il entrast en mostier,
Ne Deu ne sa croiz n'aora.
A requerre chevalerie,
Que les estranges aventures,
Les felonesses et les dures
Aloit querant, […] (ll.6143–53)

[Perceval, the story relates, had lost his memory so totally that he no longer remembered God. April and May passed five times – without him having entered a church or adored God or His Cross. Five years he remained like this, yet in spite of everything he never ceased to pursue deeds of chivalry: he sought out the most difficult, treacherous and unusual adventures. (457)]

Two essential points are made: first, Perceval, the knight elected to seek the Grail, has forgotten about God. Thus he has left aside the highest goal of chivalry, defending God and the Holy Church. Secondly, arbitrariness and knightly deeds for their own sake rather than a meaningful *avanture* lead the hero's behaviour. In the *Conte du Graal*, there are various instances of this implicit critique of meaningless chivalry, which may have been the inspiration either directly or indirectly of the Scottish poet.

Thus, although Thomas Hahn claims that in *Golagros and Gawane* violence is not detached from the courtly code (Hahn ed. 1995: 230), the arguments put forward accord better with Elizabeth Walsh's affirmation that

this fifteenth-century story challenges many of the assumptions of medieval society and culture. It also reflects some of the preoccupations of the Scottish people. In a world that took warfare for granted, the poem speaks for peace; in a world which glorified the bonds between vassal and lord, the poem speaks for freedom (Walsh 1989: 92).

The makar removes most of the linguistic ornamentation which disguises war as a knightly and gallant game to expound its reality and outcome.

The final resolution of the romance emphasises the absurdity of the confrontation even further. As well as my suggestion in Chapter 2 that Arthur experiences a partial (but not complete) learning process, the King of Britain's renunciation of Golagros's sworn fealty also poses an extra question concerning the legitimacy and usefulness of war. Golagros's territory and his subjects regain freedom. The situation returns to the existing one prior to Arthur's invasion. Therefore, like Sir David Lindsay in *Squyer Meldrum*, placing himself in a moralistic or even humanistic position, the makar implicitly questions what the point of so many wasted lives is, should the situation remain the same. The end forces Arthur and his *pax arturica* into an unsustainable position. War and subjugation of smaller free lands is not the way to peace and order but to chaos and destruction.

By the end of the narrative, the reference to late medieval Scotland becomes strong once again.

As for *cortesia*, the poem maintains the same contrast between Gawain and Kay already present in the *First Continuation*. In one of the first scenes, Kay offers to ask for some victuals in a nearby castle. His hunger augments his habitual rusticity: instead of doing his duty by asking for shelter and food, he takes a roasted bird from a dwarf and eats it (ll.79–83). "Than dynnyt the duergh, in anger and yre" (l.84). His behaviour could not be worse for a knight: not only does he steal and display bad manners but he also takes advantage of his physical superiority towards an inferior, who can do nothing to defend himself.

The characterisation of Kay is the Middle Scots romance is even more negative than in the French original, in which the dwarf does not show a very welcoming attitude to Kay: "Droit vers lui se traist Qex avant, / Et li nains li fist mal samblant" [Kay approaches him without hesitation, and the dwarf acts in an unpleasant manner] (ll.3683–84). Moreover, when Kay asks him to give him the bird, the dwarf defies Kay in an impertinent way:

"Ja Damredex ne li aït
Qui en boce le vos metra;
Miudres de vos le mangera.
De ci vos en lo a ader,
Ou ja vos en ferai aler
Tresc'a peu molt vilainement". (ll.3698–703)

["May God not help that who put it [the bird] in your mouth. Someone better than you should eat it. I'd recommend you to leave, otherwise I'll make you skedaddle shortly."]

The exclusion of these defiant words from *Golagros and Gawane* intensifies Kay's *vilania* even more. Uncourtliness and obnoxious abuse can only result in dishonourable expulsion from someone's household. By way of contrast, as Jack notes, Gawain's conduct is always fair and sometimes even charitable (Jack 1974–75: 7). His gentle and courteous demeanour is rewarded by the castle's lord, who kindly offers shelter to Arthur's party (ll.149–52). The subtle difference between both works highlights Gawain's *cortesia*, in particular, and his image as an ideal hero, in general, even more patently.

His sense of *cortesia* is tested again when Golagros asks him to feign defeat for his own sake and that of his vassals. Golagros's preference of death to dishonour deeply moves Gawain: "The sege that schrenkis for na schame, the schent might hym schend, / That mare luffis his life than lois upon erd" (ll.1077–78). Gawain's subsequent question intermingles his courtly conduct together with a deep humane feeling: "How may I succour the sound, semely in sale, / Before this pepill in plane, and pair noght thy pris?" (ll.1092–93). His acceptance of Golagros's strange and dangerous petition to accompany him to his castle faking defeat goes beyond standard *cortesia*. Jack suggests that such an attitude is grounded on spiritual concerns and operates as an illustration of genuine mercy (Jack 1974–75: 16). Therefore, in the Scottish text, Gawain's courtly and knightly behaviour is never questioned. Gawain emerges as the incarnation of the perfect knight. as in most late medieval romances written in the British Isles: in Middle English romances such as *Sir Gawain and the Green Knight*, *The Wedding of Sir Gawain and Dame Ragnell* and *The Awntyrs off Arthure*, Gawain is portrayed as the main hero.

In the *First Continuation*, this scene is slightly but significantly different. The motives expounded by the Riche Soudoyer preferring death to surrender situate the work in a distinctively courtly context:

Et quant ç'avint que il parla,
Si crïa: "Dex! qui m'ocirra?"
Puis dist: "Elle est morte et fenie,
Si ne me caut mais qui m'ocie."
[…]
"Ele est morte a estros,
Par foi, del monde la mellor.
Trop l'amoie de grant amor". (ll.6307–10; 6316–18)

[When he spoke finally, it was to shout: "God! Who will kill me?" Then he added: "She is very dead. Consequently I do not care who will kill me." […] "She is dead, unquestionably, the most perfect woman in the world. I feel this great love for her."]

The political and feudal concerns of *Golagros and Gawane* are not present in the original text. The defeat of her beloved will bring about the damsel's death (ll.6375–78). *Fin'amors* and the feminine, which are totally alien to the Scottish version, stand as essential aspects of the *First Continuation*. As Walsh points out, the courtly love motif is central to the passage of the *Chastel Orgueilleux*. Conversely, the makar reinterprets the original to create a romance in which war for its own sake in late medieval societies is questioned (Walsh 1989: 94).

Nevertheless, the reasons for the suppression of *fin'amors* in *Golagros and Gawane* are not exclusively political. The other *fin'amors* – or rather simply *amors* – scene obliterated in the Scottish text elucidates a different sort of motivation. In the French romance, this section stands between the two episodes used in the Scottish text. But the makar opts not to use it. In the *First Continuation*, Gawain has to face a set of accusations, from which at least one is totally true:

"Gavains, traïtres, n'en irois.
La mort mon pere comparrois,
Et mon oncle c'avés ocis.
Le pucelage ravés pris
De ma seror c'ui main trovastes;" (ll.4339–43)

["Gawain, traitor, you are not going to escape. You are going to pay for the death of my father and that of my uncle. Moreover, you deflowered my sister whom you have met this morning."]

Although Gawain might claim that the deaths of Bran de Lis' father and uncle occurred as a consequence of fair fight (ll.4385–97), the deflowering of the damsel cannot be denied. Despite Arthur's mediation, Gawain or the king's arguments cannot convince Bran de Lis. Not until the lady appears with a child, does the combat stop:

"Biaus ciers fius, alés orendroit
A monsignor Bran de Lis droit;
C'est vostre oncles, je sui sa suer.
Biaus fius, ne vivroie a nul fuer
S'il ocioit ne faisoit mat
Vostre pere a cui se conbat."
[…]
[the child] Puis dist : "Sire, ce dist ma mere
Que vos n'ociés pas mon pere". (ll.4923–28; 4937–38)

["My beloved son, go to Sir Bran of Lis straight away. He is your uncle, I am his sister. My son, there is no chance that I would survive it if he killed or defeated your father against whom he fights." […] [the child] then said: "Sir, my mother asks you not to kill my father."]

This revelation ends the fight. Gawain's image as a perfect knight suffers from such a shocking disclosure. Previously, the seduction scene of the Damoisele de Lis is presented as an irrelevant "geus d'amors" (l.1700), where Gawain displays his courtly and seductive manners. When he promises to return for her, it is never clear whether he is telling her what he is supposed to say according to the norms of *cortesia* or whether he really means it. The fact that the damsel tells the story to her family reveals that she was not sure about Gawain's promise either. The sudden appearance of the child and its implications redefine the context of the seduction and make the audience question Gawain's excessively *courtly* behaviour.

Gawain cannot be the incarnation of the perfect knight. He is moving dangerously into the domain of *luxuria* (aiming at the consummation of sexual desire without the spiritual fulfilment of *fin'amors*), which also connotes a lack of *mesura*. Gawain even acknowledges his fault:

"Vos deveriés plus bel parler,
Car tos sui pres de l'amender,
S'ainc vos fis honte ne damage
Ne d'ami ne de pucelage,
Au los de trestos vos amis.
Por que n'i perde honeur ne pris
Ne mi ami n'i aient honte;" (ll.1831–37)

["You should speak more politely because if I have ever inflicted an affront on you or caused you any wrong, regarding a relative or your virginity, I am completely willing to make reparation, with the consent of all your friends, so that my honour and my reputation may not be tainted or my friends may not be subjected to disgrace."]

Jean Frappier claims that Gawain's words confirm that the knight would be prepared to take on himself all the shame for what had happened to save the lady's honour. The seducer becomes the gentleman. It all responds to the refinement of courtesy and generosity (Frappier 1957–58: 339). Nevertheless, his own reputation and not that of the damsel seems to be the reason why he is disposed to redress his previous act. He refers to *his* "honeur" and "pris", two essential knightly virtues, which are at stake. The lady and her reputation are never suggested to be in the knight's mind. At a time when the legend of the Grail was becoming increasingly more religious than in Chrétien's *Conte du Graal*, the author of the *First Continuation* alerts the reader/hearer to the real perils and possible consequences of courtly games.

This suggests a second reason why the author of *Golagros and Gawane* suppresses this passage. While the *amors* episode was irrelevant owing to the martial and political focus of romance, its inclusion would have damaged Gawain's representation as a perfect knight. The makar could not allow his main hero to undergo such a devastating criticism. Moreover, the long narrative of the French text permits the author to regenerate Gawain; whereas the Middle Scots work, as a comparatively short romance, could not have possibly devoted too many lines to question and then redeem Gawain.

Constance Kelly concludes that:

> The plot, and in many cases the actual phrasing of *Golagros* were undeniably derived from the *Perceval*. The themes, characterisation, imagery, style and vocabulary here, however, belong wholly to the alliterative school. (Kelly 1975: 247).

Although her affirmation is correct, some refinements should be made. Thematically and politically, while the *First Continuation* offers a suitable story line for the Middle Scots romance, the latter's addition and suppression of central elements demonstrate how the text serves divergent literary and ideological purposes. As for Kelly's second assertion, although the poem does pertain to the "alliterative school", it is also true that the Scottish element, as opposed to the Northern English element, is palpable. As suggested in Chapter 1, the Scottish context imposed a different composition in which the image of Arthur is more deeply criticised and his idea of kingship more thoroughly questioned. As for *fin'amors*, the makar's motives in suppressing the love plot are based, first, on his martial and political discourse following the Scottish tradition and, second, on the necessity to preserve Gawain as a virtuous hero at all times.

Chapter Five

The Alexander and Charlemagne Romances

The historical figures of Alexander and Charlemagne became the main heroes of medieval epic and romance. The historical distance between the lives of both military leaders and the period in which the narratives were composed allow for less restrictive treatment of the subject matter than more contemporary figures may have received. Although the two surviving Alexander romances in Middle Scots were written in the mid-fifteenth century, their respective approach to the subject matter is very different. The anonymous *Buik of Alexander* (c.1438) is a close translation of two episodes from the Old French *Roman d'Alexandre* and Jean de Longuyon's *Voeux du Paon*. The Scottish text emphasises the tensions between epic and romance discourses. Around 1460, Gilbert Hay is supposed to have written *The Buik of King Alexander the Conquerour*, a cumulative romance, summarising the life of Alexander. Although the display of *cortesia* is not as profuse as in the French Alexander romances, there is a greater degree of elaboration of courtly manners and conduct than in most Older Scots romances. The use of the supernatural, typical of late medieval texts dealing with the East, but uncharacteristic of the Scottish romances, makes this narrative unique in the Scottish context. Finally, *The Taill of Rauf Coilyear*, composed around 1470, although not directly reliant on a French source, belongs to the Matter of France. However, the makar takes a different outlook from most French Charlemagne epics and English Charlemagne romances. A comic tone dominates the first half of the text whereas the author only reverts to the seriousness of the fight against the heathen in the second part of the romance.

The tension between epic and romance in *The Buik of Alexander*

Although the *Foray de Gadres* and Jean de Longuyon's *Voeux du Paon* (1312) often appeared together in the same manuscripts as different parts of the vast *Roman d'Alexandre* (Richie ed. 1921–9: II.

vii–viii), the Scottish translator decides to put them together to
provide the *Buik of Alexander* with a new meaning. He creates mirror
narratives and characters which offer divergent approaches to the
world of knighthood. In the *Forray*, the makar emphasises the epic
aspects traditionally associated with *chansons de geste* even more so
than in the original. Revenge, honour, loyalty, bravery without measure, and exclusively male protagonists dominate the narrative.
Conversely, in the *Avowis*, the appearance of Cassamus, a figure
without a counterpart in the *Forray*, is crucial for the development of
the newly romance-based plot. He mediates between the epic thirst of
his nephews and that of his enemies to promote a set of knightly
values typical of chivalric romances. The presence of female
characters and the heroes' courtly vows also contribute to the
establishment of a romance mood. As argued in the Introduction, I am
not suggesting a clear-cut or structuralist definition of romance.
Indeed, the epic and romance modes influenced each other greatly, to
the extent that what would be labelled as a *chanson de geste* in French
was translated into the form of romance in English. Even so, the
disposition of the narrative in the *Buik* reveals how late medieval
writers and audiences differentiated motifs more clearly associated
with epic narratives from motifs more typical of courtly texts. By the
end of the romance, after the death of Cassamus, Alexander designs a
more distinctively political discourse by the arrangement of marriages,
guaranteeing his victory and peace between his new vassals.

  In the *Forray*, the epic atmosphere, already existing in the French
original, is present from the very beginning. During the siege of Tyre,
Alexander himself is constructed as a ruthless military leader whose
demeanour is very different from that of a courtly knight:

The King thair grit defence has sene,
And maid ane aith in propir tene
That nane that was in that Cittie,
That micht be takin, sould sauit be; (*Forray*, 23–26)

Alexander's pitiless wish could easily remind the reader of Arthur's
attitude in *Golagros and Gawane* when he first sees Golagros's castle.
Yet the context is completely different. Arthur's enterprise is to go on
a crusade to expiate his sins. He replaces his spiritual goal by his
desire for power. Conversely, the *Forray* is devoid of religious
aspects. Alexander's mission and, more importantly, destiny is to

conquer the known world. His set of values differs from courtly idealism. He operates according to the much harsher rules of the battlefield. Annihilating the enemy might sound excessively cruel; yet this is what a total victory requires. The first lines of the *Forray* situate the text within the parameters of the *chanson de geste* rather than those of chivalric romance.

The *chanson* tone is rapidly enhanced by Emenidus, one of Alexander's generals. On seeing how heroically the Arabs are defending the city, he wants revenge. The use of the word in this particular context might read a little bit odd as the Greeks are the actual invaders. Nonetheless, it anticipates and consolidates one of the most recurrent themes in the *Forray*. It is not accidental that revenge is one of the most common motifs in *chansons*. Indeed, vengeance becomes the primary force, unleashing the quick succession of events in the narrative. Both Greeks and Arabs are induced into action by their desire for revenge on the adversaries. In a feudal world in which the link between men was based upon the sworn word, revenge was an inevitable component of their lives.

A long sequence of revengeful acts illustrates the character of the text and the idiosyncrasy of the protagonists. A good example of this is the series of killings involving Emenidus and Gadifer. First, Pirrus, Emenidus's nephew, kills Gadifer's nephew (*Forray*, 1455–63). In response, Gadifer full of ire takes revenge on Pirrus (*Forray*, 1485–92). Finally, Emenidus kills Gadifer (*Forray*, 3181–217). In the eminently epic world of the *Forray*, there is no space for truce, forgiveness or taking of prisoners. Death of a comrade-at-arms demands an immediate response. In the meantime, however, Gadifer is repeatedly praised for his courtly and knightly attributes even by Alexander (*Forray*, 3019–68), who refutes Ptolemy's disdain for the enemy. The *encomium* of Gadifer anticipates the confrontation and reconciliation between Alexander and Gadifer's family which will be negotiated in the courtly scenario of the *Avowis*.

The thirst for vengeance figures together with a desire to fight beyond recommendable chivalric *mesura*. Death on the battlefield is preferred not only to surrender but also to any sign of weakness. In the traditional interpretation of the earliest preserved *chanson de geste*, the *Chanson de Roland* (c.1100), the main hero shows the same commitment to heroic action out of measure to the extent of sacrificing his life and those of his men in the name of honour and heroism:

Dist Oliver: "Paien unt grant esforz;
De noz Franceis m'i semble aveir mult poi.
Cumpaign Rollant, kar sunez vostre corn,
Si l'orrat Carles, si returnerat l'ost."
Respunt Rollant : "Jo fereie que fols!
En dulce France en perdreie mun los". (83, ll.1049–54)

[Oliver said; "There is a huge army of pagans, / But mighty few of our Franks, it
seems to me. / Companion Roland, blow your horn; / Charles will hear it and the army
will turn back." / Roland replies: "That would be an act of folly; / Throughout the fair
land of France I should lose my good name. (62)][1]

According to that traditional view, this is the first of many instances in
which the more reasonable Oliver suggests Roland blowing his horn.
The French army is heavily outnumbered. Had he followed Oliver's
wise advice, many lives would have been saved, including his own
and that of Oliver. As he equals asking for help with great shame and
dishonour, it is not until he has killed many Saracens and is about to
perish that Roland finally blows his horn. Nevertheless, more recent
approaches suggest a completely different interpretation of both
Oliver's and Roland's roles. Robert F. Cook proposes that Roland is
simply carrying out the duty towards Charlemagne. His oath of loyalty
binds him to fight and, if necessary, die for his king. In this way, the
Song of Roland idealises the feudal world and its mechanisms at the
time of their progressive consolidation (Cook 1987: 220–21).

Following the conventions of *chansons de geste*, a number of
analogous situations take place in the *Forray*. Betys' army is much
larger than the Greek troops led by Emenidus: "That [the Arabs] ma
than .XXX. thousand wair, / And thai [the Greeks] bot seuin
houndreth" (*Forray*, 901–2). In seeing his men in such a dis-
advantageous position, Emenidus repeatedly asks some of the most
heroic characters in his army to tell Alexander about it so he can come
to the rescue. Following the French original quite closely, in about
four hundred lines, Emenidus gets the practically same answer from
all his soldiers:

"My haubrek salbe first to-rent,
And my helme also hewin be
In seir places, that men may se,
My sword richt in my hand bludy,

---

[1] For the *Chanson de Roland*, I am using Glyn Burgess's translation.

And I als woundit in the body
In sindrie places, or I ma
This message that ʒe carp of sa!
The King sall neuer haue na cause to say,
Na ʒit shir Ptolemere, perfay,
That I fled him for cowardise!" (*Forray*. 404–13)

These are Arreste's words but could have been uttered by any other
Greek knight insofar as the author deploys the same epic pattern in the
construction of all the replies for the increasingly desperate Emenidus.
All the warriors prefer a glorious death on the battlefield or else being
fatally injured before abandoning their comrades-at-arms even if the
reason is as good as demanding speedy assistance from their monarch.
Such an attitude accords with the two aforementioned interpretations
of the *Chanson de Roland*. In the traditional one, fear of dishonour
and of being regarded as a coward is much stronger than the threat of
death. The world of epic poetry prioritises masculine knightly virtues.
Inasmuch as male identity is defined according to such attributes,
there is an implicit apprehension about emasculation. In this example,
Arreste would not want Alexander or Ptolemy to brand him as a
coward; that is, as a failed knight, and by implication an incomplete
man. These heroes lack the knightly *mesura* Bruce deploys in the
battle of Methven in Book III of *The Bruce*, when he thinks it is much
wiser to retreat than to fight a battle which he is going to lose.
Interestingly, Cook's interpretation of the *Song of Roland* as idealising
feudalism at the time of its consolidation also works with the original
Old French of the *Forray*. The Greek heroes would understand their
duty as dying for the king rather than as searching for help. But why
would a Scottish writer translate a text celebrating feudalism in the
mid fifteenth century at a time when the feudal system had been
established for centuries? Certainly, there was no need to do that
unless he wanted to contrast the *Forray* with the overtly courtly
atmosphere of the *Avowis*.

   In contrast with the *Forray*, the *Avowis* displays a courtly tone in
which negotiation between the epic and the courtly realm is basic.
After a short introduction, the translator hastens to merge both French
narratives into one:

Qvhen Alexander, the King of prys,
Had discomfit the duke Betys
And Dedifeir, the fair citie,
Had wonnen. (*Avowis*, 1–4)

He replaces the "duc Melchis" (*Voeux*, 1) of the French text by "duke Betys". This implicit connection between the independent French works unveils the *intentio auctoris*. The makar places them together to examine the tensions between epic and romance codes and conducts, bestowing a new meaning on the newly created *Buik*.

In this context, the presence of Cassamus, who is the brother of dead Gadifer, is pivotal for the development of the courtly discourse. His image is that of the old sage with a long beard (*Avowis*, 44–47). In disparity with the characters in the *Forray*, Cassamus's thirst for revenge is short-lived (*Avowis*, 105–10). Moreover, he praises Alexander as the best monarch and knight in the world (*Avowis*, 75–76). In front of wise Cassamus, Alexander also shows a different attitude to that in the *Forray*. His not-taking-prisoners policy (*Forray*, 23–26) becomes more political and conciliatory. In fact, not only to conquer but to preserve such a vast empire, Alexander needs to promote alliances with the local leaders; otherwise, there is no way he could maintain so much territory under control just with the Greco-Macedonian army. Alexander offers to help Gadifer's children and Cassamus, who are under siege by Clarus of India after the death of their father (*Avowis*, 173–74).

Once in Ephesus, Cassamus has to persuade his nephew, Gadifer, named after his father, not to take revenge on Alexander. Young Gadifer behaves as a young and enraged knight, unable to see beyond his offended honour. At this juncture, his demeanour mirrors his deceased father's, anticipating the need for a change unless he wants to meet the same end. In the distinctly courtly world of the *Avowis*, there is no room for haughty behaviour and blind vengeance. Cassamus reminds his nephew of this:

> "Thow may na thing ingreif the King,
> And he may help the in mekill thing.
> Forʒet thy fathers dede, I rede!
> Outtragius hardement made his dede." (*Avowis*, 2961–64)

Cassamus makes two points crucial to understanding the transformation of the ideological framework and genre in the *Avowis*. Ideologically, Alexander's help is the only possibility to keep Gadifer in power even if that means becoming the emperor's vassal. Confrontation with him will most possibly result in death. Generically, the lack of *mesura* in epic heroes (as witnessed in old

Gadifer or Roland) can only lead to a heroic death. In a courtly milieu, *mesura* is necessary both on the battlefield and at court in exchanges with ladies.

After this scene, it is just a question of Alexander's ingenious deployment of rhetoric to convince Gadifer to be his ally. The emperor's language of *cortesia* disguises feudal concerns not of equal-to-equal alliance but of implicit vassalage. Alexander's offer of courteous "freinship" (*Avowis*, 3137) is in reality a proposal of submission to his overlordship in exchange for help against Clarus, Gadifer's dangerous foe. Gadifer follows his uncle's recommendation:

"Schir," said Gaudifeir, "ȝour meiknes,
ȝour courtasy and ȝour largnes
Is bot mesure; that wait men weill.
I sall do as ȝe deim, ilk deill!" (*Avowis*, 3141–44)

Again, feudal bonds are expressed in the terms of romance idealisation. Gadifer's praise of Alexander's courtly virtues also reveals the way in which he would like Alexander to treat him in his new condition of liege man. Immediately afterwards, the king refers to him as "vassale" (*Avowis*, 3150). Previously, in the bellicose atmosphere of the *Forray* courtly attributes were just mentioned en passant and were never central to the main discourse of military action. By way of contrast, in the *Avowis* courtly interrelationships play a fundamental role in the development of the plot and consolidation of feudal relationships.

Porrus, one of King Clarus's four sons, is a valiant but daredevil knight. When the Indian army is retiring after its first defeat against Alexander, Porrus thinks that this is not an honourable procedure. In a manoeuvre consonant with the *Forray* and epic values, he decides to return to the fight on his own. After a series of heroic single-handed combats, he is finally surrounded. Again, it is Cassamus's intervention that saves Porrus's life; he is taken prisoner instead of being killed. The old sage is once more crucial in the implementation of courtly values in young and hot-blooded warriors on both sides. Without Cassamus, both his nephew Gadifer and Porrus would have died. By the end of the romance, the two youngsters will play a central role in the establishment of the *pax alexandrina* in a overtly courtly atmosphere. Therefore not only does Cassamus transform the epic tone of

the *Forray* into the more courtly one in the *Avowis* but this reformu-
lation of values is essential for the outcome of the romance too.

Ironically but also necessarily, in the final battle, Cassamus dies
at the hands of Porrus, who is avenging the killing of his father,
Clarus. Although this seems to relocate the narrative in the domains of
epic revenge in the same exact terms as in the *Forray*, a set of chivalric vows mediate the battle, which is devoid of the dramatic realism of
the *Forray*. While captive, Porrus kills a peacock with an arrow
(*Avowis*, 5100–04). Following an autochthonous tradition, every
single knight has to make a chivalric vow, which he must accomplish
on the battlefield. In front of the ladies, the knights endeavour to
impress them with the most daredevil and chivalric deeds they can
imagine. Such feats do not concern the overall interests of either
Alexander or Clarus, but the personal *pretz* of individuals. It is, for
example, very difficult to comprehend how Perdicas's vow to fight on
foot (*Avowis*, 8111–26) will contribute to Alexander's enterprise. Yet
in the courtly and highly idealised atmosphere of the *Avowis*, such
oaths seem normative. Even Alexander seems to support these oaths
rather than oppose them even if they are against his military ambitions.

The author therefore has to reconcile the courtly vows of the
knights with Alexander's expansion of his empire. At first, on the
battlefield, both the King's men and Porrus and the Bauderane are
more concerned about accomplishing what they promised than about
the outcome of the war. The narrator, however, avoids commenting on
the tension between the epic and the courtly discourses, but leaves the
interpretation to the audience. Perdicas and Betys's decision to fight
on foot is praised, underlining the comradeship of the two: "It semit
togidder thay brether ware" (*Avowis*, 8757). Even more striking is the
attitude of Cassamus, who tells his vassals not to attack King Clarus,
his major enemy. Cassamus's way of action is certainly more
shocking than anyone else's. If he is the one who introduces the
courtly code in the narrative, preventing the young heroes Gadifer and
Porrus from death, now he is taking his courtly commitment to the
extreme. Not only is King Clarus besieging his nephew's territory, but
he also wants to marry his niece, Fesonas, against her will. Only in the
ideal and unrealistic world of *roman courtois* can such a paradox
occur. As a consequence, the mediation of the war through an idealistic set of courtly conventions dissociates the battle scenes from the

dramatic urgency of the *Forray*. By placing together both texts, the makar mirrors two diametrically opposed visions of the knightly world, one based upon attaining honour in the theatre of war, in which the masculine attributes of warriors are prioritised; and the other stemming from the social interactions between the nobility, in which the courtly code rules over the knights' behaviour not only at court, but also at war.

Once Cassamus has helped Clarus, he feels liberated from his vow. The next time they encounter one another on the battlefield, Cassamus kills him, reproving Clarus while he is dying:

"Thow wald haue had to thy behufe
My nece halely agane hir will!
Now mon thow thole, all lyke the ill,
That another by hir ly
And bruke hir blis and hir droury!" (*Avowis*, 9568–72)

Again, it is revealing that Cassamus's admonishment centres on Clarus's uncourtly demeanour towards the former's niece rather than on Clarus's much more important military enterprise, the conquest of the domains of Cassamus's nephew, Gadifer. The old sage, Cassamus, proves he is probably not that wise owing to his total attachment to the courtly code. He condemns Clarus's way of action, but not his goal. If Clarus wants to marry Fesonas is precisely as a means to legitimise his objective, the invasion of Ephesus. By slaying Fesonas's two brothers and forcing her to marry him, Clarus would become the *rightful* ruler of Ephesus.

The killing of Clarus exposes Cassamus to one the most recurrent topoi of the *chanson de geste* and the leitmotif of the *Forray*: venge-ance. Nonetheless, Porrus's revenge on his father lacks the immediacy of those in the *Forray*. First he thinks of Cassamus, then of Fesonas, whom he loves, and finally of attaining his vow (*Avowis*, 9691–704). When he sets his priorities in this context, not surprisingly, he chooses to accomplish his chivalric undertaking first. To impress his beloved Fesonas becomes more significant than avenging his father. Only after unhorsing Alexander himself, does Porrus confront and kill Cassamus. Conveniently, for the outcome of the narrative, both Porrus and the Bauderane fall prisoners for a second time.

By the end of the romance, Alexander becomes the central character for the first time. A politicised series of feudal alliances follow under the disguise of courtly interchanges and sophistication. As opposed to the *Forray*, to put an end to a war, the Macedonian Emperor relies on feudal agreements rather than on the total annihilation of the enemy. He marries Fesonas to Porrus and Ideas to the Baudenare, reinforcing the links between former foes, who have now become Alexander's vassals. His apparent magnanimity and *largeza* respond to his plans to conquer the entire known world. The *Forray*'s ideology of blood is replaced by an astute political framework mediated through courtly discourses. To be the emperor of such a vast territory, incessant battles against the inhabitants of those lands would only lead to the exhaustion of his own troops. The epic dialectics of the *Forray* are no longer valid. The *pax alexandrina* conforms to the submission of former enemies through the negotiation of the existing tensions between them. The new vassals will now govern their own countries in the name of Alexander.

The juxtaposition of the *Forray* and the *Avowis* creates a number of knightly tensions between opposite approaches to warfare. The exclusive epic action of the *Forray* works within the bellicose framework of the text. Yet, when extrapolated to a larger warlike conflict and life at court, the epic discourse of the *Forray* based on honour, revenge and heroic thirst unveils its deficiencies. Cassamus's mediation through the courtly dialectics proves effective only to a certain extent. Although it brings peace between his people and Alexander, it also perverts the natural course of military action. The personal enterprise for *pretz* and the ladies' favour subverts the main goal of the war. Even if, when the battle is over, the narrative reconciles the individual ambitions with the military purpose, the makar has already exposed the inadequacy of a total commitment to the courtly code through Cassamus. His death and that of Clarus, whose attachment was to epic action, symbolises the end of the old order, which is replaced by Alexander and the young knights and ladies. As neither the epic nor the romance discourses will provide a satisfactory outcome, Alexander political strategies are necessary to attain an adequate ending.

As opposed to the Scottish historical, Arthurian and Charlemagne modes of romance, the Alexander texts elaborate on the representation of *cortesia* to a large extent if only to question its validity in real warfare. As should be expected in the *Buik of Alexander*, the courtly atmosphere is fully developed in the *Avowis* whereas its display in the *Forray* is as schematic and functional as it is customary in the Scottish romance corpus. The sporadic references to *cortesia* in the latter contrast with the long sections devoted to the courtly interchanges between knights and ladies in the *Avowis*. In them, *fin'amors* and *cortesia* explore the social facet of knightly life at length. They also mediate the narrative outcome of epic feats through a series of courtly vows undertaken to attain the ladies' favour. In these scenes, the exoticism typical of French Alexander texts is also present. The comments of the female characters on the incidents on the battlefield also impose a completely different interpretation of the epic mood from that in the *Forray*.

The eminently epic discourse of the *Forray* leaves little room for courtly interchanges. There is not a single female character. From time to time, the author makes general allusions to the knights' courtly virtues, but they are reduced to three or four lines at most:

Philot was of mare quantite,
Of ioyous and of blyth manere,
With stout visage and lauchand chere,
Richt kynd, courtes and amorous; (*Forray*, 1008–11)

The makar forces the reader to believe his words although there is no indication in the narrative of Philot's courtly manners apart from the author's claim. This shows the dialogic nature of late medieval literature in which different genres borrow elements from each other. Epic heroes needed courtly attributes even if they were attached to them in a vague fashion like in the case of Philot. Similarly, courtly romances incorporated essentially epic motifs such as the protagonist's desire for revenge in their narratives.

The functional deployment of courtly attributes in the *Forray* permits the author to confer more of those features to Alexander's enemy Gadifer than to any of the Macedonian Emperor's knights. Indeed, the only instance of a *fin'amors* relationship is bestowed on Gadifer:

Vpon his [Gaudifeir's] gilt helme, for drowrie,
Was put the sleif of ane lady,
The Kingis dochter of Nuby. (*Forray*, 3202–4)

Yet neither his courtly virtues nor his love affair are developed at all. The King of Nuby's daughter, who is unnamed, is never mentioned again. When Emenidus kills Gadifer the only one lamenting his death is Alexander; there is no reference to the mysterious princess. Revealingly, Alexander's grieving *encomium* on Gadifer concentrates on his knightly attributes, which are those extensively shown in the narrative.

The functionality of the courtly world in the *Forray* contrasts with its centrality in the *Avowis*. The idealised and colourful setting, the presence of female characters, and their courtly conversations with knights portray a different representation of *cortesia* and the feminine in the *Avowis*. In Ephesus, all the knights, including the prisoners Porrus and the Bauderane, meet the ladies at the Chamber of Venus. Its name itself suggests an enclosed space detached from the combat zone, the world of Mars. It also implies a meeting place for knights and ladies for playful courtly interactions, ranging from *fin'amors* and *cortesia* to mischievous games of seduction. The depiction of the chamber denotes the exoticism of a prosperous distant place of mysterious beauty:

At the fute of the mekill tour,
Wnder the flurist siccamour,
Was spred into ane harbure grene
Carpettis of silk and siluer schene. (*Avowis*, 3685–88)

What would be a conventional picture of Arabian richness in European Alexander and Charlemagne romances and *chansons* such as *Sir Ferumbras* or *Otuel* becomes an exceptional feature in a Scottish text. Out of around fifteen fragmentary or complete romances preserved in Early and Middle Scots, only the two Alexander narratives and *Clariodus* present elaborate portrayals of courtly life and idealised settings.

In the *Buik of Alexander*, this creation of idyllic sophistication is enhanced even further when the knights asked for a chessboard. The pieces are made of emeralds, sapphires, topazes and rubies. In opposition to the free adaptations of *Golagros and Gawane* and *Lancelot of the Laik*, in the *Buik* the translator follows the French original very closely, enjoying the exhaustive description of details. The presence of the chessboard, as a game of feigned war, displaces the violence of the epic action from the centre of the narrative. In the Chamber of

Venus feigned war becomes one of the many pastimes for knights and ladies.

McDiarmid claims that, in the *Buik of Alexander*, the scenes at court are less successfully developed that those on the battlefield (McDiarmid 1988: 31). Certainly, if compared with Scottish texts such as *Eger and Grime* and the historical, Charlemagne and Arthurian romances, the long courtly passages in the *Buik* read very differently and may seem to slow down the agile succession of events characteristic of the abovementioned narratives. Nonetheless, the presence of these passages determines the equilibrium and tension between the *Forray* and the *Avowis*. The Chamber of Venus is the perfect place for flirtatious conversations and *fin'amors*. The imprisonment of the Bauderane and Porrus facilitates the courteous interactions between the Indian warriors and the ladies of Ephesus. Fesonas is rapidly attracted to Porrus. She is the first to address the prisoner:

> "Schir, ȝe haue me greued sare
> To-day, sa God me keip fra care!
> For greuous panes I saw ȝow dre.
> Carles are euill folk and vnsle;
> Had ȝe nocht all the better bene,
> Thay had ȝow slane, that men had sene;
> Bot wonder hie worship and bounte
> Delyuered ȝow of thare pouste!" (*Avowis*, 4749–56)

Chrétien had already created female characters who took the initiative in their dialogues with knights. In the *Chevalier de la Charrette*, for example, one of the tests which Lancelot has to pass to prove his self-control and fidelity to Guenevere consists of rejecting the overtly sexual advances of an obstinate lady (ll.940–45). At any rate, active female figures who take the first step such as Fesonas are generally associated with romances focussing on Arabia and the East. They are less reserved and more willing take the initiative in the games of *amors* than Christian ladies. These stereotypes are mostly found in Charlemagne and Alexander narratives which contributed to what in the twentieth century Edward Said defined as the Western "invention" of the Orient (Said 2003: 5). Fesonas's approach to Porrus is subtle, but direct; first expressing her concern about the knight and then her admiration by praising his prowess. Cassamus also highlights Porrus's demeanour at war. At this juncture, Porrus feels "sum deill aschamit"

(*Avowis*, 4765). The most outstanding warrior loses the initiative in the courtly interactions. There is a reversal of roles: Porrus, the subject of action while fighting becomes the object of veneration at court, whereas Fesonas, instead of being the courtly object of adoration, becomes the subject who makes advances towards the knight.

The other prisoner, the Bauderane, becomes interested in Ideas, who in turn is also attracted to him. Cassamus tells the Bauderane about Ideas's captivating allure, whilst Fesonas sparks Ideas's attraction towards the Bauderane. Yet this is by no means disinterested *fin'amors*. Feudal matters lie behind Cassamus's intentions. As the mediator of the courtly discourse, his concerns are confined to the feudal world. In a later conversation with Ideas, he reveals his plan:

> "Maydin, this man is richt douchty
> And lord is of great senȝeory,
> And he is ȝoung, fare and plesand,
> Courtes, fetas and auenand.
> Lufe him and hald him [in] dante". (*Avowis*, 2107–11)

Typical courtly attributes such as courteous and *joven* (young disposition towards love) intermingle with his position of authority and richness.

Just before the interchange of prisoners, the Baudenare offers Ideas his love and possessions, accentuating the realistic economic advantages of such a relationship: she will be a "lady of great dignite" (*Avowis*, 6907). Love by itself would probably not be enough. Only after reassuring her of his high position, does he adopt a more idealised role as a *fin amant*:

> "And heir I leif ȝow vterly
> My hart, but parting, halely
> To duell in ȝour sueit seruage,
> And here to ȝow I mak homage!" (*Avowis*, 6910–13)

The Bauderane conventionally enters the service of love. Yet this *fin'amors* has little to do with its origins in the poetry of the troubadours. The language remains the same, but the context is diametrically opposed. Its transgressive nature regarding the religious and social norms is absent. Instead, it is redefined in the realm of acceptable and constructive social behaviour, leading not only to marriage, but also to feudal alliances and political power.

There are no long disquisitions about the joys and sorrows of love. The only character who debates, if only for a few lines, the nature of *fin'amors*, is Alexander himself. First, he admits that thinking of the beloved makes him happy. His description of such a person basically deals with physical attributes which indicates a rather superficial and functional approach to the subject. In the romance, love is not an end in itself but a means to attain social and, in the case of Alexander, also imperial stability. In fact, when Idorus asks the sovereign what the three main virtues attached to love are, Alexander surprises Idorus by referring not to "swete hart, gay and ioly", but to "God him-self, the lele luffar, / Beris witnes in lele lufing" (*Avowis*, 2538; 2544–45). The Macedonian Emperor relocates the notion of love at its highest possible level: *caritas*, divine love. Alexander's statement suddenly shakes the courtly context in which the action takes place. However, after this brief appreciation, the scene returns to its courtly atmosphere without any further comment. This seems to indicate that the role of this isolated remark serves to enhance Alexander's moral worth in a concrete Christian context, which is absent from the original. In *Les Voeux de Paon*, the monarch does not mention God but he alludes to "scïence" (1.1869), that is, knowledge or wisdom.

Thus, the *Buik* explores the possibilities and defects of epic and romance narratives. In the *Forray*, the epic discourse, analogue to that of *chansons de geste*, confines the action to the battlefield. Revenge and honour dominate a masculine-centred narration in which there is no space for courtly embellishment or for the presence of female characters. In the particular framework of the *Forray*, total war and not negotiation are the ideal solution to military conflict. Yet, within Alexander's overall goal, the conquest of the known world, such a bloodthirsty way of action posits many questions. If there is no negotiation with local leaders, the submission of those lands would never be complete. In the *Avowis*, this negotiation does take place. Whilst the appearance of Cassamus injects a courtly tone in the narrative where interactions between ladies and knights become possible, the battlefield scenes are perilously mediated by the courtly discourse. The knights' vows take precedence over the motivations of the war itself, the defence of Ephesus. Only by the end of the narrative, when Alexander finally becomes the central figure, does the Macedonian Emperor bridge the gap between epic and romance through a political discourse of matrimonial alliances which secures peace among former enemies who have now become his vassals.

Knighthood and the marvels of the east in the *Buik of King Alexander the Conquerour*

Gilbert Hay's *Buik of King Alexander the Conquerour* (c.1460) is an accumulative romance which has survived in a later version or reworking (c.1500). It shifts between the prominently epic narrative of the conquering of the known world and the sporadic courtly inter-changes between knights and ladies – and also between the realistic battlefield settings and the supernatural associated with the Marvels of the East. Changes of scenario allow Alexander's characterisation to develop as an ideal leader of his people, a model ruler, a subtle politi-cian and a courtly knight. In the epic battles, dominating more than half of the narrative, Alexander shows his leadership qualities and bravery on the battlefield. As well as richly describing the exotic and supernatural features of Orient, the sections dealing with the Marvels of the East recreate two more facets of the Macedonian Emperor: the tamer of uncanny beasts and the attentive observer of the working of destiny beyond his earthly domains of power and control.

The knightly characterisation of Alexander follows the patterns of any other great military leader of late medieval literature. Even before he has had much time to exhibit his warrior skills on the battle-field or his ruling ability in political affairs, he shows his maturity and *sapientia* from a young age. The topos of a knight controlling the supernatural is repeated several times owing to Alexander's encoun-ters with the Marvels of the East. The first instance of this takes place during his youth. At fifteen, he manages to tame Bucephalus, a horse "With tuskis and hornis lyk till ane bull his hed" (1.601), which no other person could handle. The steed, from then on, will become his brave and loyal horse. Not only does this demonstrate the supremacy of the human intellect over animals but such an act serves to different purposes. First, it anticipates the success in his future adventures when faced with supernatural creatures. It also singles out the young hero to be of more worth than any of King Philip's soldiers. King Philip him-self realises how special his son is and concedes that "'Now am I sicker þairof for þow art he / To myne are succeid suld efter me'" (ll.655–56). The taming of Bucephalus also certifies the glorious future of Alexander as someone whose knightly virtues are superior to any other human being. In fact, the horse proves to be a faithful and brave companion to Alexander. When Graudefere unhorses him (ll.3777–81), leaving him defenceless on the ground, Bucephalus does not permit anyone to get any near his owner. Thanks to this, the twelve peers have time to come to rescue him. Therefore, like the giant Beligog, in the Tristan romances, the subjugation of the supernatural also entails the future service of the subjugated to the subjugator.

Shortly after domesticating Bucephalus, Alexander takes advantage of his favourable position in the eyes of the king to ask him to become chief commander and governor in front of King Nicholas, who wants to invade Little Armenie. The maturity of young Alexander's words and firmness amaze Nicholas (ll.759–60). Like Hary's Wallace, a point Joanna Martin also makes, Alexander is represented as a *puer senex* (Martin 2006: 79 and 2008: 65). Therefore, these two early instances begin to shape Alexander as the perfect knight and king even before he enters a fight. They also anticipate two of the main developments of the romance: his encounters with the supernatural full of real and unreal beasts and his most important enterprise, the conquest of the known world, through which he will have both to confront and to negotiate with numerous regional leaders and mighty sovereigns.

Alexander's metamorphosis from a young prince into a courageous knight and leader is represented through different textual strategies from Alexander's attire to his way of action, surrounding himself with brave and loyal generals:

Quhan Alexander haid ordand his battell attyre,
And all was payit of wage and of hyre,
Than sett he for to mak his ordinance
Off officieris to keip his obseruance, (ll.895–98)

In his *Buke of the Governaunce of Princis*, Gilbert Hay also refers to the importance of a monarch's clothing:

Alexander, faire sone, it effeiris till magestee ryale to be ever stately cled and honourably in preciouse vestimentis and in fair maner grathit. And that suld be abone all otheris of his subjectis bathe in richesse in fassone and in fairenesse […] sa that he suld appere abone and before all otheris in knaulage of dignitee, so that throu the nobilitee of him, his ornaments and estate, all his contree war the mare prisit, lovit lufit and honourit. (p. 92)

The symbolism of the "battell attyre" transforms Alexander's teenage body into a regal body. There is a metaphoric transformation from a youthful person into figure of power and authority. It is then that Alexander can give orders and device his own policies:

And in þe first, twelf duzeperis he made,
Of þe heist lordis and of þe gretest haid,
At quhilk lordis he wald counsell tak, (ll.899–901)

His first decision reveals that his maturity and wisdom are greater than what normally characterises a boy of his age. At a time of rivalries and treason within and outside Macedonia and Greece, Alexander surrounds himself with people he can trust: loyal and valiant warriors and generals upon whom the success of his enterprise and sometimes even his life will depend.

The twelve peers will help Alexander to gain military dominance and prestige. As well as entrusting them with a consulting role (1.901), owing to the epic tone of more than half of the narrative, they will become key figures in Alexander's exploits. Indeed Alexander makes them his twelve peers just before a battle against his most perilous foe, King Darius. It is no coincidence that the narrator subsequently refers to the disposition of an army in battle:

Syne maid he his luftennend-generall,
That is to say, þe duke of his battall:
The duke of battall suld þe vangarde haue,
The leftennend suld gouern all þe laue,
And with þe counsall of þe duzepeiris
Suld set all offeiciaris as to þame affeiris;
The king in nothing occupeit suld be,
Bot in gret caus of all noueltie.
Off marascalis þai ordand alwayis tua,
On euirie syde þe battell ane of tha,
[…]
The admirall, and maister of ablestre,
Befoir þe duk in battall suld þai be,
With armis cartis, crapald, and colubringis – (ll.903–12; 915–17)

The twelve peers' military feats at the service of Alexander establish their significance in the narrative. Nonetheless, there is no specification as to which role each of the peers is going to carry out, but only general references to the rank, duty and disposition of a formation facing the enemy. The absence of names universalises the functions of the leaders on the battlefield. In the same way, this detailed account in the context of this romance, in which the author very often opts to condense the action, operates as an exemplary, didactic lesson to the courtly audience, in particular to the monarch himself. If, as previously argued, Aristotle's counsels follow the advice to princes tradition teach not only Alexander but anyone reading or listening to the text, these lines also have a similar objective: to instruct the reader/listener in the duties of a king at war. As customary in most Scottish romances, the collective effort is more important to the enterprise than individual deeds. Thus the formation of the army plays a central role both in romances and in historical conflicts to win the day.

The author underlines the importance Alexander attaches to the twelve peers again at a time when his succession to Philip is not completely guaranteed yet. While his military fame is already spreading, Alexander knows how to strengthen his position further. The future emperor gives all the lands of King Nicholas to one of his twelve peers, Ptolemy. Alexander also avers his forthcoming plans: "With grace of God, I think throw conquessing / To mak my douzeperis euerie man ane king" (ll.2011–12). Such a statement is full of both knightly and political nuances. In knightly terms, Alexander recognises the magnitude of his men's contribution to his conquering ambitions. The best way to demonstrate his recognition is by providing them with lands, riches and power. Politically, he makes sure that the newly occupied territories are under his direct control through the appointment of his own trustworthy men. Like its manifestation in Robert Bruce in *The Bruce* and King Arthur in *Lancelot of the Laik*, *largeza* serves to reinforce the present and future loyalty of subjects as well as constituting an act of liberality and the acknowledgement of contribution to the sovereign's cause. Thus, the reward for their loyal services is not reduced to being the acquisition of exclusively material possessions, but also comes with political responsibility. The twelve peers will have the power to rule over the new conquered territories, but they will still be Alexander's trustworthy liegemen. Although in theory King Philip would be the overlord of these lands, Alexander effectively conceals the power thanks to *his* twelve peers. In front of King Philip, Alexander would no longer be a defenceless child, but an intimidating adversary in case (as it will happen) of a confrontation between the two of them. These circumstances recall an early passage in which Samson feels closer to Alexander who "hes me dycht / In stait of prince, and hes me dubbit knycht" (ll.1123–24), than to his uncles Darius and Nicholas, who have behaved dreadfully to him. Therefore, in the *Conquerour*, the vow of loyalty towards one's lord becomes much more important than family links. As already seen in previous chapters, this is a typical trait of most Scottish romances: they lay remarkable emphasis on the knightly virtue of loyalty, which recovers the same central role as in earlier epic *chansons de geste*.

As well as loyalty, *largeza* is equally promoted in the romance. When Porrus flees after confronting the Macedonian Emperor, the two worthy attributes which the author immediately highlights are "His [Alexander's] grete renoun, his larges and fredome", which "gart halely the cuntre till him cum" (ll.11,078–88). Thus the value of *largeza* is accentuated with a double reference to two synonyms: "larges and fredome". The subsequent lines explain the makar's insistence on the extolling of this virtue:

Than schupe he him to entir in þat citie;
The ordinance þai made was ioye to se,
For commounis ioyis ay of lordschip newe,
For commounis ar sone turnit and vntrew: (ll.11,091–94)

In contraposition with knights' loyalty, the members of the Third Estate's volatility demands the rapid intervention of the king so that the early enthusiasm for a new lord does not cease with the same speediness with which it has commenced.

Another illustration of Alexander's *largeza* takes places just after Darius's defeat. Although he might be tempted to devastate his major enemy's lands after vanquishing him, Alexander deploys more intelligent tactics:

Bot tak the place in his protectioun,
And put to kepe men of religioun,
And rentit þame with landis mychtelie,
For thare honoure þat had bene sa wourthy. (ll.6278–81)

Even if, as the narrator says, Alexander wanted to honour the men of religion, there seems to be a less altruistic political intention behind the Macedonian Emperor's attitude. While Alexander appropriates all the lay institutions of power, he also needs to reach an agreement with the appointed, religious controllers of the faith. When both the legal and spiritual ruling organisations are united, it becomes easier to dominate the Third Estate. If he obliterates regal, regional and local secular authority, he requires to maintain the fiction of the existence of old traditional institutions to which the different strata of society may still feel attachment. Alexander's *largeza* in this instance is employed to create powerful political links with the church to implement a stable government after occupying Darius's territories. As a conquering hero, Alexander must gain the newly conquered people's approval with celerity to avoid any sort of resentment or revolts. Therefore, Alexander's *largeza* plays a pivotal role in the management of affairs during his conquest of the known world. As well as giving power to his men, Alexander, like the Alexander of *The Buik of Alexander*, seeks alliance with local authorities either political or religious. Even if he was going to die before the success of his plan had been proved, through a combination of foreign imposition and indigenous pacts, Alexander would have implicitly endeavoured to maintain his authority and pacify his vast empire.

Subsequent to Darius's defeat and death, Alexander accomplishes his objective of conquering the entire known world. At this point, the tone of the narrative must necessarily shift to accommodate the new territorial disposition. Alexander is no longer the epic conqueror but must act as a pacifying lord within his own domains. The epic dimension of his *avanture* is transformed into a more local and localised good administration of power. The heroic leader must adapt to act as a feudal lord if he wants his enterprise to be successful. Indeed, had he remained alive for a longer period of time, his success would have been measured against his capacity to retrain himself as an efficient administrator of power in such a large empire. For example, a lord called Gracian rides to Alexander to complain about a "tyran lord":

"He is sa tyrand and sa cuvatus,
And in his living als is sa vicius,
That he haldis myne heretege me fra,
And heryit me, as he has done to ma;

And syne, becaus I askit him ressoun,
He has me haldin ane lang tyme in presoun". (ll.16,551–56)

This has little to do with the epic dimension of the problems he has
had to face previously. Not only does Alexander kill Duke Melchy,
the tyrant, but he also arranges the marriage of his daughter, an act
which will legitimise his taking of the land.

Alexander's valiant feats of arms, however, do not only take
place in the realm of realistic warfare. As it was customary of the
Alexander romances all over Europe, the supernatural and the
depiction of the Marvels of the East were an unavoidable part of
Alexander's adventures. The exoticism and richness of the Orient,
together with the appearance of uncanny and mythological animals
and the dangerous but seductive presence of Amazons, captured the
imagination of Western audiences. Even in Scotland, where romance
writers were not particularly keen on the supernatural, Gilbert Hay
had no qualms about profusely elaborating on the Marvels of the East
of his originals, where his two most important sources were the
Roman d'Alexandre and the *Historia de Preliis* (Cartwright 1986:
230; Martin 2006: 78).

Yet, the first supernatural instance in the *Conquerour* occurs, not
in the Orient, but even before Alexander is born. Like many classical
and medieval heroes, such as Hercules, Arthur or Tristan, Alexander's
conception is far from conventional. King Philip has two visions of
the originally Egyptian god Ammon (the equivalent of the Greek
Zeus), descending in the shape of a dragon and kissing Queen Olympias (ll.37–66). Subsequently, the king has another dream about a bird,
an egg and a snake, which Aristotle interprets:

"Lord, traist weill þat þow sall haue ane air,
That efter þe sall regn heir and repair;
This warld he sall all conques and ourepas,
And quhan he sua þe warld ourconquest hes,
And wald agane cum in his cuntre,
In his maist welth and gloir þan sall he de". (ll.107–12)

Alexander's future is sealed even before his birth through the elucida-
tion of a premonitory vision. Although this just confirms what the
audience knew in advance, it bestows a mysterious tone to the narrative: Alexander becomes a more-than-human epic hero. Even if stylistically and thematically the *Buik of King Alexander the Conquerour*

shares many elements with most Older Scots romances, such a distinctive beginning, even from the *Buik of Alexander*, attests the text's focus on the supernatural in a much more sustained manner than was typical of the genre in Scotland.

The makar's predilection for the supernatural and exoticism is even more remarkable in the variety of beasts which Alexander confronts. Real and mythological animals come together: "þe dragouns, / Baith vnicornes, serpentis, and liouns" (ll.11,559–60) and also "griffouns" (l.11,662). Alexander's fight with a dragon exemplifies the meaning and significance of these animals:

Thare was na hous sa-mekill in ony toun;
Quhilk till ane dragoun like scho had a snowtt,
And all hir sydis skalit wat about;
Hir leggis grete and armit war alsua,
Ay schotand flauchtis of fire, quhare-evir scho ga.
[…]
Thay war sa basit, þir lordis all bedene,
Thay wend that scho ane feynd of Hell had bene.
[…]
Scho was of diuers hewis and cullouris,
And with that scho made all men sic horrouris. (ll.11,612–16; 11,621–22; 11,627–28)

The detailed picture of the beast merges terrifying elements and exotic features, making the dragon at once frightening and attractive to the audience's imagination. The dragon's fire is conventionally associated with the fire of Hell. While everybody is fearful, Alexander will not only fight the beast but will also be the eradicator of evil from the region. The topos of the civilising knight performs a very precise function within the overall framework of the *pax alexandrina*: Alexander brings peace and order to the newly conquered lands.

Another apposite element of representation of the Marvels of the East is the richness of the places described which merges realistic and fantastic features and locations. Darius's palace illustrates the highly idealistic and exotic flavour of such dwellings. The narrator takes some time to devote to the sumptuousness of the place. Nevertheless, its opulence is not just celebrated for its own sake but also reveals significant aspects of Darius's kingdom. The political pre-eminence Darius enjoyed over his and adjacent territories is encapsulated in the functionality of the palace: "Quhare all the princis semblit þare to him" (l.6956). The beauty of the walls, which are marble and alabaster with images of gold (ll.6963–64), operates as a reminder of the prosperity of Darius's reign. Similarly, the pillars "full of ymagery, / Off batallis and of storeis of ancestry" (ll.6968–69), reveal the Persians' predilection for art as well as respect and admiration for their past.

The mythological Amazons also appear in the narrative. However, they are not sensually portrayed according to the exotic Muslim princess stereotype of Arabian romances which might have aroused the audience's imagination. Instead, the confrontation between Alexander and Palisseda, Queen of the Amazons, becomes a rhetorical debate on ideas and expectations about gender roles. Alexander sends a letter to Palisseda, stating that:

"It settis nocht ladyis batalis for to lede,
Na conquest landis, na to manteine na fede,
Na maistres oure þare husbandis for to be,
Na governe croun, na realme, na dignetie –
The man is hede to woman, and ledare,
And at his biddin suld be euermare;" (ll.11,773–78)

Queen Palisseda's epistolary reply does not show any sign of her having been intimidated by the Macedonian Emperor's reliance on late medieval visions of the sexes. The vindication of the Amazon way of life has nothing to do with the comic tone of the Wife of Bath's defence of transgressive female attitudes in the *Prologue* to her tale or that of the widow in Dunbar's *Tretis of the Twa Mariit Wemen and the Wedo*. The Queen's words proclaim her queenship over her domains on the customary bases of 'tradition' and 'right' which they would defend with their lives as any other Christian monarch, such as Robert I in *The Bruce* (I. 157–64), would have done:

"It war folie sic wourschip to diffaid,
And of sic governance oure-selff to degrade;
Sen oure forebearis, quhilk war wise conqueriouris,
Manteineit thare richt, and vpheld þare honouris,
And we of power and prosperetie
For to defend oure richt in all degrie,
We think it war na witt, bot grete foly
To giff oure suggettis oure ws ony maistry,
For war oure husbandis of witt to governe ws,
We had nocht tane the maistry till ws þus,
The quhilk we sall manteine quhill we liff may
Aganis all men, to de on a day". (ll.11,805–16)

The only difference with archetypal discourses on kingship is Queen Palisseda's emphasis on sex difference which should not be taken into account on the grounds of the good government the female rule of the Amazons has exercised – as good as any male regime could be.

Subsequently, the Queen complains that as knights Alexander and his men should "succoure, favore, and defend" women, rather than menace to conquer them (ll.11,825–28). At this point, Cartwright argues that any possible first impression of "a radical proto-feminist challenge to the patriarchal assumptions" vanishes (Cartwright 1991a: 340). Even if Cartwright is right, what is important about these lines is Palisseda's manipulation of language. After condemning Alexander's claim being based on an essentialist superiority of men over women, she resorts to the chivalric code for which the Macedonian Emperor stands. She reminds him that, owing to his patriarchal image of women, he should never invade the country of the Amazons but be chivalrous to them. Palisseda matches Alexander's command of rhetoric, using his arguments and ideology to her own benefit.

Despite the political tone of the letter to Palisseda, Alexander also makes use of the language of *cortesia*. Interestingly, earlier in the narrative, the first time he deploys the sophisticated vocabulary of courtly interchanges, he refers to his mother Olympias, unveiling the close affection existing between the two of them. Alexander receives a letter, expounding his mother's state: she is very ill and in danger of death. He is understandably shaken:

"And that I pas nocht hir swete pappis to kis,
Bot for scho in a deidlie seiknes is,
To comforte hir, as sone suld for to do,
As gude nature and kynd drawis to". (ll.4796–99)

The language here is deliberately ambiguous: it could indicate either Alexander's filial love for his mother or insinuate some kind of Oedipal attraction between the two. Her quick recovery when Alexander goes to visit her (ll.4836–39) accentuates the ambiguity of their affection. The nature of the disease is never explained but the non-naturalistic improvement in her health suggests that her sufferings were due to Alexander's absence rather than to any physical deterioration. Such a situation recalls the affliction of *fins amants* when apart.

In other instances, *fin'amors* is unambiguously presented. In Venus's Chamber, an episode which is much more developed in the anonymous *Buik of Alexander*, the Macedonian Emperor enumerates the good and bad things about love. For about sixty lines (ll.8259–322), a long exposition of *loci communes* about a *fin amant's* behaviour indoctrinates Alexander's knights and, by implication, the audience of the romance. Such a didactic exposition is closer in tone to Aristotle's or Hay's political counselling and teaching than to the elaborate love scenes of a *roman courtois*. The functional depiction of *fin'amors* is complemented by a later disquisition, also uttered by Alexander, on what a woman should be like:

> "womannis honoure is mare tendir and sliddir,
> And ethar for to bleke, be mekill thing,
> As farast rois will sonest tak fading.
> And woman ever sould schame haue, and raddoure,
> Ewir dredand þe thing þat micht be dishonoure,
> Ay full of pietie and humeletie,
> And litill of langage, bot grete mystir be;
> Nocht loude of lauchter, na of langage cours,
> And euer be doand sum gude to the hous,
> Nocht vsitt to sitt with tractilling in þe toun,
> Na favoure nane þat spekis dishonoure". (ll.8488–98)

There is nothing particularly innovative is this rather conventional description of a courtly lady's demeanour. Again, as well as being a lesson to the damsels at Venus's Chamber, Alexander's oration functions as a message aimed at the ladies in the audience. After listening to these words, it is not surprising that Alexander could not understand the abovementioned Amazons, who appear as a threat not only to patriarchal authority, but also to Alexander's hierarchical vision of the world.

This functional approach to *fin'amors* is also evident in Alexander's response to Floridas's sadness because of the death of his beloved. The King, instead of showing any worry about his man, is displeased and promises him to find him a new wife (ll.16,834–41). After the taking of Carras, the king of this city's daughter, who is not even given a name, is married to Floridas. Fortunately,

> quhan Floridas saw the madyn fare,
> Quhilk was þe lordis dochter and his are,
> He was enamorit sa of hir farnes,
> Fer mare na euer he with þe tothir was. (ll.16,854–57)

Alexander's practical conceptualisation of love does not allow warriors to spend any time lamenting their fortune. The swiftness with which the Macedonian Emperor solves Floridas's situation could be seen in a rather ironic light. Love, even if more preeminent here than is most Scottish romances, lacks the capacity to impart profound psychological insights in the lovers' minds. If a knight is diverted from his duties owing to love's interference, Alexander will find a way, quite detached from sentiment, to redirect his man to serve the military cause. Yet Alexander is not wholly devoid of humane feelings. When Darius's wife dies of grief after being captured with most of her family, Alexander honours her with a funeral which many sovereigns attend. As in the case of Wallace in Hary's narrative, these scenes serve to complete the hero's image as a courtly figure.

Like most Scottish romances, *The Buik of King Alexander the Conquerour* emphasises the military aspects of knightly life. Alexander's leadership and his knights' loyalty place the narrative in the same tradition as Barbour's *Bruce* and Hary's *Wallace*. At the same time, however, owing to the subject matter, the makar also develops themes traditionally absent from the Older Scots romances, such as the supernatural within the milieu of the Marvels of the East. The Macedonian Emperor successfully deals with the uncanny, redefining the role of the civilising knight in a political context: he is not only bringing civilisation and the Christian world to places where they did not exist but he is also enforcing his vision of government and peace in those territories. At any rate, *fin'amors*, which could have easily been developed within the exotic Oriental context, is drastically reduced and given a rather practical function. Such a combination of particular Scottish and more widely European elements makes the *Conquerour* an idiosyncratic text.

Rauf Coilyear: from humorous *Cortesia* to serious spirituality

The fifteenth-century *Taill of Rauf Coilyear* stands as the only surviving medieval Scottish romance dealing with the Matter of France. Although the main concern of the Charlemagne Romances is the fight against the heathen, the Scottish text treats this issue only in its final stanzas. The core of the poem concentrates on the discrepancies between the *cortesia* of Charlemagne and his knights and the blunt honesty of the collier. Yet the humorous outcome of this contrast and its implications go beyond laughter. In the last section of the poem, the religious significance brings about a change of mood from humour to seriousness.

The beginning of the romance establishes a comic tone in which the theme of giving shelter is central to the development of the plot. This serves to confront two visions of *cortesia*. Rauf's understanding of the concept stems from his own experience based upon a series of values typical of his social stratum. His position stands out against the set of determined conventions which codifies courtly behaviour:

The coilyear, gudlie in feir, tuke him [Charlemagne] be the hand
And put him befoir him, as ressoun had bene.
Quhen thay come to the dure the king begouth to stand,
To put the coilyear in befoir maid him to mene.
He [Rauf] said, "Thow art uncourtes, that sall I warrand!"
He tyt the king by the neck, twa part in tene.
"Gif thow at bidding suld be boun or obeysand,
And gif thow of courtasie couth, thow hes foryet it clene.
Now is anis!" said the coilyear. "Kynd aucht to creip!
Sen ellis thow art unknawin
To mak me lord of my awin!
Sa mot I thrive, I am thrawin,
Begin we to threip! (stanza 10)

This long stanza summarises the main concerns of the first part of the romance. Rauf imposes his own conceptualisation of *cortesia*. His words reveal his ignorance of courtly standards. He does not allow for the existence of any other sort of civil conduct, but only the one he knows. In his perception of the world as a member of the Third Estate, the collier cannot imagine or comprehend the otherness of the chivalric world. The *hero* of the romance alienates and is alien to the customary codes of the genre: Rauf's matter-of-fact realism displaces and substitutes literary courtly conventions. Subversion of the norm produces a comic outcome.

The fact that Charlemagne is his guest entitles Rauf to apply his own rules, which, he believes, no-one should question. As an outsider, the King seems to accept the host's authority, even his violent rusticity.[2] For instance, in stanza 12, he hits the king for his lack of *cortesia* once more. When Charlemagne invites him to his court, Rauf's answer is enlightening:

He said, "I have na knawledge quhair the court lyis,
And I am wonder wa to cum quhair I am unkend". (stanza 20)

Rauf's ignorance is not only of the geographical location of Charlemagne's court, but also implies his unfamiliarity with the norms of the knightly society from which the Frankish Emperor comes.

His anger and personal display of manners create another conflict in his first meeting with Roland. Mutual understanding is patently impossible. They both speak the same language but do not share the same conception of the world. Communication is hardly possible. Shepherd's interpretation of these lines as social critique stems from the idea that behind the obvious comic tone, there is an insightful observation of the demise of *cortesia* as a marker of social prejudice (Shepherd 1991: 286):

"In faith," said the coilyear, "yit was I never sa nyse!
Schir Knicht, it is na courtasie communis to scorne.
Thair is mony better than I cummis oft to Parys
That the king wait not of, nouther nicht nor morne.
For to towsill me or tit me, thocht foull be my clais,
Or I be dantit on sic wyse, my lyfe salbe lorne!"
"Do way," said Schir Rolland, "me think thow art not wise!
I rid thow at bidding be, be all that we have sworne,
And call thow it na scorning, bot do as I the ken". (stanza 34)

Although Shepherd argues that the impossibility of understanding between the two men points to social critique, this instance shows that the prejudices are reciprocal. Rauf never intends to submit to the knight; instead, he endeavours to impose his own criteria once again. Rauf is as aggressive as (or even more than) Roland in his language. When Roland just wants to escort him to Paris, the collier takes that as an offence and accuses the knight of lacking *cortesia*. Not even when Rauf admires the rich attire of the knight and evaluates the latter's

---

[2] Shepherd suggests that these instances state that Charlemagne is aware of his own fallibility (Shepherd 1991: 290). His fallibility reveals a very similar approach to kingship to those in the historical and Arthurian and Charlemagne romances, which places *Rauf Coilyear* in the same literary tradition.

worth as a warrior (stanza 36–37), does he desist from defying Roland if he tries to interfere with his journey: "Thow and I sall dyntis deill quhill ane of us be deid, / For the deidis thow hes me done upon this deir day!" (stanza 40).

Once in Charlemagne's court, there is a sudden change: the collier who has been a dominant and overtly confident character at his house and in his verbal confrontation with Roland feels intimidated by this new world. The discovery of the true identity of the Frankish emperor enhances his fears even more:

"In faith, he [Charlemagne] is of mair stait than ever he me [Rauf] tald.
Allace, that I was hydder wylit,
I dreid me sair I be begylit."
The king previlie smylit
Quhen he saw that bald. (stanza 55)

While in the collier's dwelling the margins of courtly society were transformed into the centre, in Paris the court recovers its centrality and Rauf's homeland becomes the periphery. His rusticity and rude manners are no longer valid; any possibility of the narrator articulating a subversive discourse disappears. The scenario serves to outline the evolution from the comic narrative to the knightly and chivalric context and the ultimate Christian message. This shift characterises the second part of the romance.

In fact, the most remarkable aspect of Rauf's characterisation is not his personal sense of *cortesia* or his aggressiveness against Charlemagne and Roland but his natural nobility and *gentilesse*. As Chaucer tells us:

Vyce may wel be heir to old richesse,
But ther may no man, as men may wel see,
Bequethe his heir his vertuous noblesse
(That is appropred unto no degree
But to the firste fader in magestee,
That maketh hem his heyres that him queme),
Al were he mytre, croune, or diademe. ("Gentilesse", ll.15–21)

Rauf possesses the nobility of the soul to which Chaucer refers, the origin of which is divine and not aristocratic. Such a spiritual attribute predisposes him to provide lodging for Charlemagne. Although this is also a romance motif, Rauf is a member of the Third Estate and not the typical *varvassor* or burgess. His humble origin accentuates his charity. This is a basic feature of the story, which typifies the collier's representation as a good Christian. As R.D.S. Jack and P.A.T. Rozendaal assert, in Matthew 25. 31–46, Christ, on the mount of olives, affirmed that the foremost test for corporeal mercy was to give shelter to those in need (Jack and Rozendaal ed. 1997: 58n). Despite his rudeness, then, Rauf willingly offers his house to Charlemagne quite:

"I wait na worthie harberie heir neir hand
For to serve sic ane man as me think the –
Nane bot mine awin hous, maist in the land,
Fer furth in the forest, amang the fellis hie.
With-thy thow wald be payit of sic as thow fand,
Forsuith, thow suld be welcum to pas hame with me,
Or ony uther gude fallow that I heir fand". (stanza 6)

Rauf's attitude to offer his humble home, not only to Charlemagne but to whoever may need help, projects an image of the collier as an exemplary Christian in the spiritual realm and a man of natural *cortesia* and *largeza* in the earthly domain. This will be a key aspect of the narrative in its later development. Rauf will not have to wait for the other life for his charity to be rewarded. Although it has little to do with a spiritual gift, Charlemagne's gratitude will be materialised in financial and social improvement for the collier: "Befoir mony worthie he dubbit him knicht". The Frankish Emperor also tells Rauf that "Ilk yeir thre hundredth pund assigne the I sall" (stanza 59).

Then, although Shepherd claims that the construction of Rauf can be regarded as that of a serious spokesman for social issues, defending the stratum of society to which he belongs (Shepherd 1991: 287), Rauf's conduct after being knighted seems to contradict the scholar's affirmation. By virtue of becoming a knight, the former collier's demeanour is non-naturalistically dignified:

"For to hald that I have hecht I hope it be the best,
To yone busteous beirne that boistit me to byde.
Amang thir galyart gromis I am bot ane gest,
I will the ganandest gait to that gay glyde.
Sall never lord lauch on loft quhill my lyfe may lest
That I for liddernes suld leif, and levand besyde". (stanza 61)

Suddenly the rustic commoner who knew nothing about the chivalric world behaves and speaks as a knight. No learning process is required. The makar uses this artifice to conform to the *decorum* that a noble-man should show through his conduct. Rauf's language and words reveal the internalisation of his new role in society through such a dramatic, but knightly, assertion that death is better than living in dishonour. More importantly, he realises his position as an outsider and will do his best to integrate. Social critique, then, does not work any longer in the last section of the romance.

The text redefines itself by recreating the context of the typical Charlemagne romances: the fight against the heathen. Although the comic tone predominates during the major part of the narrative, offering a transgressive approach to chivalric values (Jack and Rozendaal ed. 1997: 58), the passage in which a Muslim emir is converted regains the seriousness that such a momentous scene requires. Rauf fights the emir according to the knightly norm: first on horseback (stanza 63), and then on foot with his sword (stanza 64). He is not, and does not behave as, a member of the Third Estate any longer. His way of action and language are the same as those of Charlemagne's knights. Nevertheless, it is not until Roland's intervention that the Saracen is convinced that he should convert to Christianity:

"Na", said Schir Rolland, "that war na resoun.
I trow in the mekle God, that maist of michtis may.
The tane is in power to mak the presoun;
For that war na vassalage, sum men wald say,
I rid that thow hartfully forsaik thy Mahoun.
Fy on that foull fiend, for fals is thy fay;
Becum Cristin, schir knicht, and on Christ call!" (stanza 69)

Although Rauf is already a knight, the writer significantly reverts to the most famous of the twelve peers and his command of rhetoric to persuade the enemy. This narrative strategy highlights the religious significance of such a moment both in the romance and at a spiritual level.

In conclusion, the romance is divided into two thematically and tonally distinctive parts. The first one contrasts the natural *cortesia* of Rauf with the mannered *cortesia* of the upper classes in a humorous manner. Charlemagne accepts the authority of Rauf on the basis of being the latter's guest. Once in the Frankish Emperor's court, however, it is the collier who feels displaced and finally submits to courtly manners and behaviour. The potentially socially disruptive message of the first part disappears, implicitly indicating the superiority of courtly life. In the second part, the makar deals with the central theme of the Matter of France: the struggle against the infidel. All the humour of the previous sections is substituted by the seriousness of the Muslim emir's conversion. Lastly, it is also noteworthy that the display of *cortesia* and nobility is not recreated in a detailed manner as was customary in the French romances. Thematically, then, the author belongs to an established Scottish tradition whereby the depiction of social ceremony is reduced to the minimum.

Conclusion

The Scottish Romance Tradition

When commissioned to compose *The Bruce*, John Barbour went far beyond the commemoration of Robert I's heroic deeds. Through this foundational romance, he disseminated specific ideological tenets and literary conventions which established a national literary tradition in the writing of romances. His cultivated background, including his familiarity with French, Anglo-Norman, English, Latin and Scottish material (now not extant), allowed him to readapt existing traditions. The makar appropriated and redefined epic and romance *loci communes* to fashion a distinctive and ambitious project.

The ideological influence of *The Bruce* on the writing of medieval Scottish romances was considerable. In these works, the debates on good government and kingship are central to the evolution of the narrative, intimately connecting them with the wider Scottish advice to princes tradition. The commonwealth of the nation replaces the individual knightly enterprise of earlier *roman courtois*. The hero's conflict is not generated by the desire to find a place within society but to make his feats of arms serve the interests of the community. This means that it is invested with no less than the importance of the survival and the future of a people – a feature traditionally associated with epic rather than romance. Hence, the individual crisis of the protagonist found in romances such as those of Chrétien de Troyes becomes a collective quest: the traditional quest for identity and a place within feudal society is transformed into a search for the consolidation of shared values. In the historical and Arthurian romances, national and territorial aspirations to freedom comprise the primary instigator of the action rather than the protagonist's idealised love for a lady. Even in *Lancelot of the Laik*, while Lancelot is said to be fighting for the love of Guenevere, his combats are redefined in the epic context of a country's fight to resist foreign subjugation. In this bellicose milieu, the construction of national identity originates from the conflict with invading power which puts forward the need for a unifying definition of commonality and community to overcome a militarily superior force.

All these aspects are directly or indirectly connected with the contemporary political realities of Scotland. The conflictive nature of Anglo-Scottish relationships all through the late Middle Ages determines the high degree of politicisation in these texts. The close heroic past of the Wars of Independence is reshaped to gather support for the reign of Robert II in *The Bruce*, whereas *The Wallace* angrily responds to James III's matrimonial policies with England. In *The Bruce*, the image of the King of Scots is constructed along the lines of a *speculum principis*, and that of Douglas as the ideal of knightly conduct which the nobility should adopt in regards to Robert II. In Hary's *Wallace*, the legendary figure of William Wallace and his comrades-at-arms revive the long lived animosity towards the English at a time when the royal policy of James III favoured a friendly and collaborative approach to the traditional foe. The Arthurian and Alexander romances also problematise the foundations of good kingship and the autonomy of the people. The selections and alterations of particular passages of the French originals convey a different reading in which the Scottish reference is both historically and ideologically present. Even *Rauf Coilyear* represents a Charlemagne who is aware of the limitations of royal power: while at court and on the political arena he is the ideal Frankish leader, his submission to the Rauf's rules at his house enacts the Emperor's respect for individual freedom. The past is deployed to problematise the political tensions of the present.

Although the philosophical and religious bedrock of the Scottish texts lies in the broad Aristotelian tradition as adapted to Christian thought, the heroes' inner progression is inescapably linked to notions of good kingship and the collective welfare of a people. Spiritual awareness grows hand in hand with the protagonist's necessity to understand the intricacies of just government on behalf of all the strata of society. This is not a radical redefinition of late medieval politics since the upper classes are still privileged. The main premise is that, as long as everyone fulfils his/her role in society according to the medieval division of labour, they should be treated fairly. In this way, whereas the heroes' evolution facilitates the integration of some romances such as Hay's *Conquerour* or *Lancelot of the Laik* within the larger corpus of the Scottish advice to princes tradition (owing to their overt debates on the nature of kingship), the other texts also expressed a similar, if less explicit, concern with the state of government. In *The Bruce*, Bruce does not simply evolve to become a perfect knight questing after ethereal ideals. Rather he is transformed into a self-aware sovereign who must prioritise his nation's needs. In the Arthurian romances, Arthur's progression goes beyond literary convention. He is not introduced as a young man but as a mature king who has forgotten the real significance of *pax arturica*. He must undergo a regeneration process as much relating to his inner self as to the respect of Golagros's lands and autonomy in *Golagros and Gawane*, or to the preservation of his kingdom in *Lancelot of the Laik*. The Aristotelian-Boethian element is more accentuated than in the original French texts. In the Alexander romances, the inclusion of Hay's own translation of *Buke of the Governaunce of Princis* accentuates the import of the Macedonian Emperor's kingly learning. In *The Wallace*, the spiritual journey is structurally different. Hary, inspired by the representations of saints' lives, does not portray Wallace as the typical knight who evolves from impulsive young age to wise maturity. Instead, the figure of the *puer senex* is translated into the language and thematic strategies of romances. His progression is about awareness of the paramount importance of the national cause. His personal revenge is first redefined politically and ethically (the defence of Scotland), then allegorically (the struggle becoming a quasi-sacred *avanture* supported by Saint Andrew and the Virgin Mary), and finally anagogically (his sacrifice as a martyr leading to his afterlife salvation). Structurally different though they might be, in the Scottish romances the spiritual or ethical evolution of the heroes cannot be dissociated from their political consciousness on a national level.

On a different level of spirituality, the demise of the heroes in the historical romances is presented via conventional Christian symbolism; this symbolism is in typological correspondence with Christ's death at a time when living a proper life was as important as dying a holy death. This representation appears in most serious late medieval European romances such as the Anglo-Norman *Chanson de Guillaume le Maréchal* or the French *Vie de Saint Louis*. After the protagonists solve their terrestrial, political duties, they die in a way in which they secure a place in heaven. Following this *locus classicus*, both Bruce and Wallace instruct David II and Bruce respectively so that the succession in the leadership of Scotland guarantees the autonomy and good functioning of the nation.

Barbour also defined the literary parameters of *cortesia* and knighthood. He had the advantage of having at his disposal a fully developed range of forms and motifs from which to select the most suitable for his ambitious project. His subject matter (and that of Hary and the anonymous makars of *Lancelot of the Laik* and *Golagros and Gawane*) required the accentuation of knightly virtues rather than of courtly demeanour. However, had any of the makars wanted to include the sophistication of a courtly atmosphere, it would not have been at all difficult to represent the figures of Bruce or Wallace along these lines. In fact, in the Arthurian romances not only did the authors minimise such features but they got rid of many of the courtly scenes appearing in the originals. While courtliness plays an important role in the Alexander romances, it is still re-codified within the parameters of knighthood. The *Buik of Alexander* explores the limitations of both an exclusively epic narrative and an exclusively courtly text. Only the final intervention of Alexander reconciles the two discourses through the language and ways of action of practical politics, bringing the text to a more realistic conclusion of feudal pacts than either the *Forray* or the *Avowis* could suggest. Again, politics are central to the development of knighthood in the *Buik of King Alexander the Conquerour*. The Battlefield scenes and Alexander knightly virtues, as in most Scottish romances, are at the service of the common good, and closely related to the king's duties.

The profound redefinition of courtly literary devices and forms of expression may appear to be part of a larger British tradition. Like the Scottish texts, Anglo-Norman and fourteenth-century English alliterative romances do not generally elaborate on ornamented descriptions of life at court or the intricacies of *fin'amors* as much as their French counterparts. Nevertheless, the earlier and contemporary English Arthurian romances lack the exact thematic, political focus of the Scottish compositions: Anglo-Norman and English romances tend to scrutinise the tensions between the barony and the king whereas the Scottish works adopt a much more national perspective whereby the government of the country was intimately related to the fortunes of its people in the context of international rather than simply feudal conflicts. It is precisely this narrative axis that may have induced Barbour to simplify or suppress long digressions on courteous manners and erotic entanglement. If individual quests and the fulfilment of *fin'amors* were no longer at the core of the story line, their inclusion became optional (and even distracting from the main narrative) rather than indispensable. *Fin'amors* is nothing but a marginal feature which does not contribute to the protagonists' evolution in either historical or chivalric romances. In *The Bruce*, Barbour subverts the *amor et militia* topos by displacing the love plot to the English side. Its outcome, with the death of an English knight who wanted to please his lady's requests, questions the validity of such an attitude in real warfare. In *The Wallace*, love is integrated into the nationalistic dialectics of the text. The killing of Wallace's wife brings about further revenge against the English. In the Arthurian works, Lancelot's love for Guenevere is placed at the service of the liberation of Arthur's territories whereas in *Golagros and Gawane* love is completely removed from the narrative. As a consequence, the number of female figures, who played a basic role in courtly interchanges and the love plot, is drastically reduced too. This re-codification of *cortesia*, *fin'amors*, and the feminine becomes a fundamental trait of the Scottish romance tradition. Displays of *cortesia* are reduced to a minimum. Although the terminology of courtly behaviour is kept, it is very schematically represented. It serves to complement the image of the heroes but is never one of their primordial attributes. Even in the Alexander romances, *cortesia* and *fin'amors* are secondary to territorial and national concerns, unlike the central role which they play in other European traditions. In the *Conquerour*, in which the number of courtly scenes is superior to any other Older Scots romance studied in this book, *fin'amors* is mainly confined to Alexander's moralistic interpretation. His knights' amorous encounters are permitted as long as they do not interfere with the Macedonian Emperor's conquering plans.

In this context, the knightly feats and conduct dominate the narrative. The adaptation of these thematic motifs and modes of expression configures the literary character of the Scottish romances. The preference for the masculine domain of knighthood to the feminised courtly world leads to the predominance of martial exploits. The language deployed endorses rapid narrative pace of events. The dearth of long descriptions of the pomp of tournaments and courtly feasts, and of psychological expositions of the lovers' inner state, also contributes to the creation of an agile narratorial evolution within the texts. Apart from the *Conquerour's* cumulative narrative, there are no elaborate digressions from the central theme. The result is a compact romance both narratorially and ideologically. This difference becomes especially obvious when the adaptations of the originals in the Arthurian works are considered. The long French texts, in which many different actions come together, are drastically modified. Firstly, the narrative is very compact; secondly, the value system is altered: courtliness and *fin'amors* are reduced to a large extent; and thirdly, the political aspects are underlined. The exception to this rule is *Clariodus* whose adaptation preserves all the ornamentation and psychological debates of the original. Even *Eger and Grime*, with its substantially different subject matter from that of the historical, Alexander and Arthurian romances, follows the precise syncretism favoured in the Scottish corpus.

All these shared thematic, philosophical and ideological components constitute the late medieval Scottish romance tradition. In comparison to French romances, the lack of courtly elements and the long disquisitions on the nature of *fin'amors* should not be seen as some kind of deficiency but as a stylistic and thematic choice based on the overtly political implications of the texts at a national level. It is precisely this national concern which differentiates the Scottish tradition from the also overtly ideological Anglo-Norman and Middle English romances, which opt to discuss political affairs from the point of view of the barons' perspective. Even when in Scotland romances such as Hary's *Wallace* put forward ideas closer to the interests of a noble faction rather than those of the royal house, the narratives adapt a national perspective. As well as a differentiated romance tradition in the European milieu, the romances offer an alternative but interlacing literary tradition to that of the great makars even if the former do not share is their metrical disposition. In fact, as claimed earlier, this might be the main reason why they have not been considered as belonging to the same corpus so far. Yet the great makars, Henryson, Dunbar and Douglas, deployed different modes of expression at the same time that no-one would question as being part of the same late medieval Scottish practice. For this reason, formal aspects should not hinder us from regarding the romances as constituents of the same literary tradition. It is necessary to understand the importance of the romances to have a more complete vision of Older Scots literary culture. Indeed, Hary and the anonymous authors of *Lancelot of the Laik* and *Golagros and Gawane* show the interrelationship between the courtly and the romance traditions. The Prologue of the Scottish

Lancelot and numerous passages in *The Wallace* are still reminiscent of the highly sophisticated literary culture of the Scottish court in the late Middle Ages. In this light of reciprocity, Douglas's masterpiece, the translation of the *Aeneid*, can be considered the culmination of John Barbour's literary efforts to create a distinctive vernacular tradition in Scots.

Bibliography

Primary Texts

Adomnán, Saint. 1995. *Life of Saint Columba* (tr. R. Sharpe). London: Penguin.

Agustín, San. *La ciudad de Dios*. México: Editorial Porrúa, 1998.

Andreas Capellanus. 1982. *On Love* (tr. P.G. Walsh). London: Duckworth.

Aneirin. 1994. *The Gododdin* (tr. S. Short). Felinfach: Llanerch Publishers.

Ambroise. 1897. *Le Estoire de la Guerre Sainte*. Paris: Imprimerie Nationale.

—. 1941. *The Crusade of Richard Lion-Heart* (tr. M.J. Hubert). New York: Columbia University Press.

Aristotle. 1940. *Art of Poetry* (tr. I. Bywater). Oxford: Clarendon Press.

—. 1892. *The Nicomachean Ethics* (tr. ed. J.E.C. Welldon). London: MacMillan and Co.

—. 1909. *Rhetoric* (tr. R.C. Jebb). Cambridge: Cambridge University Press.

Augustine, Saint. 1948. *The City of God* (tr. ed. M. Dods). 2 vols. New York: Hafner Publishing Company.

—. 1956. *The City of God and Christian Doctrine* (tr. M. Dods and J.F. Shaw). Michigan: W.M.B. Eerdmans Publishing Company.

The Awntyrs off Arthure at the Terne Wathelyne. 1969. (ed. R.J. Gates). Philadelphia: University of Pennsylvania Press.

Barbour, John. 1790. *The Bruce* (ed. J. Pinkerton). 3 vols. London: H. Hughs.

—. 1869. *The Bruce* (ed. J. Jamieson). Glasgow: Maurice Ogle & Co.

—. 1894–95. *The Bruce* (ed. W.W. Skeat). 3 vols [First Series 31, 32, 33]. Edinburgh and London: The Scottish Text Society.

—. 1909. *The Bruce* (ed. W.M. McKenzie). London: A. & C. Black.

—. 1981–85. *The Bruce* (ed. Matthew P. McDiarmid and J.A.C. Stevenson). 3 vols [Fourth Series, 15, 12, 13]. Edinburgh: Scottish Text Society.

—. [1907] 1996. *The Bruce* (tr. G. Eyre-Todd). Edinburgh: The Mercat Press.

—. 1997. *The Bruce* (tr. ed. A.A.M. Duncan) [Canongate Classics 78]. Edinburgh: Canongate Books.

Bede. 1990. *Ecclesiastical History of the English People* (tr. L. Sherley-Price). Harmondworth: Penguin Books.

Beroul. 1989. *The Romance of Tristan*. (tr. ed. N.J. Lacy) [The Garland Library of Medieval Literature, Series A 36]. New York and London: Garland.

Blind Hary. 1884–89. *The Wallace* (ed. J. Moir). 3 vols [First Series 6, 7, 17]. Edinburgh and London: Scottish Text Society.

—. 2003. *The Wallace* (ed. Anne McKim) [Canongate Classics 112]. Edinburgh: Canongate Books.

Boethius. 1999. *The Consolation of Philosophy* (tr. P.G. Walsh). Oxford: Oxford University Press.

The Brut or The Chronicles of England. 1906. (ed. F.W.D. Brie). 2 vols [Original Series 131, 136]. London: Early English Text Society.

The Buik of Alexander. 1921–29. (ed. R.L.G. Ritchie). 4 vols [Second Series 12, 17, 21, 25]. Edinburgh and London: Scottish Text Society.

Chandos Herald. 1975. *La Vie du Prince Noir*. (ed. Diana B. Tyson). Tübingen: Max Niemeyer Verlag.

La Chanson d'Aspremont. 1923–24. (ed. L. Brandin). 2 vols. Paris: Librairie Ancienne Honoré Champion.

La Chanson de Girart de Roussillon. 1993. (ed. M. de Combarieu de Grès and G. Gouiran). Paris: Librairie Générale Française.

La Chanson de Roland. 1990. (tr. ed. Ian Short). Paris: Lettres Gothiques.

Chaucer, Geoffrey. 1988. *The Riverside Chaucer* (ed. L.D. Benson). Oxford: Oxford University Press.

Le chevalerie Ogier de Danemarch. [1832–48] 1969. 2 vols [Romans des Douze Pairs de France 8, 9]. Genève: Slatkine Reprints.

Chrétien de Troyes. 1990. *El conte del Graal* (tr. ed. Martí de Riquer). Barcelona: Quaderns Crema.

—. 1991. *Arthurian Romances* (tr. William W. Kibler and Carleton W. Carroll). Harmondsworth: Penguin.

—. 1994. *Romans*. Paris: Livre de Poche.

Christine de Pizan. 1977. *Ditié de Jehanne d'Arc* (ed. A.J. Kennedy and K. Varty). Oxford: Society for the Study of Mediaeval Languages and Literature.

—. 1997. *The Selected Writings of Christine de Pizan* (ed. R. Blumenfeld-Kosinski, tr. R. Blumenfeld-Kosinski, and Kevin Brownlee). New York and London: W.W. Norton & Company.

—. 1998. *Le Livre du corps de la policie* (ed. A.J. Kennedy). Paris: Honor Champion.

Clariodus: A Metrical Romance. 1830. (ed. Edward Piper). Edinburgh: the Maitland Club.

Cleriadus et Meliadice: Roman en prose du XVe siècle. 1984. (ed. Gaston Zink). Paris: Librairie Droz.

The Cloud of Unknowing. 1973. (tr. C. Wolters). Harmondsworth: Penguin Books.

Cuvelier. 1990. *La Chanson de Bertrand du Guesclin* (ed. J.C. Faucon). 3 vols. Toulouse: Éditions Universitaires du Sud.

Dunbar, William. 1996. *Selected Poems* (ed. Priscilla Bawcutt). London and New York: Longman.

Early Popular Poetry of Scotland. 1895. (ed. David Laing). 2 vols. London: Reeves and Turner.

Eger and Grime: A Parallel-Text Edition of the Percy and the Huntington-Laing Versions of the Romance. 1933. (ed. J.R. Caldwell) [Harvard Studies in Comparative Literature IX]. Cambridge: Harvard University Press.

Enéas. 1891. (ed. Jacques Salverda de Grave). Halle: Max Niemeyer.

Eneas, A Twelfth-century French Romance. 1974. (tr. John A. Yunck). New York: Columbia University Press.

Froissart, Jean. 1838–42. *Les Chroniques de Jean Froissart* (ed. J.A.C. Buchon). 3 vols. Paris: Société du Panthéon Littéraire.

Froissart, John. 1859. *Chronicles of England, France, Spain and the Adjoining Countries: From the Latter Part of the Reign of Edward II to the Coronation of Henry IV* (tr. T. Johnes). 2 vols. London: Henry G. Bohn.

—. 1979. *Dits et Débats* (ed. F. Fourrier) [Textes Littéraires Français, 274]. Genève: Librairie Droz.

Geoffrey of Monmouth. 1928. *History of the Kings of Britain* (tr. S. Evans). London: J.M. Dent & Sons.

Geoffrey of Vinsauf. 1971. *The Poetria Nova and Its Sources in Early Rhetorical Doctrine* (tr. ed. E. Gallo) [De Proprietatibus Litterarum, Series Maior 10]. The Hague: Mouton.

Geoffroi de Charny. 1996. *The Book of Chivalry* (ed. R.W. Kaeuper and E. Kennedy). Philadelphia: University of Pennsylvania Press.

Guillaume le Clerc. 1983. *The Romance of Fergus* (ed. W. Frescoln). Philadelphia: W.H. Allen.

—. 1991. *Fergus of Galloway: Knight of King Arthur* (tr. D.D.R. Owen). London: Dent.

Guy of Warwick. 1883, 1887, 1889. (ed. J. Zupitza). 3 vols [Extra Series 42, 49, 59]. London: Early English Text Society.

Hamilton of Gilbertfield, William. 1998. *Hary's Wallace.* Edinburgh: Luath Press Ltd.

Hary. 1968. *The Wallace* (ed. Matthew P. McDiarmid). 2 vols [Fourth Series 4, 5]. Edinburgh and London: Scottish Text Society.

—. 2003. (ed. Anne McKim) [Canongate Classics 112]. Edinburgh: Canongate Books.

Le Haut Livre du Graal: Perlesvaus. 1932–37. (ed. W.A. Nitze, and T.A. Jenkins). Chicago: University of Chicago Press.

Hay, Sir Gilbert. 1986. *The Buik of King Alexander the Conquerour* (ed. J. Cartwright). 3 vols [Fourth Series 16, 18]. Aberdeen: Scottish Text Society.

Haye, Gilbert of the. 1901–14. *Gilbert of the Haye's Prose Manuscripts* (ed. J.H. Stevenson). 2 vols [First Series 44, 62]. Edinburgh and London: Scottish Text Society.

Horace. 1874. *The Works of Horace.* (tr. J.G. Lonsdale and S. Lee). London: Mac-Millan and Co., Ltd.

Hugh of Saint Victor. 1961. *Didascalicon: A Medieval Guide to the Arts* (tr. ed. J. Taylor) [Records of Civilization, Sources and Studies 64]. New York: Columbia University Press.

Jaufré: Roman arthurien du XIIIe siècle en vers provençaux. 1943. (ed. C. Brunel). 2 vols. Paris: Société des Anciens Textes Français.

Jean le Ménestrel. 1891–1901. *L'Histoire de Guillaume le Maréchal* (ed. P. Meyer). 3 vols. Paris: Société de l'Histoire de France,

Johannes de Irlandia. 1925–90. *The Meroure of Wyssdome* (ed. C.J. Macpherson, F. Quinn and C. McDonald). 3 vols [New Series 19; Fourth Series 2, 19] Edinburgh: Scottish Text Society.

John of Salisbury. 1927. *Policraticus* (tr. J. Dickinson). New York: Alfred A. Knopf.

Joinville, Jehan. 1977. *La Vie de Saint Louis* (ed. N.L. Corbett). Sherbrooke: Éditions Naaman.

Karlamagnús Saga: The Saga of Charlemagne and his Heroes. 1975. (tr. C.B. Hieatt). 3 vols. Toronto: The Pontifical Institute of Mediaeval Studies.

Lancelot do Lac: The Non-Cyclic Old French Prose Romance. 1980. (ed. E. Kennedy). Oxford: Clarendon Press.

Lancelot of the Laik. 1912. (ed. Margaret M. Gray) [Second Series 2]. Edinburgh and London: Scottish Text Society.

Lancelot of the Laik. 1865. (ed. W.W. Skeat) [Original Series 6]. London: Early English Text Society.

Lancelot of the Laik. 1839. (ed. J. Stevenson). Edinburgh: Maitland Club.

Lancelot of the Laik and Sir Tristrem. 1994. (ed. A. Lupack). Kalamazoo: Medieval Institute Publications.

Lancelot. Roman en prose du XIIIᵉ siècle. 1978–83. (ed. A. Micha). 9 vols. Gevève: Droz.

Langland, William. 1995. *The Vision of Piers Plowman* (ed. A.V.C. Schmidt). London: Everyman.

La Sale, Antoine de. 1995. *Jehan de Saintré* (ed. J. Blanchard). Paris: Libraire Générale Française.

Legends of the Saints. 1886–96. (ed. W.M. Metcalfe). 6 vols [First Series 13, 18, 23, 25, 35, 37]. Edinburgh: Scottish Text Society.

Lindsay, Sir David. 1959. *Squyer Meldrum* (ed. J. Kinsley). London and Edinburgh: Thomas Nelson.

—. 1989. *Ane Satyre of the Thrie Estaitis* (ed. R. Lyall) [Canongate Classics 18]. Edinburgh: Canongate Publishing Limited.

Llull, Ramon. 1987. *Llibre d'Evast e Blanquerna* [Millors Obres de la Literatura Catalana, 82]. Barcelona: Edicions 62.

—. 1988. *Llibre de l'orde de cavalleria* [Els Nostres Clàssics, Col·lecció A 127]. Barcelona: Barcino.

—. 1992. *Libre del orde de cavayleria.* Valencia: Biblioteca Valenciana.

Lull, Ramon. 1926. *Blanquerna: A Thirteenth Century Romance.* (tr. E.A. Peers). London: Jarrolds.

—. 1926. *The Book of the Ordre of Chyualry* (tr. William Caxton). London: Early English Text Society.

—. 1976. *The Book of the Ordre of Chyvalry or Knyghthode.* (tr. William Caxton). Amsterdam: Theatrum Orbis Terrarum, Ltd.

Machaut, Guillaume de. 1908–21. *Oeuvres de Guillaume de Machaut* (ed. E. Hoepffner). 3 vols [Société des Anciens Textes Français, 57]. Paris: Didot and Librairie Ancien Edouard Champion.

Macrobius. 1952. *Commentary on the Dream of Scipio.* (tr. W.H. Stahl). New York: University of Columbia Press.

Martorell, Joanot. 1990. *Tirant lo Blanc i altres escrits* (ed. Martí de Riquer). Barcelona: Editorial Ariel.

McClure, J. Derrick. 1979. "The *Florimond* Fragment" in *Scottish Literary Studies*, Supplement, 10: 1–10.

Mézières, Philippe de. 1969. *Le Songe de Vieil Pelerin* (ed. G.W. Coopland). 2 vols. Cambridge: Cambridge University Press.

La Mort le Roi Artu. 1954. (ed. J. Frappier). Genève; Librairie Droz.

Plato. [1938] 1950. *Phaedo* in *Portraits of Socatres* (tr. B. Jowett, ed. R.W. Livingstone). Oxford: Clarendon Press.

—. 1888. *The Republic* (tr. ed. B. Jowett). Oxford: Clarendon Press.

Poesia trobadoresca. 1982. (tr. A. Badia) [Millors Obres de la Literatura Universal 14]. Barcelona: Edicions 62.

Première Continuation de Perceval. 1993. (W. Roach). Paris: Librairie Générale Française.

Shakespeare, William. [1951] 1992. *The Complete Works of William Shakespeare* (ed. P. Alexander). London and Glasgow: Collins.

Sir Beves of Hamtoun: A Metrical Romance. 1838. (ed. W.B.D.D. Turnbull) [Maitland Club, 44]. Edinburgh: Maitland Club.

Sir Gawain and the Green Knight, Pearl, Cleanness, Patience. 1996. (ed. J.J. Anderson). London: Everyman.

Sir Gawain: Eleven Romances and Tales. 1995. (ed. Thomas Hahn). Kalamazoo: Medieval Institute Publications.

Sir Tristrem. 1886. (ed. G.P. McNeill) [First Series 8]. Edinburgh and London: Scottish Text Society.

Sir Tristrem: A Metrical Romance of the Thirteenth Century. 1806. in Scott, Sir Walter (ed.). *The Poetical Works of Sir Walter Scott, vol. V*. Edinburgh: Ballantyne and Co.

Scottish Alliterative Poems. 1896. (ed. F.J. Amours) [First Series 38]. Edinburgh and London: Scottish Text Society.

Stewart, Marion. 1972. "A Recently-Discovered Manuscript: 'ane taill of Sit colling ye kny'" in *Scottish Studies* 16: 23–39.

—. 1973. "*King Orpheus*" in *Scottish Studies* 17: 1–16.

Thomas à Kempis. 1972. *The Imitation of Christ* (tr. L. Sherley-Price). Harmondsworth: Penguin Books.

Thomas Aquinas. 1988. *St. Thomas Aquinas on Politics and Ethics* (tr. ed. P.E. Sigmund). New York: W.W. Norton & Company.

Thomas Aquinas. 1989. *Summa Theologiae* (tr. ed. T. McDermott). London: Eyre and Spottiswoode and Methuen.

Los trovadores: Historia literaria y textos. 1975. (tr. ed. Martín de Riquer). 3 vols. Barcelona: Editorial Planeta.

Virgil. 1903. *The Works of Virgil* (tr. J. Lonsdale and S. Lee). New York: The MacMillan Company.

—. 1969. *Opera* (ed. R.A.B. Mynors). Oxford: Clarendon Press.

Le Voyage de Charlemagne a Jérusalem et Constantinople. 1965. (ed. P. Aebischer). Genève: Librairie Droz.

The Vulgate Version of Arthurian Romances. 1908–16. (ed. H.O. Sommer). 8 vols. Washington: Carnegie Institution.

Wace. 1962. *La Partie Arthurienne du Roman de Brut* (ed. A.I. Arnold and M. Pelan). Paris: Librairie L. Klincksieck.

Wace and Layamon. 1962. *Arthurian Chronicles* (tr. Eugene Mason). London: Dent.

Wedderburn, Robert. 1979. *The Complaint of Scotland* (ed. A.M. Stewart) [Fourth Series 11]. Edinburgh: Scottish Text Society.

Secondary Texts

Adler, Alfred. 1959. "Eneas et Lavine: *puer et puella senes*?" in *Romanische Forschungen* 71: 73–91.

Alexander, Flora. 1975. "Late Medieval Scottish Attitudes to the Figure of King Arthur: A Reassessment" in *Anglia* 93: 17–34.

Auerbach, Erich. 1965. *Literary Language and its Public in Late Latin Antiquity and in the Middle Ages* (tr. Ralph Manheim). London: Routledge.

—. 1953. *Mimesis: The Representation of Reality in Western Literature*. (tr. W.R. Trask). Princeton: Princeton University Press.

Barber, Richard. 1995. *The Knight and Chivalry*. Woodbridge: The Boydell Press.

Barrell, Andrew D.M. 2000. *Medieval Scotland.* Cambridge: Cambridge University Press.

Barron, W.R.J. 1963. "*Golagrus and Gawane:* A Scot's Conception of Love and Honour" in *Bibliographical Bulletin of the International Arthurian Society* 15: 131–32.

—. 1974. "*Golagros and Gawain*: A Creative Redaction" in *Bibliographical Bulletin of the International Arthurian Society* 26: 173–85.

—. 1987. *English Medieval Romance.* London and New York: Longman.

Barrow, G.W.S. 1979 "The Idea of Freedom in Late Medieval Scotland" in *The Innes Review* 30: 16–34.

—. [1965] 1988. *Robert the Bruce and the Community of the Realm of Scotland.* Edinburgh: Edinburgh University Press.

Bawcutt, Pricilla. 1976. *Gavin Douglas.* Edinburgh: Edinburgh University Press.

—. 2001–2. "English Books and Scottish Readers in the Fifteenth and Sixteenth Centuries" in *Review of Scottish Culture* 14: 1–12.

Beaumont, Jacqueline. 1981. "The Latin Tradition of the *De Consolatione Philosophiae*" in Gibson, Margaret (ed.) *Boethius: His Life, Thought and Influence.* Oxford: Basil Blackwell Publisher Ltd. 278–305.

Bawcutt, Priscilla and Janet Hadley Williams (eds). 2006. *A Companion to Medieval Scottish Poetry.* Cambridge: D.S. Brewer.

Beer, Gillian. *The Romance.* 1970. [The Critical Idiom 10]. London: Methuen and Co. Ltd.

Benson, Larry D. 1980. "The Tournament in the Romances of Chrétien de Troyes and *L'Histoire de Guillaume le Maréchal*" in Benson, L. D. and J. Leyerle (eds) *Chivalric Literature.* Kalamazoo: Medieval Institute Publications. 1–24.

Berlin, Isaiah. 1958. *Two Concepts of Liberty: An Inaugural Lecture Delivered before the University of Oxford on 31 October, 1958.* Oxford: Clarendon Press.

Blacker, Jean. 1994. *The Faces of Time: Portrayal of the Past in Old French and Latin Historical Narrative of the Anglo-Norman Regnum.* Austin: University of Texas Press.

Bloch, Marc. 1939. *La société féodale: La formation des liens de dépendance.* Paris: Éditions Albin Michel.

—. 1961. *Feudal Society* (tr. L.A. Manyon). London: Routledge & K. Paul.

Boase, Roger. 1977. *The Origin and Meaning of Courtly Love: A Critical Study of European Scholarship.* Manchester: Manchester University Press.

Boardman, Steve. 2002. "Late Medieval Scotland and the Matter of Britain" in Cowan, Edward J. and Richard J. Finlay (eds) *Scottish History: The Power of the Past.* Edinburgh: Edinburgh University Press. 47–72.

Bogdanow, Fanny. 1972. "The Treatment of the Lancelot-Guenevere Theme in the Prose *Lancelot*" in *Medium Aevum* 41: 110–20.

Brewer, D.S. (ed.). 1966. *Chaucer and Chaucerians.* London and Edinburgh: Nelson.

Broun, Dauvit, Richard J. Finlay and Michael Lynch (eds). 1998. *Image and Identity: The Making and Remaking of Scotland through the Ages.* Edinburgh: John Donald.

Brown, J.T.T. 1900. *The Wallace and The Bruce Restudied.* Bonn: P. Hanstein.

Bruckner, Matilda Tomaryn. 2001. "The Shape of Romance in Medieval France" in Krueger, Roberta L. (ed.) *The Cambridge Companion to Medieval Romance.* Cambridge: Cambridge University Press. 13–28.

Burlin, Robert B. 1995. "Middle English Romance: The Structure of Genre" in *Chaucer Review* 30: 1–14.

Caie, Graham et al. (eds). *The European Sun: Proceedings of the Seventh International Conference on Medieval and Renaissance Scottish Language and Literature*. Glasgow: Tuckwell Press.

Calin, William. 1962. *The Old French Epic of Revolt: Raoul de Cambrai, Renaud de Montauban, Gormond et Isembard*. Genève: E. Droz.

—. 1994. *The French Tradition and the Literature of Medieval England*. Toronto: University of Toronto Press.

Cartwright, John. 1986. "Sir Gilbert Hay and the *Alexander* Tradition" in Strauss, Dietrich and Horst W. Drescher (eds) *Scottish Language and Literature, Medieval and Renaissance: Fourth International Conference 1984*. Frankfurt and New York: Peter Lang. 229–38.

—. 1991a. "Basilisks, Brahmins and Other Aliens: Encountering the Other in Sir Gilbert Hay's *Alexander*" in *Studies in Scottish Literature* 26: 334–42.

—. 1991b. "Sir Gilbert Hay's *Alexander*: A Study in Transformations" in *Medium Aevum* 60(1): 61–72.

Cazelles, Brigitte. 1996. *The Unholy Grail. A Social Reading of Chrétien de Troyes's Conte Du Graal*. Stanford: Stanford University Press.

Clanchy, M.T. [1979] 1987. *From Memory to Written Record: England 1066–1307*. London: Edward Arnold.

Coleman, Janet. 1981. *English Literature in History, 1350–1400: Medieval Readers and Writers*. London: Hutchinson.

Copleston, F.C. [1955] 1991. *Aquinas*. London: Penguin Books.

Cormier, Raymond J. 1973. *One Heart one Mind: The Rebirth of Virgil's Hero in Medieval French Romance*. Valencia: Romance Monographs, inc.

Cowan, Edward J. 1998. "Identity, Freedom and the Declaration of Arbroath" in Broun, Dauvit, Richard J. Finlay and Michael Lynch, (eds) *Image and Identity: The Making and Remaking of Scotland through the Ages*. 38–68.

Craigie, William A., A.J. Aitken and James A.C. Stevenson (eds). 1931–2002. *A Dictionary of the Older Scottish Tongue: From the Twelfth Century to the End of the Seventeenth*. Chicago: University of Chicago Press.

Crane, Susan. 1986. *Insular Romance: Politics, Faith, and Culture in Anglo-Norman and Middle English Literature*. Berkeley: University of California Press.

Crosby, Ruth. 1936. "Oral Delivery in the Middle Ages" in *Speculum* 11: 88–110.

Curtius, Ernst Robert. [1953] 1990. *European Literature and the Latin Middle Ages* (tr. W.R. Trask) [Bollingen Series 36]. Princeton: Princeton University Press.

Denomy, Alexander J. 1947. *The Heresy of Courtly Love*. New York: The Declan X. McMullen Company, Inc.

Desmond, Marilynn. 1994. *Reading Dido: Gender, Textuality, and the Medieval Aeneid* [Medieval Cultures 8]. Minneapolis: University of Minnesota Press.

Dickinson, W.C., G. Donaldson and I.A. Milne (eds). 1952–53. *A Source Book of Scottish History*. 2 vols. London: Thomas Nelson and Sons Ltd.

Dickson, Thomas and James Balfour Paul (eds). 1877. *Accounts of the Lord Higher Treasurer of Scotland*. Volume 1. Edinburgh: H.M. General Register House.

Dronke, Peter. 1968. *The Medieval Lyric*. London: Hutchinson University Library.

Duby, Georges. 1978. *Les trois ordres, ou, l'imaginaire du féodalisme*. Paris: Gallimard.

—. 1980. *The Three Orders: Feudal Society Imagined* (tr. A. Goldhammer). Chicago: The University of Chicago Press.

—. 1984. *Guillaume le Maréchal ou le meilleur chevalier du monde*. La Flèche: Fayard.

Dufournet, Jean (ed.). 1975. *Relire le "Roman d'Enéas"*. Paris: Librairie Honoré Champion.

Dumézil, Georges. 1995. *Mythe et epopée*. Paris: Gallimard.

Ebin, Lois A. 1971–72. "John Barbour's *Bruce*: Poetry, History and Propaganda" in *Studies in Scottish Literature* 9: 218–42.

Edington, Carol. 1995. *Court and Culture in Renaissance Scotland: Sir David Lindsay of the Mount (1486–1555)*. East Linton: Tuckwell Press.

—. 1998. "Paragons and Patriots: National Identity and the Chivalric Ideal in Late-Medieval Scotland" in Broun, Dauvit, Finlay Richard J. and Lynch, Michael (eds) *Image and Identity: The Making and Remaking of Scotland Through the Ages*. 69–81.

Edwards, A.S.G. 2000. "Contextualising Middle Scots Romance" in Houwen, L.A.J.R., A.A. MacDonald and S.L. Mapstone (eds) *A Palace in the Wild: Essays on Vernacular Cultural and Humanism in Late-Medieval and Renaissance Scotland*. Peeters: Mediaevalia Groningana. 61–73.

Evans, Deanna Delmar. 2001. "Re-evaluating the Case for a Scottish Eger and Grime" in Caie, Graham et al. (eds) *The European Sun: Proceedings of the Seventh International Conference on Medieval and Renaissance Scottish Language and Literature*. Glasgow: Tuckwell Press, 276–87.

Fanon, Frantz. [1967] 1980. *The Wretched of the Earth* (tr. C. Farrington). Harmondsworth: Penguin Books.

Faris, David E. 1981. "The Art of Adventure in the Middle English Romance: *Ywain and Gawain, Eger and Grime*" in *Studia Neophilologica* 53: 91–100.

Field, Rosalind. 1999. "Romance in England 1066–1400" in Wallace, David (ed) *The Cambridge History of Medieval English Literature*. Cambridge: Cambridge University Press. 152–76.

Finlayson, John. 1980 "Definitions of Middle English Romance" in *Chaucer Review* 15: 44–62.

Forde, Simon et al. (eds). 1995. *Concepts of National Identity in the Middle Ages*. Leeds: School of English, University of Leeds.

Foucault, Michel. 1979–90. *The History of Sexuality* (tr. R. Hurley). 3 vols. Harmondsworth: Penguin Books.

Fox, Denton. 1966. "The Scottish Chaucerians" in Brewer, D.S. (ed.) *Chaucer and Chaucerians*. London: Thomas Nelson and Sons. 164–200.

Frappier, Jean. 1957–58 "Le personnage de Gauvain dans le *Première Continuation de Perceval*" in *Romance Philology* 11: 331–44.

—. 1964. "Le personnage de Galehaut dans le *Lancelot en prose*" in *Romance Philology* 17(3): 535–54.

Gaunt, Simon. 2001. "Romance and Other Genres" in Krueger, Roberta L. (ed.) *The Cambridge Companion to Medieval Romance*. Cambridge: Cambridge University Press. 45–59.

Gaunt, Simon and Sarah Kay (eds). 1999. *The Troubadours: An Introduction*. Cambridge: Cambridge University Press.

Gerould, Gordon Hall. 1916. *Saint's Lives*. Boston and New York: Houghton Mifflin Company.

Gilbert, Jane and Ad Putter (eds). 2000. *The Spirit of Medieval English Popular Romance*. Harlow: Longman.

Gibson, Margaret (ed.). 1981. *Boethius: His Life, Thought and Influence*. Oxford: Basil Blackwell Publisher Ltd.

Gilson, Étienne. 1936. *The Spirit of Medieval Philosophy* (tr. A. H. C. Downes). London: Sweed & Ward.

Goldstein, R.J. 1991. "The Women of the Wars of Independence in Literature and History" in *Studies in Scottish Literature* 26: 271–82.

—. 1993. *The Matter of Scotland*. Lincoln and London: University of Nebraska Press.

Grillo, Peter R. 1968 "The Courtly Background in the *Roman d'Enéas*" in *Neuphilologische Mitteilungen* 69: 688–702.

Guenée, Bernard. 1985. *States and Rulers in Later Medieval Europe* (tr. J. Vale). Oxford: Basil Blackwell.

Hahn, Thomas. 2001. "Gawain and Popular Chivalric Romance in Britain" in Krueger, Roberta L. (eds) *The Cambridge Companion to Medieval Romance*. Cambridge: Cambridge University Press. 218–34.

Hall, Stefan Thomas. 2004. "'Quham dowis thow Scot' Scottish Identity in Blind Hary's *Wallace*" in *Studies in Scottish Literature* 33–34: 177–94.

Harding, Alan. 1980. "Political Liberty in the Middle Ages" in *Speculum* 55: 423–43.

Hardman, Phillipa. 2002. *The Matter of Identity in Medieval Romance*. Woodbridge: D.S. Brewer.

Harf, Laurence. 1984. "Lancelot et la Dame du Lac" in *Romania* 105: 16–32.

Harward, Vernon. 1972. "Hary's *Wallace* and Chaucer's *Troilus and Criseyde*" in *Studies in Scottish Literature* 10: 40–50.

Hasler, Antony J. 2000. "Romance and its discontents in *Eger and Grime*" in Gilbert, Jane and Ad Putter (eds) *The Spirit of Medieval English Popular Romance*. Harlow: Longman, 200–18.

Henderson, T.F. 1910. *Scottish Vernacular Literature: A Succinct Study*. 3rd rev. ed. Edinburgh: John Grant.

Hewitt, David and Michael Spiller (eds). 1983. *Literature of the North*. Aberdeen: Aberdeen University Press.

Hobsbawm, E.J. 1990. *Nations and Nationalism since 1780: Programme, Myth and Reality*. Cambridge: Cambridge University Press.

Huchet, Jean-Charles. 1984. *Le Roman médiéval*. Paris: Presses Universitaires de France.

Huizinga, Johan. 1990. *The Waning of the Middle Ages* (tr. F. Hopman). London: Penguin Books.

Iser, Wolfgang. 1978. *The Act of Reading: A Theory of Aesthetic Response*. London: Routledge and Kegan Paul Ltd.

Jack, R.D.S. 1972. *The Italian Influence on Scottish Literature*. Edinburgh: Edinburgh University Press.

—. 1974–75. "Arthur's Pilgrimage: A Study of *Golagros and Gawane*" in *Studies in Scottish Literature* 12: 3–20.

—. (ed.) 1988. *The History of Scottish Literature 1: Origins to 1660*. Aberdeen: Aberdeen University Press.

—. 2000. "'A! fredome is a noble thing': Christian Hermeneutics and Barbour's *Bruce*" in *Scottish Studies Review* 1: 26–38.

—. 2001. "Discoursing at Cross Purposes. *Braveheart* and *The Wallace*" in Göbel, W. and B. Ross (eds) *Renaissance Humanism – Modern Humanisms*. Heidelberg: Universitätsverlag. 41–54.

Jack, R.D.S. and P.A.T. Rozendaal (eds). 1997. *The Mercat Anthology of Early Scottish Literature 1375–1707*. Edinburgh: Mercat Press.

Jackson, W.T.H. 1982. *The Hero and the King*. New York: Columbia University Press.

Jamison, D.F. 1864. *The Life and Times of Bertrand du Guesclin: A History of the Fourteenth Century*. London: Trüberand and co.

Kay, Sarah. 1995. *The Chansons de Geste in the Age of Romance: Political Fictions*. Oxford: Clarendon Press.

—. 2001. "Courts, Clerks, and Courtly Love" in Krueger, Roberta L. (ed.) *The Cambridge Companion to Medieval Romance*. Cambridge: Cambridge University Press. 81–96.

Keen, Maurice. 1973. *England in the Later Middle Ages*. London: Methuen.

—. 1984. *Chivalry*. London: Yale University Press.

Keller, Hans-Erich. 1989. "De l'amour dans le *Roman de Brut*" in Lacy, Norris J. and Gloria Torrini-Roblin (eds) *Continuations, Essays on Medieval French Literature and Language*. Birmingham: Summa Publications, inc.. 63–81.

Kelly, Constance S. 1975. "The Northern Arthur". PhD thesis. University of Edinburgh.

Kelly, Tomas E. 1974. *Le Haut Livre du Graal: Perlesvaus. A Structural Study*. Genève: Librairie Droz.

Kennedy, Elspheth. 1986. *Lancelot and the Grail*. Oxford: Clarendon Press.

Ketrick, Paul J. 1931. *The Relation of the Golagros and Gawane to the Old French Perceval*. Washington D.C.: Catholic University of America.

Kinghorn, A.M. 1968–69. "Scottish Historiography in the XIVth Century: A New Introduction to Barbour's *Bruce*" in *Scottish Studies in Literature* 6: 131–45.

Kliman, Bernice W. 1973. "The Idea of Chivalry in Barbour's *Bruce*" in *Medieval Studies* 35: 477–508.

—. 1973–74. "The Significance of Barbour's Naming of Commoners" in *Scottish Studies in Literature* 11: 108–13.

—. 1975. "Speech as a Mirror of *Sapientia* and *Fortitudo* in Barbour's *Bruce*" in *Medium Aevum* 44: 151–61.

—. 1977. "John Barbour and Rhetorical Tradition" in *Annuale Mediaevale* 18: 106–35.

Kolve, V.A. 1984. *Chaucer and the Imagery of Narrative: The First Five Canterbury Tales*. London: Edward Arnold.

Kratzmann, Gregory. 1980. *Anglo-Scottish Literary Relations*. Cambridge: Cambridge University Press.

Krueger, Roberta L. (ed). 2001. *The Cambridge Companion to Medieval Romance*. Cambridge: Cambridge University Press.

Kurath, H., S.M. Kuhn, J. Reidy and R.E. Lewis (eds). 1951–. *Middle English Dictionary*. Ann Arbor and London: University of Michigan Press and Oxford University Press.

Lacy, Norris. 1977. "The Form of *The Brut's* Arthurian Sequence" in Rute, H.R., H. Niedzielski and W.L. Hendrickson (eds) *Jean Misrahi Memorial Volume: Studies in Medieval Literature*. Columbia: French Literature Publication Company. 150–58.

—. 2001. "The Evolution and Legacy of French Prose Romance" in Krueger, Roberta L. (ed.) *The Cambridge Companion to Medieval Romance*. Cambridge: Cambridge University Press. 167–82.

Lawrence, C.H. 1984. *Medieval Monasticism: Forms of Religious Life in Western Europe in the Middle Ages*. London: Longman.

Legge, M. Dominica. 1956. "In fere of were" in *Scottish Historical Review* 35: 20–25.

—. 1963. *Anglo-Norman Literature and its Background*. Oxford: The Clarendon Press.

—. 1969. *The Significance of Anglo-Norman* [University of Edinburgh, Inaugural Lecture, no. 38]. Edinburgh: T. and A. Constable Ltd.

Lévi-Strauss, Claude. 1978. *Myth and Meaning*. London: Routledge & Kegan Paul Ltd.

Lewis, C.S. [1936] 1988. *The Allegory of Love*. Oxford: Oxford University Press.

Loomis, R.S. (ed.). 1959. *Arthurian Literature in the Middle Ages*. Oxford: The Clarendon Press.

López Couso, María José. 1994. "Some Editions of *The Bruce*: A Comparative Account" in *SELIM* 4: 48–58.

Lyall, Roderick J. 1976. "Politics and Poetry in Fifteenth and Sixteenth Century Scotland" in *Scottish Literary Journal* 3(2): 5–29.

—. 1989. "The Lost Literature of Medieval Scotland" in McClure, J. Derrick and Michael R.G. Spiller (eds) *Bryght Lanternis: Essays on the Language and Literature of Medieval and Renaissance Scotland*. Aberdeen: Aberdeen University Press. 33–47.

Lynch, Michael. [1991] 1997. *Scotland: A New History*. London: Pimlico.

—. 1993. "Scottish Culture in its Historical Perspective" in Scott, Paul H. (ed.) *Scotland: A Concise Cultural History*. Edinburgh: Mainstream. 15–45.

MacQueen, John. 1967. "Some Aspects of the Early Renaissance in Scotland" in *Forum for Modern Languages Studies* 3: 201–22.

—. 1977. "The Literature of Fifteenth-Century Scotland" in Brown, Jennifer M. (ed.) *Scottish Society in the Fifteenth Century*. New York: St. Martin's Press. 184–208.

Mainer, Sergi. 2003. "Identity under Threat: Origin Myths as a Device of National Affirmation in Catalonia and Scotland" in *Catalan Review* 17: 67–78.

—. 2005. "Reinventing Arthur: Representations of the Matter of Britain in Medieval Scotland and Catalonia" in Purdie, Rhiannon and Nicola Royan (eds) *The Scots and Medieval Arthurian Legend* [Arthurian Studies 61]. Woodbridge: D.S. Brewer. 135–47.

Mainster, Phoebe A. 1987. "Folkloric Element in Barbour's *Bruce*" in *Michigan Academician* 19(1): 49–59.

Mapstone, Sally. 1986. *The Advice to Princes Tradition in Scottish Literature*. D. Phil thesis. University of Oxford.

—. 1991. "Was There a Court Literature in Fifteenth-Century Scotland?" in *Studies in Scottish Literature* 26: 410–22.

—. 2001. "The Scots, the French, and the English: An Arthurian Episode" in Caie, Graham et al. (eds) *The European Sun: Proceedings of the Seventh International Conference on Medieval and Renaissance Scottish Language and Literature.* Glasgow: Tuckwell Press. 129–44.

Martin, C.J.F. 1996. *An Introduction to Medieval Philosophy.* Edinburgh: Edinburgh University Press.

Martin, Joanna. 2002. *Readings of John Gower's* Confessio Amantis *in Fifteenth- and Early Sixteenth-Century Scotland.* D. Phil thesis. University of Oxford.

—. 2006. "'Of Wisdome and of Guide Governance': Sir Gilbert Hay and *The Buik of King Alexander the Conquerour*" in Bawcutt, Priscilla and Janet Hadley Williams (ed.) *A Companion to Medieval Scottish Poetry.* Cambridge: D.S. Brewer. 75–88.

—. 2008. Kingship and Love in Scottish poetry, 1424–1540. Aldershot: Ashgate.

Martines, Vicent. 1995. *Els cavallers literaris: Assaig sobre literatura cavalleresca catalana medieval.* Madrid: Universidad Nacional de Educación a Distancia.

Minnis, A.J. and A.B. Scott (eds). [1988] 2000. *Medieval Literary Theory c.1100– c.1375: The Commentary Tradition.* Aldershot: Scholar Press.

McClure, J. Derrick and Michael R.G. Spiller (eds). 1989. *Bryght Lanternis: Essays on the Language and Literature of Medieval and Renaissance Scotland.* Aberdeen: Aberdeen University Press.

McDiarmid, Matthew P. 1979. "The Kingship of the Scots in their Writers" in *Scottish Literary Journal* 6: 5–18.

—. 1983. "The Northern Initiative: John Fordun, John Barbour and the Author of the *Saints' Legends*" in Hewitt, David and Michael Spiller (eds) *Literature of the North.* Aberdeen: Aberdeen University Press. 1–13.

—. 1988. "The Metrical Chronicles and Non-Alliterative Romance" in Jack, R.D.S. (ed.) *The History of Scottish Literature 1: Origins to 1660.* Aberdeen: Aberdeen University Press. 27–38.

—. 1991. "*Rauf Colyear, Golagros and Gawane,* Hary's *Wallace*: Their Themes of Independence and Religion" in *Studies in Scottish Literature* 26: 328–33.

—. 1993. "Concerning Sir Gilbert Hay, the authorship of *Alexander the Conquerour* and *The Buik of Alexander*" in *Studies in Scottish Literature* 28: 28–54.

McIntosh, Angus. 1989. "Is Sir Tristrem an English or a Scottish Poem?" in McKenzie, J. Lachlan and Richard Todd (eds) *Other Words: Transcultural Studies in Philology, Translation, and Lexicology Presented to Hans Heinrich Meier on the Occasion of His Sixty-Fifth Birthday.* Dordecht: Foris Publications. 85–95.

McKenzie, J. Lachlan and Richard Todd (eds). 1989. *Other Words: Transcultural Studies in Philology, Translation, and Lexicology Presented to Hans Heinrich Meier on the Occasion of His Sixty-Fifth Birthday.* Dordecht: Foris Publications.

McKim, Anne M. 1980. "*The Bruce*: A Study of John Barbour's Heroic Ideal". PhD thesis. University of Edinburgh.

—. 1981. "James Douglas and Barbour's Ideal of Knighthood" in *Forum for Modern Languages Studies* 17: 167–80.

—. 1989. "'Gret Price of Chewalry:' Barbour's Debt to Fordun" in *Scottish Studies in Literature* 24: 7–28.

Mohl, Ruth. 1933. *The Three Estates in Medieval and Renaissance Literature*. New York: University of Columbia Press.

Morse, Ruth. 1991. *Truth and Convention in the Middle Ages: Rhetoric, Representation and Reality*. Cambridge: Cambridge University Press.

Nederman, C.J. and K.L. Forhan (eds). 1993. *Medieval Political Theory. A Reader: The Quest for the Body Politic, 1100–1400*. London: Routledge.

Newman, F.X. (ed.). 1968. *The Meaning of Courtly Love*. Albany: The Research Foundation of State University of New York.

Nicholson, Ranald. 1974. *Scotland: The Later Middle Ages* [The Edinburgh History of Scotland, Volume 2]. Edinburgh: Oliver & Boyd.

Paris, Gaston. 1883. "Études sur les romans de la Table Ronde: *Lancelot du Lac*" in *Romania* 12: 459–534.

Pearsall, Derek. 1977. *Old English and Middle English Poetry*. London: Routledge & Kegan Paul.

—. 2003. *Arthurian Literature: A Short Introduction*. Oxford: Blackwell.

Petit, Aimé. 1985. *L'anachronisme dans les Romans Antiques du XIIe siécle*. Lille: Centre d'Études Médiévales et Dialectales de l'Université de Lille III.

Pocock, John. 1975. "England" in Ranum, Orest (ed.) *National Consciousness, History, and Political Culture in Early-Modern Europe*. Baltimore and London: The John Hopkins University Press.

Purdie, Rhiannon. 2002. "*Clariodus* and the Ambitions of Courtly Romance in Later Medieval Scotland" in *Forum for Modern Languages Studies* 38(4): 449–61.

—. 2005. "The Search for Scottishness in *Golagros and Gawane*" in Purdie, Rhiannon and Nicola Royan, (eds) *The Scots and Medieval Arthurian Legend*. Woodbridge: D.S. Brewer. 95–107.

—. 2006. "Medieval Romance in Scotland" in Bawcutt, Priscilla and Janet Hadley Williams (eds) *A Companion to Medieval Scottish Poetry*. Cambridge: D.S. Brewer. 165–77.

Purdie, Rhiannon and Nicola Royan (eds). 2005. *The Scots and Medieval Arthurian Legend* [Arthurian Studies 61]. Woodbridge: D.S. Brewer.

Putter, Ad and Jane Gilbert (eds). 2000. *The Spirit of English Popular Romances*. Harlow: Longman.

Queruel, Danielle (ed.). 1995. *Amour et chevalerie dans les romans de Chrétien de Troyes*. Paris: Annales littéraires de l'Université de Bescaçon.

Ramsey, Lee C. 1983. *Chivalric Romances: Popular Literature in Medieval England*. Bloomington: Indiana University Press.

Rand, Edward Kennard. [1928] 1957. *Founders of the Middle Ages*. New York: Dover.

Ranum, Orest (ed.). 1975. *National Consciousness, History, and Political Culture in Early-Modern Europe*. Baltimore and London: The John Hopkins University Press.

Raynaud de Lage, Guy. 1961. "Les romans antiques et la représentation de l'antiquité" in *Le Moyen Age* 67: 247–91.

—. 1993. *Introduction a l'Ancien Français*. Paris: Sedes.

Riddy, Felicity. 1974. "*Squyer Meldrum* and the Romance of Chivalry" in *The Yearbook of English Studies* 4: 26–36.

—. 1991. "Reading England: Arthurian Literature and National Consciousness" in *Bibliographical Bulletin of the International Arthurian Society* 43: 314–32.

Rieger, Dietmar. 1988. "Le motif de viol dans la littérature de la France médiévale entre norme courtoise et réalité courtoise" in *Cahiers de civilisation médiévale* 31: 241–67.

Riquer, Martí de. 1964. *Història de la literatura catalana*. 4 vols. Barcelona: Edicions Ariel.

Rollo, David. 1998. *Historical Fabrication, Ethnic Fable and French Romance in Twelfth-Century Britain*. Lexington: French Forum.

Robertson, D.W. 1963. *A Preface to Chaucer*. Princeton: Princeton University Press.

Ruck, E.H. 1991. *An Index of Themes and Motifs in Twelfth-Century French Arthurian Poetry* [Arthurian Studies 25]. Cambridge: D.S. Brewer.

Rumble, T.C. 1959. "The Middle English *Sir Tristrem*: Towards a Reappraisal" in *Comparative Literature* 11: 221–28.

Said, Edward W. [1978] 2003. *Orientalism*. London: Penguin.

Scheps, Walter. 1967–68. "Thematic Unity of *Lancelot of the Laik*" in *Studies in Scottish Literature* 5: 167–75.

Schmolke-Hasselmann, Beate. 1983. "The Round Table: Ideal, Fiction, Reality" in *Arthurian Literature* II: 41–75.

Schwend, Joachim. 1986. "Religion and Religiosity in *The Bruce*" in Strauss, Dietrich and Horst W. Drescher (eds) *Scottish Language and Literature*. Frankfurt: Peter Lang. 207–16.

Scott, Paul H. (ed.). 1993. *Scotland: A Concise Cultural History*. Edinburgh: Mainstream.

Scott, Tom. 1966. *Dunbar: A Critical Exposition of the Poems*. Edinburgh: Oliver & Boyd.

Shepherd, Stephen H.A. 1991. "'Of Thy Glitterand Gyde Have I Na Gle': *The Taill of Rauf Coilyear*" in *Archiv für das Studium der Neueren Sprachen und Literaturen* 228: 284–98.

Skeat, Walter W. 1911. "The Author of *Lancelot of the Laik*" in *Scottish Historical Review* 8: 1–4.

Smith, Anthony D. 1998. *Nationalism and Modernism*. London and New York: Routledge.

Smith, Janet M. 1934. *The French Background of Middle Scots Literature*. Edinburgh: Oliver and Boyd.

Snell, F.J. 1899. *The Fourteenth Century*. Edinburgh: Blackwood.

Spearing, A.C. 1976. *Medieval Dream-Poetry*. Cambridge: Cambridge University Press.

Stevenson, Katie. 2003. "Knighthood, Chivalry and the Crown in Fifteenth-Century Scotland, 1424–1513". PhD thesis, University of Edinburgh.

—. 2006. *Chivalry and Knighthood in Scotland 1424–1513*. Woodbridge: The Boydell Press.

Stock, Brian. 2001. *After Augustine: The Meditative Reader and the Text*. Philadelphia: University of Pennsylvania Press.

Strauss, Dietrich and Horst W. Drescher (eds). 1986. *Scottish Language and Literature, Medieval and Renaissance: Fourth International Conference 1984*. Frankfurt and New York: Lang.

Strohm, Paul. 1977. "The Origin and Meaning of Middle English *Romaunce*" in *Genre* 10:1–28.

Sweetser, Franklin P. 1989. "L'amour, l'amitié et la jalousie dans le *Lancelot en prose*" in *Travaux de Littérature* 2: 23–29.

Tanner, Roland. 2001. *The Late Medieval Scottish Parliament: Politics and the Three Estates, 1424–1488* [Scottish Historical Review Monographs Series no. 12]. East Linton: Tuckwell.

Thomson, Derick. 1993. "Gaelic Literature" in Scott, Paul H. (ed.) *Scotland: A Concise Cultural History*. Edinburgh: Mainstream. 127–43.

Topsfield, Leslie Thomas. 1975. *Troubadours and Love.* Cambridge: Cambridge University Press.

—. 1981. *Chrétien de Troyes: A Study of the Arthurian Romances.* Cambridge: Cambridge University Press.

Turville-Petre, Thorlac. 1977. *The Alliterative Revival.* Cambridge: D.S. Brewer.

Utz, Hans. 1969. "If Freedom Fail... 'Freedom' in Barbour's *The Bruce*" in *English Studies* 50: 151–65.

Van Duzee, Mabel. 1963. *A Medieval Romance of Friendship: Eger and Grime* [Selected Papers in Literature and Criticism no. 2]. New York: Burt Franklin.

Vogel, Bertram. 1943. "Secular Politics and the Date of *Lancelot of the Laik*" in *Studies in Philology* 40: 1–13.

Wagner, David. 1983. *The Seven Liberal Arts in the Middle Ages.* Bloomington: Indiana University Press.

Walker, I.C. 1963–64. "Barbour, Blind Hary and Sir William Craigie" in *Studies in Scottish Literature* 1: 202–6.

Wallace, David (ed.). 1999. *The Cambridge History of Medieval English Literature.* Cambridge: Cambridge University Press.

Walsh, Elizabeth. 1979. "*The Tale of Rauf Coilyear*: Oral Motif in Literary Guise" in *Scottish Literary Journal* 6(2): 5–19.

—. 1984. "Hary's *Wallace*: The Evolution of a Hero" in *Scottish Literary Journal* 11(1): 5–19.

—. 1989. "*Golagros and Gawane*: A Word for Peace" in McClure, J. Derrick and Michael R.G. Spiller (eds) *Bryght Lanternis: Essays on the Language and Literature of Medieval and Renaissance Scotland.* Aberdeen: Aberdeen University Press. 90–103.

Watson, Fiona. 1998. "The Enigmatic Lion: Scotland, Kingship and National Identity in the Wars of Independence" in Broun, Dauvit, Richard J. Finlay and Michael Lynch (eds) *Image and Identity: The Making and Remaking of Scotland through the Ages.* Edinburgh: John Donald. 18–37.

Watt, Diane. 1994. "Nationalism in Barbour's *Bruce*" in *Parergon* 12(1): 89–107.

Webster, Bruce. 1997. *The Making of an Identity.* London: MacMillan Press.

White, Hayden. 1975. *Metahistory: The Historical Imagination in Nineteenth-Century Europe.* Baltimore: Johns Hopkins University Press.

—. 1985. *Tropics of Discourse: Essays in Cultural Criticism.* Baltimore: Johns Hopkins University Press.

Wilson, Grace G. 1990. "Barbour's *Bruce* and Hary's *Wallace*: Complements, Compensations and Conventions" in *Studies in Scottish Literature* 25: 189–201.

Wittig, Kurt. 1972. *The Scottish Tradition in Literature.* Westport: Greenwood Press.

Wolfzettel, Friedich (ed.). 1995. *Arthurian Romance and Gender.* Amsterdam: Ropodi.

Wulf, Charlotte A.T. 1995. "A Comparative Study of Wace's Guenevere in the Twelfth Century" in Wolfzettel, Friedich (ed.) *Arthurian Romance and Gender.* Amsterdam: Ropodi. 66–78.

Zumthor, Paul. 1972. *Essai de poétique médiévale.* Paris: Éditions du Seuil.

—. 1992. *Towards a Medieval Poetics* (tr. Philip Bennett). Minneapolis and London: University of Minnesota Press.

Index

Aeneas, 115, 165, 179, 192

Aeneid, 38, 115, 161, 165, 179, 263

Albanactus, 52

Alexander III (King of Scots), 44, 81, 118

Alexander the Great (Macedonian Emperor), 41, 50–51, 76–78, 80, 85–87, 97–98, 104, 129, 132, 146–54, 159, 223–34, 237–49, 260–61

Amustans, 133

Amytans, 71, 95, 99, 119, 129, 132–39, 141, 143–45, 148, 200, 206, 211

Anderson, Benedict, 42

Aquinas, Thomas, 45–46, 70, 122, 150

Arbre des Bataille, 162

Arbuthnet, Alexander, 31

Aristotle, 15, 50, 77, 81, 104, 146–52, 154, 175, 241, 244, 248

Arreste, 227

Arthur (King of Britain), 20, 21, 26, 31, 34–35, 47–50, 55, 71, 73, 76, 89–91, 95–96, 99–101, 104, 109, 119, 121–46, 149, 155, 159, 195–97, 200–1, 203, 206, 208–12, 216–17, 219, 221, 224, 241, 244, 259, 261

Auerbach, Erich, 13, 20

Augustine of Hippo, Saint. *See* Saint Augustine of Hippo

Auster, Paul, 14

Awntyrs off Arthure, The, 218

Aymer, Sir, 168

Ball, John, 168

"Ballat of Our Lady, Ane", 38

"Ballat of the Fenyeit Freir of Tungland, Ane", 142

Ballat of the Nine Nobles, Ane, 160

Balliol, John, 52, 54, 61, 66, 73–77, 81, 83–84, 98, 136, 159–60

Ban (King of Albenak), 99, 100, 194, 197

Barbour, John, 13, 28–31, 33–34, 37, 41, 45–46, 49, 51, 54–56, 58–61, 65–70, 74–88, 92–93, 98, 101, 103, 112–16, 120, 140, 154, 157–77, 183, 185–86, 192–93, 249, 257, 260–61, 263

Barron, W.R.J., 15

Barrow, G.W.S., 44, 54–56, 80, 84

Bataille Loquifer, 19

Bauderane, the, 230–31, 234–36

Bede, 89–90

Beer, Gillian, 14

Bellenden, John, 38

Betys, Duke, 32, 78, 226–28, 230

Bisset, Baldred, 52, 55

Blind Hary, 13, 33, 36–37, 41, 45, 51–52, 54–55, 61, 65–68, 76, 87–89, 91–92, 98, 101, 103–7, 110–12, 157–58, 175–80, 182–86, 190, 192–93, 239, 249, 258–60, 262

Boardman, Steve, 34

Boccaccio, Giovanni, 25

Boece, Hector, 34, 38, 45, 91

Boethius, Anicius Manlius Severinus, 61, 119, 125, 127, 175

Bonet, Honoré, 162

Boniface VIII, Pope, 52

Book of the Duchess, The, 176, 180

Bower, Walter, 34, 45, 65, 175

Bran de Lis, 212–13, 219

Bruce, Edward (the), 165

Bruce, Robert. *See* Robert I (King of Scots)

Bruce, The, 28–29, 38–39, 41–42, 46–49, 51, 53, 56–57, 59–61, 65–70, 73–80, 85–86, 98, 102, 104, 112–13, 115–17, 136, 140, 146, 148, 154–55, 157–59, 161, 164, 166–68, 171–72, 175–77, 184–87, 193, 227, 241, 246, 257–59, 261

Brutus, 44, 52, 89–91

Buchanan, George, 38

Buik of Alexander, 31–33, 39, 78, 80, 104, 129, 132, 134, 139, 223–24, 232, 234–35, 243, 245, 248, 260

Buik of King Alexander the Conquerour, 31–32, 39, 41, 50,

53, 85, 97, 104, 146, 155, 223,
    238, 244, 249, 260
Buke of the Governaunce of Princis,
    146, 149, 152, 239, 259
Buke of the Law of Armys, 162
Buke of the Ordre of Knychthede,
    158, 162, 164
Caesar, Gaius Julius, 76, 159
Calin, William, 107, 194
Canterbury Tales, The, 117, 175, 180
Capellanus, Andreas, 25
Cassamus, 141, 224, 228–32, 235,
    236–37
Chandos, John, Sir (Chandos Herald),
    174
Chanson de Bertrand du Guesclin,
    53, 91
Chanson de Roland, 184, 225–27
Charlemagne (King of the Franks),
    18, 28, 223, 226, 232, 234–35,
    249–54, 258
Charteris, Henry, 38
Chaucer, Geoffrey, 25, 30, 105, 116–
    17, 175–78, 180–81, 185, 189,
    199, 252
Chepman, Walter, 34, 36
Chevalier au lion, Le (Yvain), 12
Cicero, Marcus Tullius, 43, 129, 134
City of God, 145
Clariodus, 26, 39, 159, 234, 262
Clarus, King, 104, 129, 132, 134–35,
    139–42, 228–32
Cleopatra, 50, 85
Cleriadus et Meliadice, 39
Cligès, 12, 21–22
Cochrane, Robert, 30
Compleynt of Mars, The, 105, 175
Comyn, John, 74, 76–77, 113–15,
    136
Conte du Graal, Le (Perceval), 12,
    21, 23, 215–16, 220
Cook, Robert F., 226
Cowan, Edward, 45, 55
Craigfergus, Lady of, 188, 190–91
Crane, Susan, 24, 58
Criseyde, 181
Cuvelier, 91–92
Daiches, David, 56

Darius I (King of Persia), 77, 85–87,
    240, 242–43, 245–46, 249
Darsie, Anthony, Sir, 94
David II (King of Scots), 27, 44, 98,
    259
De Bello Civili, 158
De Civita Dei. See City of God
De Consolatione Philosophiae, 61,
    119, 125, 127, 134, 175–76
De Doctrina Christiana, 134
De regimine principum, 45
Declaration of Arbroath, 41–42, 45,
    55, 60, 72, 74, 84, 86, 97, 151
Dido, 179, 192
"Dirai vos senes duptansa", 205
Dit dou Vergier, Le, 180
Douglas, Archibald (Earl of Angus),
    33
Douglas, Gavin, 13, 30, 35, 38, 56–
    58, 65, 77, 78, 82, 120, 262, 263
Douglas, James, 102
Dreme, The, 38, 186
Duby, Georges, 166
Dunbar, William, 13, 30–31, 35–38,
    44, 142, 246, 262
Ebin, Lois, 58, 66, 89, 114
Edington, Carol, 31, 39, 186, 190,
    192
Edward I (King of England), 35, 44,
    46, 49, 52, 54, 57, 59, 62–63, 66–
    68, 73, 75–76, 78, 81–82, 84, 88,
    98, 128
Edward II (King of England), 67,
    167–68
Edward III (King of England), 44
Edward IV (King of England), 44
Edward, the Black Prince, 174
Eger and Grime, 14, 39, 235, 262
Emenidus, 225–27, 234
Eneados, 38
Erec et Enide, 12, 174
Erlingsson of Bjarkey, Lord Bjarni,
    28
Erskine, Thomas, Lord, 31–32
Fanon, Frantz, 66–67, 90
Fesonas, 135, 141, 230–32, 235–36
Field, Rosalind, 15
Fierabras, 29

First Continuation of Perceval, 35, 36, 193

Floire et Blacheflor, 19

Fonteinne Amoureuse, 180

Fordun, John, 34, 45, 55, 91, 120

Foucault, Michel, 63

Frappier, Jean, 220

Freiris of Berwick, The, 37

Froissart, Jean, 175, 180, 199

Fulgentius, Duke, 34

Gadifer (father), 225, 228–29, 233–34

Gadifer (son), 228–31

Galehot, 96, 135, 146, 206–9

Galiot, 47, 96, 100, 123, 129, 131–32, 136–37, 139–40, 144, 146, 201–3, 206–7, 215

Gawain, 12, 15, 22, 25, 34, 72, 95–96, 101, 116–17, 124–25, 136, 209–11, 214, 217–19, 220–21

Gaythelos, 31, 34

Geoffrey of Charny, 158

Geoffrey of Monmouth, 20, 89

Geoffrey of Vinsauf, 79, 105

Girart de Roussillon, 18

Gleneagles, Lady of, 191–92

Golagros, 22, 35–37, 39, 41, 47–50, 53–54, 72–73, 95, 97, 99–101, 104, 121–28, 136, 142, 153–54, 186, 189, 211–12, 214, 216–19, 221, 224, 234, 259–62

Golagros and Gawane, 22, 35–37, 39, 41, 47–48, 50, 53–54, 72–73, 95, 97–98, 100, 104, 121–22, 126, 136, 142, 153–54, 186, 189, 211–12, 214, 216–19, 221, 224, 234, 259–62

Goldstein, R.J., 51, 54–55, 58–60, 63, 64, 67, 75, 77, 83, 110, 158, 160, 168, 181, 185

Gower, John, 25

Gray, Thomas, Sir, 29

Guenée, Bernard, 43, 97

Guenevere, 21, 23, 26, 35, 96, 100, 124, 130, 133, 189, 196–97, 201, 203–11, 235, 257, 261

Guesclin, Bertrand du, 53, 91–92

Guillaume le Clerc, 11, 28

Gyflet fils Do, 49, 122

Hahn, Thomas, 216

Hamilton of Gilbertfield, William, 34

Harf, Laurence, 195

Havelok the Dane, 24

Hay, Gilbert, 31–33, 36, 41, 50, 70, 77, 85, 87, 97–98, 104, 108, 146–52, 155, 158, 162, 166, 173, 184, 223, 238–39, 244, 248, 258–59

Haye, Gilbert of the, 68, 108, 120, 164, 166, 173

Henry II (King of England), 23

Henry IV (King of England), 44

Henry VI (King of England), 44, 151

Henryson, Robert, 13, 30, 37, 65, 262

Hercules, 244

Histoire de Guillaume le Maréchal, 154, 171

Historia de Preliis, 244

Historia Regum Britanniae, 20, 89

Historie of Squyer Meldrum, The, 38, 157, 186

History of the Kings of Britain. See Historia Regum Britanniae

Hobsbawm, E.J., 42

"How sould I Governe me?", 142

Hugh of St Victor, 103

Ideas, 232, 236

Ipomedon, 24, 171

Iseut, 21

Isidore of Seville, 43

Jack, R.D.S., 22, 42, 60, 104–5, 111, 113, 120–21, 123, 180, 217–18, 253

James I (King of Scots), 27, 30–31, 98, 159

James II (King of Scots), 27, 30, 44, 78, 98

James III (King of Scots), 30, 33, 35, 72, 88, 98, 258

James IV (King of Scots), 15, 30, 34, 98, 142

James V (King of Scots), 38–39, 93–94

Jameson, Frederic, 19

Jaufre, 16

Jehan de Saintré, 173

John of Salisbury. *See* Salisbury, John of

Karlamagnús saga, 28
Kay, 127, 211, 217
Kay, Sarah, 17, 19
Kelly, Constance, 49, 221
Kennedy, Elspeth, 196
Kennedy, Walter, 30
Kenneth I. *See* MacAlpin, Kenneth
Ketrick, Paul, 212
Kingis Quair, 30
Kliman, Bernice W., 79, 114–15, 161, 163
"Knight's Tale, The", 25, 177
Lacy, Norris, 22–23
Lady of the Lake, 194–97
Lai of Havelok, 24
Lancelot, 21, 26, 35–36, 95–96, 99–100, 136, 146, 179, 189–90, 193–98, 201–11, 235, 257, 261
Lancelot en prose. See Prose Lancelot
Lancelot of the Laik, 22, 35–36, 39, 41, 47, 49, 53–54, 71, 95–96, 98, 100–1, 104, 119, 129, 131–32, 135, 137, 140–42, 148–49, 152, 155, 189, 193–95, 197, 199, 201–3, 211, 234, 241, 257–58, 260, 262
"Laurentius", 111
Layamon, 89
Le Chevalier de la charrette, Le (Lancelot), 12
Legend of Good Women, The, 198
Leigni, Godefroi de, 22
Lekpreuik, Robert, 34, 37
Lévi-Strauss, Claude, 34
Lewis, C.S., 211
Liddale, James, 33
Lindsay, David, Sir, 11, 13–14, 38–39, 70–71, 92–94, 142, 146, 151, 157–58, 186–87, 189–92, 216
Livy (Titus Livius), 38
Llibre de l'orde de cavalleria, 158
Llull, Ramon, 158, 172–73
Locrine. *See* Locrinus
Locrinus, 52
Longuyon, Jean de, 31, 223
Lorne, John of, 113
Lorris, Guillaume de, 12
Loth (Lord of Lothian), 34
Louis IX (King of France), 118–19

MacAlpin, Kenneth, 41, 43
Machaut, Guillaume de, 25, 180, 199
MacQueen, John, 30–31, 34–37
Macrobius, Ambrosius Theodosius, 129
Major, John, 38
Malcolm II (King of the Scots), 43
Malory, Thomas, Sir, 25
Malveisin, William, 11
Mapstone, Sally, 35, 51, 97, 132, 136–37, 142, 146–47, 149–52
Marcabru, 205
Marciane, 132, 139–42
Margaret, Maid of Norway, 28
Martin, Joanna, 32–33, 36, 97, 195, 239
McDiarmid, Matthew P., 28–29, 31–33, 37, 55, 60–61, 88, 104–5, 181, 235
McKim, Anne, 58, 163
Meldrum, William, 38
Melyhalt, Lady of, 145
Menteith, John de, Sir, 110
Merlin, 34
Meun, Jean de, 12
Mézières, Philippe de, 131, 143
Modred, 34, 91, 138
Morall Fabillis, 37
Morte Arthur, 26
Morte Arthure, 26
Morte le Roi Artu, La, 138
Mowbray, Philip, Sir, 58
Myllar, Androw, 34, 36
Oliver, 226
Olympias, Queen, 85, 154, 244, 247
"Order of Combats for Life in Scotland, The", 159
Orygynale Cronykil of Scotland, 34
Otuel, 234
Palisseda (Queen of the Amazons), 246–47
Paris, Gaston, 13, 27, 251
Perceval, 22, 216, *See* Conte du Graal, Le
Percy, Lord, 165
Perlesvaus, 23
Petrarch, Francesco, 25
Phaedo, 150

Philip (King of Macedonia), 50–51, 85–86, 98, 238, 241–42, 244
Physiognomy, 147
Plato, 150
Pleading, The, 52, 55
Pocock, John, 68
Poetics, 15
Policraticus, 46, 64, 85, 128, 149, 185
Politics, 150
Porrus, 140, 229–32, 234–35, 242
Prose Lancelot, 22, 35, 47, 72, 95–96, 100, 130, 133, 136, 138, 142, 155, 193–95, 200–3, 205, 208, 209, 211
Ptolemy, 78, 225, 227, 241
Purdie, Rhiannon, 123
Quare of Jelusy, The, 35
Queste de le Sainct Graal, La, 138
Ramsay, John, 34
Randolph, Thomas (Earl of Moray), 162–64, 169
Rauf Coilyear, 250–54
Rauf Coilyear, See Taill of Rauf Coilyear, The
Remede de Fortune, 199
Remigius of Auxerre, 125
Republic, 150
Rhetoric, 50, 173
Richard II (King of England), 49, 151
Riche Soudoyer, 49, 97, 122, 128, 212, 214, 218
Richie, R. Graeme, 31
Riddy, Felicity, 38
Rimour, Thomas, 28
Riquer, Martí de, 210
Robert I (King of Scots), 13, 27, 29, 33, 38, 41, 43–44, 46, 48–49, 51, 54–58, 60–67, 69, 72, 74–87, 98–99, 102, 112–20, 136, 140, 146, 154, 157, 159, 160–64, 166–68, 170–72, 174, 177, 183–85, 227, 241, 246, 257, 259–60
Robert II (King of Scots), 27, 34, 46, 82, 84, 258
Robert III (King of Scots), 27, 44
Roland, 184, 226, 229, 251–52, 254
Roland Furious, 37

Roman d'Alixandre, 29
Roman d'Enéas, 19, 161
Roman de Fergus, 11, 28
Roman de Horn, 24
Roman de la Rose, 12, 25
Roman de la violette, 19
Roman de Thèbes, 19
Roman de Troie, 19
Roman History, 38
Rozendaal, P.A.T., 120, 253
Said, Edward, 235
Saint Andrew, 108–9, 259
Saint Augustine of Hippo (Aurelius Augustinus), 134, 145, 150
Sainte-Maure, Benoît de, 19
Saisnes, Les, 19
Sale, Antoine de la, 173
Salisbury, John of, 46, 85, 128, 150, 185
Samson, 78, 242
Satyre of the Thrie Estaitis, Ane, 38, 93, 142, 146, 151, 186
Scalachronica, 29
Scheps, Walter, 200
Schir Thomas Norny, 38
Scota, 34, 52, 55
Scotichronicon, 34, 65
Scott, Tom, 197
Secreta Secretorum, 147, 152
Shakespeare, William, 64
Sir Ferumbras, 234
Sir Gawain and Dame Ragnell, 12, 218
Sir Gawain and the Green Knight, 12, 15, 25, 218
Skeat, W.W., 35
Smith, Anthony D., 43
Smith, Janet M., 174
Snell, F.J., 113
Socrates, 150
Songe du Vieil Pelerin, Le, 131
Spearing, A.C., 198, 208
Spynagros, 100, 123
Stewart of Baldynneis, John, 37
Stewart, Alexander (Duke of Albany), 33
Stirling of Keir, 93
Straw, Jack, 168

Sweetser, Franklin P., 207
Taill of Rauf Coilyear, The, 37–39, 223, 249, 251, 258
Talbart, Master, 186–88
Talis of the Fyve Bestis, The, 37
Teseida, 25
Testament of Cresseid, 30
Thomas, 24
Thomas Aquinas, Saint. *See* Aquinas, Thomas
Thomas of Britain, 171
Thomas of Canterbury, 92
Thomas of Erceldoune, 106–8
Thomas the Rhymer. *See* Thomas of Erceldoune
Three Priests of Peebles, The, 37
"Timor Mortis Conturbat Me", 36
Tragedie of the Cardinal, The, 39
Tretis of the Twa Mariit Wemen and the Wedo, 38, 246
Tristan, 21, 28, 179, 239, 244
Tristram. *See* Tristan
Troilus, 179, 181, 189
Troilus and Criseyde, 175, 179, 189
Troyes, Chrétien de, 12–14, 19–23, 138, 157, 174, 193–94, 196, 201–2, 209–11, 215, 220, 235, 257

Tyler, Wat, 168
Umphraville, Ingram, Sir, 67, 169
Ventadorn, Bernart de, 20
Vie du Prince Noir, 154, 174
Virgil (Publius Vergilius Maro), 38, 115, 161
Virgin Mary, 108–9, 184, 259
Voeux du Paon, 31, 223
Vogel, Bertram, 72
Wace, 89
Wallace, The, 33–34, 37–39, 41, 51–53, 60, 67–68, 73–74, 79, 87–88, 91, 98, 102–4, 107, 109, 112, 129, 136, 144, 154–55, 157, 175–76, 178–79, 184–87, 193, 258–59, 261, 263
Wallace, William, Sir, 13, 33, 36, 38, 41, 54–55, 61–66, 87–88, 91, 98–99, 102, 104–12, 144, 157, 176–86, 190, 239, 249, 258–62
Walsh, Elizabeth, 216
Watson, Fiona, 67, 76
Webster, Bruce, 43
Webton, John, Sir, 174
William I (King of Scots), 83
Wyntoun, Andrew of, 34, 175
Ywain and Gawain, 25

ASLS

The Association for Scottish Literary Studies

Founded in 1970, the Association for Scottish Literary Studies promotes the study, teaching and writing of Scottish literature and the languages of Scotland. To these ends, ASLS publishes classic works of Scottish literature in our **Annual Volumes** series. Papers on literary criticism and cultural studies, along with in-depth reviews of Scottish books, are published biannually in our journal **Scottish Literary Review** (formerly Scottish Studies Review); scholarly studies of language in **Scottish Language**; and short articles, features and news in the ASLS newsletter **ScotLit**. **New Writing Scotland**, our annual anthology, contains new poetry, drama and short fiction in Scots, English and Gaelic. Our **Scotnotes** series of school- and college-level study guides provides invaluable background information to a range of major Scottish writers. We also produce collections of essays in our **Occasional Papers** series. Our website contains a substantial and growing body of downloadable essays, articles, papers and classroom notes. Other free online resources include the peer-reviewed **International Journal of Scottish Literature** and the ezine **The Bottle Imp**.

Each year, ASLS produces and distributes over 3,500 publications to its subscribers, and a further 2,800 to secondary schools and libraries. Approximately 3,000 books are sold each year through the trade. We hold annual conferences on Scottish writers in such diverse locations as Glasgow, Kirkwall, Edinburgh, Dumfries and Skye. We also take the **Scottish Writing Exhibition** to the **Modern Language Association** conventions in the USA and to **European Society for the Study of English** conferences in Europe.

Along with other Scottish literary organisations, and supported by the Scottish Arts Council, ASLS campaigns for a greater appreciation, both at home and abroad, in schools, colleges and universities, of Scotland's literary culture.

www.asls.org.uk

Scottish
Arts Council